MANUSCRIPT RELEASES

From the Files of the Letters and Manuscripts Written

by

Ellen G. White

Volume Eleven

1993

E. G. White Estate
12501 Old Columbia Pike
Silver Spring, Maryland 20904
U.S.A.

A WORD OF EXPLANATION

When Ellen White died in 1915, she left her manuscripts and letters in the custody of a small group of ministers and administrators in the Seventh-day Adventist church whom she had appointed to serve as trustees of her estate. As the years passed, these trustees and their successors became increasingly aware of the potential usefulness to the church of this gold mine of unpublished materials. Procedures were developed whereby church entities, or even individuals, could request the "release" of specified excerpts from Ellen White's writings for use in books, articles, class lectures, or sermons. For details of the release process the reader is referred to the Preface to Manuscript Releases, vol. 1.

As in the earlier volumes, materials currently available elsewhere in published form have not been included in the present volume. In a few cases materials under consideration and assigned a release number were not processed, and the number was not reassigned. Until 1983, only the excerpts requested for public use were "released." Starting with Manuscript Release No. 970, the White Estate began "releasing" entire letters or manuscripts, so far as possible, even if only particular paragraphs were requested.

Copy for this volume has been sent to the publisher camera-ready, which means that any typographical mistakes or other inaccuracies which may appear are the responsibility of the White Estate, not the publisher.

We take pleasure in making these materials available in this form, and trust that the counsels, warnings, and principles put forth by the author will bring a blessing to every reader.

The Trustees of the Ellen G. White Estate
Washington, D.C.

CONTENTS

A Word of Explanation

ELLEN WHITE IN NEW ZEALAND

Dear Brethren in America: I am thankful to be able to write to you that I am improving in health. Although I have passed this winter in the city of Wellington which has not a healthful climate because of constant storms and high winds, yet the Lord has blessed me. I was nearly prostrated for some weeks, about two months past.

I had an appointment at Petone and the subject I thought to speak upon was the necessity of growth in grace, but it was taken from me. In its place a most solemn warning was given me for the congregation in regard to the withdrawal of the Spirit of God from the world, and the judgments of God which were plagues of sickness, disasters by sea and by land, destruction everywhere in our world by fire and floods, and earthquakes in "divers places." In the words of Christ: [Luke 17:26-30 quoted].

I felt deeply the power of God resting upon me as I warned the people that the end of this earth's history was soon to close, and we could see the fulfillment of the words of warning of the Lord Jesus Christ. And we are indeed in the time which Christ has foretold would be the state of our world.

The Spirit of the Lord was upon me, and from that time I have had physical strength. For a while I was unable to write. My mental machinery was about ready to stop, but it was quickened by the power of God. I praise His holy name for what He has done for me in giving me the "balm of Gilead," and the healing power of the great Physician.

We see a great work to be done in this field, and long to have facilities to work with. I will speak of Wellington. It is a place where churches are abundant and plenty of ministers. But I have never been in a place where prejudice was so perseveringly and determinedly carried on as it is in this place. This is the capital and great center of New Zealand. A mission should be established here. A church, if ever so humble, should be erected. It will take money to do this.

It is not God's plan, although the gold and silver are His own, to send His angels from heaven to build churches in any town or city. He has made man His almoner, His steward of trust, and the Lord's field is a very extensive one. "But ye shall receive power, after that the Holy Ghost is come upon you: and ye shall be witnesses unto Me both in Jerusalem, and in all Judea, and in Samaria, and unto the uttermost part of the earth" (Acts 1:8). This was the commission given to the disciples, and here has been a place where the people have determined that the banner of truth should not be lifted.

There is a branch of the International Tract and Missionary Society established here, but there is no house of worship. There is no one who obeys the truth, of any means, with the exception of one man, Brother Mountain, and there are none who have a house they own. We have to be dependent upon halls and the church members will not come to these halls. There is a skating rink, where temperance meetings and religious meetings were held in the summer season, but this is owned by a proprietor of a brewery, and all these things are barriers in the way.

Ministers tell their congregations that there is danger of their going to hear the Adventists. They tell them that the Adventists have not any special interest in Wellington, that they have no one who will believe in their doctrines. If they should make some church members believe in their doctrines, where will they go to worship? They have no place of worship. They are only adventurers. They will come to the place and preach their pernicious doctrines, and mislead the minds of the people, and then go away and leave them. Then "where would you be should you be deceived by these strange doctrines?"

And yet God has a people in this place. How can we reach them? Only through a steady persevering effort, carried on judiciously. A humble house of worship should be erected, so the people will know that they are not to be left out in the cold. Many minds are half persuaded, but they dare not make the final decision. Workers are needed, and money is needed to erect a house of worship. If we can get a hold here then the door is opened to get a hold in other cities. Dunedin and Christchurch are prominent places.

Brother Masters and family live in Dunedin, and are doing quite a large work in canvassing for our books. He is sure and safe, and true as steel in his business with the office in Wellington. The money is always ready to be returned when the books are delivered. We have been holding meetings in Elder Israel's house. We have done everything possible to get the people out to the halls, but they would not come.

Sister Dr. Caro, a dentist, came from Napier, a ten hours' journey on the cars, to Wellington to extract my teeth, to prepare the way for an underset of teeth which I greatly needed. There was a minister on the cars from Ormondville, where Brother McCullagh is laboring, and who opposed him fiercely. He was in conversation with a minister from Wellington, and they were comparing notes. One said that McCullagh was doing much harm in Ormondville, but he thought that he had thoroughly settled the business with him. The minister from Wellington said that there had been a Mrs. Starr and a Mrs. White in Wellington trying to fasten their heresies upon the people. But they warned their congregations not to go in to hear. Well, said the minister from Ordmondville, "I heard they had no success in Wellington." And the reply was, "No, but we find the minds of the people are unsettled, and they managed to get the people uneasy, and they are plying us with questions hard to be answered."

This was the substance of the conversation related by these ministers, that Sr. Caro overheard on the train coming here. And we know that there are quite a number interested and inquiring and "unsettled."

Sr. Tuxford and I were walking out one day when an aged man, venerable in appearance, came toward me with every expression of joy upon his countenance. He grasped my hand and said, "How glad I am to see you. My son just saw you from his grocery store and said, 'There is Mrs. White coming down the hill.'" Said he, "I did not wait one minute. I rushed out to meet you and speak with you. I heard you preach several times in Auckland. And I thank the Lord your words went right to my heart." The son came up and introduced the aged gentleman as his father. The son is also interested in the truth. He has a license as an exhorter from the Wesleyan church.

I had a favorable interview with the father, Mr. Langford, and his son requested an interview with me. I gave the father Steps to Christ and

Patriarchs and Prophets to take with him to Auckland. His family are bitterly opposed to him.   They are Wesleyans, and he is a believer in some
other doctrine as well, for he believes in the gifts being in the church.
He wrote after his return home that his wife and daughter were reading the
books given by Sr. White and they were greatly changed in spirit. We expect
that they will attend the meeting in Auckland in October or November.

Then there were several who attended our meetings regularly, who are
businessmen. They believe the truth, but are halting, having not decided to
obey. If we could have a house of worship we think a church could be raised
up here without a doubt. But without one thing to give character to the
work here we cannot see how these people will be warned. The ministers are
active, and Satan's seat seems to be in this place. But it is too important
a place to be yielded without a strong effort, and this cannot be without
some evidence. The truth will be vindicated and sustained in Wellington.

I cannot express my feelings. Sometimes I think it is best for me to
return to America,for we can do so little. When our people in America shall
feel that this field is as important as the fields in America, and that
souls are as precious here as there, I think they would not take the whole,
or nearly all the money from the treasury to add building to building, and
in the face of all our pleading carry so light a burden for these foreign
fields, tying our hands so we can work only to the greatest disadvantage.
We have nothing wherewith we can make even a start by calling out the
people.

Unless something more is done than our brethren have yet done in these
fields, I wish to return to America and leave the burden of responsibility

upon the conference. I think a few of the responsible men had better visit this part of the world and get their eyes open and their view extended to see there are many places where nothing is being done. If they should send a few thousand dollars that are being invested where the truth has a firm hold, and give us something to work with, to give us even a standing place to unfurl the banner of truth that others may rally around the standard, it would be wholly in accordance with the commission of Jesus Christ. The important missionary work ought to have more money and more workers.

We have come here to this country, with my workers. This has cost me, personally, an extra two thousand dollars from my own means, besides the large extra expense of the conference to do a work, but without furnishing us the facilities we have earnestly pled for. I entreat of you to extend your vision and broaden your ideas in place of investing so largely in your supposed necessities and swallowing up all the available means in the treasury. Give us something that we may work with in cities where there are not any souls who have an interest in the truth. They must be warned and aroused, and the kingdom of God shall be built up.

God does not purpose to do your work, but He requires that you give some chance that the seeds of truth may be sown in places where the soil has never been broken. The seed sown in these cities will be watered by the Lord of heaven, and there will be an increase. The leaven of truth must be first hidden in the meal before it will leaven the lump. Once get the truth planted in new fields, in cities where they have never heard, and then the increase and progress will follow.

The people know nothing of the truth. They know nothing of the reasons of our faith. They believe what the church ministers tell them. Is there then to be no effort made that they shall know what the truth is for this time? What can be done in these cities, without money, to start the work? If you continually see places where you think you can use means to advantage, must these countries be left and the ground not plowed nor sown? Will the Lord be pleased with this kind of neglect?

The field is the world. America is not the whole world, only a little piece of it. I know there are many calls for means in all foreign countries, but here there is such a condition financially that we cannot depend on means coming from these fields until we have some facilities to till the soil and sow the seed.

I think I shall have to turn my face homeward and go among our churches in America, and see if I cannot arouse an interest that something shall be done. I never expect to return myself to this field, but I can see that some workers, even private families, shall get the missionary spirit and come this way.--Letter 9a, 1893, pp. 1-7. (Written August 1, 1893, at Wellington, New Zealand.)

Appeal to Attend the Camp Meeting--Dear Brethren and Sisters in New Zealand: I have an appeal to make to our churches to attend the coming camp meeting in Wellington. You cannot afford to lose this opportunity. We know that this meeting will be an important era in the history of the work in New Zealand. There should be particular efforts made to get a representation of those who believe the truth to this meeting, for the very reason we are so few in numbers, and the additional help of everyone is called for. The enemies of truth are many in numbers. On such an occasion as this we want to present as good a front as possible. Let not your business detain you. You individually need the benefits of this meeting. . . .

I fear quite a number will say, It is expensive to travel, and I had better save the money to use in advancing the cause and work where it is so much needed. No, no! God calls for you to take your rank and file, and strengthen the work all you possibly can by your personal presence. Let not one say, I attended the camp meeting in Napier, and that will answer; I will remain and let somebody else go. We want you and the somebody else as well. Let no stay-away argument be used. We have need of every spiritual advantage we can possibly have. We know that believers are scattered, but we want you to make no excuses.

The Lord wants you to come to the meeting and to bring your families, except the little ones who would only tie your hands. Put forth extra exertions. Better, far better, let the business suffer than to neglect the opportunity to hear the messages that God has for you at this time.

You need every jet of light you can obtain. You are acquainted with the truth in a measure, but you ought to become better acquainted with the reasons of our faith. Come with your Bible in your hand, for you ought to have a better knowledge of the sanctifying influence of truth upon heart and character. You cannot afford to lose one such privilege as you are now favored with. You must not now disappoint us. We look to this time as important to have everyone come up "to the help of the Lord, to the help of the Lord against the mighty" (Judges 5:23).

We see that the forces of the enemy are strengthening, and that the ministers in every place are making earnest efforts to oppose the truth, and more so in Wellington than any place I ever visited. Everything is said to present Seventh-day Adventists as only a few in number, and inferior in every respect, possessing little influence. And shall we not on this occasion represent the believing rank and file the very best that we possibly can? Will our brethren not come up to the feast of tabernacles? How zealously should everyone guard the way that leads to the city of God! If we treat the work as an indifferent matter, and the army of the Lord is not on the ground to represent the cause and work in New Zealand, God will not be pleased with your neglect. Will you plead excuses, and at such a time?

One of the reasons why we have the meeting in Wellington is because we have put forth much effort in that city, and ministers stood directly in our way by holding their congregations from coming out to hear us. Now we want to get the truth before the people of Wellington, and we want to make the very best impression possible upon them. The only way we could see to accomplish our purpose was to have a camp meeting appointed which would create an interest and call the attention of the people to the truth. We want everyone to come, praying and making God their trust.

These cities must be warned, and should we break down the existing prejudice which ministers of churches have created among the people of Wellington, then we have a key to unlock Christchurch, Dunedin, Auckland, and other places. The Lord calls you to put on the armor of righteousness, and come to this second camp meeting to be held in New Zealand. Come, brethren and sisters, if you have to make a sacrifice to do so. The Lord will bless you in your efforts.

God holds you personally responsible for the advancement and honor of His cause in this country. Bear in mind God's plan was that His people should assemble together to worship not less than three times a year. The Lord has not signified it to be your duty to do this, but He calls you. He wants you to come up "to the help of the Lord, to the help of the Lord against the mighty."

The Lord has need of you. He does not do His work without the cooperation of the human agent. The truth, God's down-trodden law, is to be uplifted; Christ and His righteousness are to be presented to souls that are perishing. The blindness, the spiritual blindness upon the people today is greater even than when Christ was upon the earth. The help of every man and woman is needed. Let us now rally around the standard, and angels which minister unto those who shall be heirs of salvation will accompany you.

Make every effort to get your friends to come, not in your place but to accompany, to stand on God's side, under God's command. At the very best our numbers will not be large, but if the individual members of the church will come to the Wellington camp meeting, with a mind and will to work to the best of their ability, God will do the rest. We cannot but see the schemes and working of the enemies of our faith. Let the prayers go forth from unfeigned lips, "Hear, O our God; for we are despised." "Think upon me, my God, for good." "Now therefore, O God, strengthen my hand." (Neh. 4:4; 5:19; 6:9.)

We must use every power with which God has endowed us to make this meeting a success, and every way adapted for all who shall come to the meeting. The work of the Lord is above every temporal interest, and the Lord's cause, in any case, must not be misrepresented by those who claim to believe the truth. Watching, waiting, working, is our position. There need not be any fainthearted ones. There will be unbelief and accusers in Wellington, but we fear them not if the Lord God of Hosts shall be with us. Every soul needs now to awake out of sleep, to put on the whole armor.

There is great need of personal religion and family piety, and then there will be a clear understanding of the part each one will be called to act in the grand and important work of building up the cause of God in our world, and vindicating His downtrodden law, and uplifting the Saviour as the "Lamb of God which taketh away the sin of the world."

We want the Holy Spirit of God, that our works shall be consistent with our faith. Oh, what a work, what a sacred work is before us. The parents need enlightenment, a divine touch, that they may understand their work in the home life, to send forth from the home sanctuary Christian children, morally trained and educated to let their light shine forth to the world. We need to understand in regard to the work to be carried forward in New Zealand. There need to be subdivisions of labor combined with harmony of aim and execution of the work which is to be set in operation.

Each one is to concentrate his energies on the portion of the wall he is required to build, that no labor may be lost, that there may be no jostling of the workers, no crossing one another's path on the part of the workers, and that the laborers together with God shall put forth consecrated tact to do their utmost without waste of means or energies, each individual rejoicing in the success of his fellow workers, with a full sense that they are cooperating to the advancement of the cause of truth under the generalship of Jesus Christ.

"For we are labourers together with God: ye are God's husbandry, ye are God's building" (1 Cor. 3:9), each strengthening the hands of the other. It is full time that our brethren and sisters made an advance move. We will meet every form of opposition. Every hindrance will be placed in the way of the work, for history will be repeated. It is not evidence that the enemies and opposers of the truth want. They have fierce hatred of the truth itself, for they cannot controvert it. There are organized and sleepless adversaries from without who are determined to stop the work of God, but let us move forward with well-concentrated effort amid all the discouragements. We must reach the people. The reproach cast upon God's messengers must be counteracted, and it will be.

I again urge you for the truth's sake, for Christ's sake, to come up to this meeting. Elder Olsen will be at the meeting and other helpers from America, and we want a heavenly sitting together in Christ Jesus, and a rich reward in blessing will come to the people. I leave these lines with you, and beg of you response. We want to see the salvation of God. There must be a waking up among believers. Each may be so imbued with the spirit of the work that he will be a Nehemiah, possessing holy energy and faith and hope, thus strengthening one another's hands, depending wholly on God, the great and mighty Worker.--Letter 8a, 1893. (Written October 31, 1893, at Gisborne, New Zealand.)

Bring Your Children to the Camp Meeting--Dear Sr. Brown and Household: We sincerely hope that you will not lose this opportunity of attending the meeting brought so near your own door. Come, mother and children, and

Sister Lounge. We want to enjoy this holy convocation with you. Bring all the children you can spare from the home place, for this meeting is that which you all need to strengthen and confirm your faith, and you want to hear the message which God has for you. Come and let us meet with God on this encampment. We are amid the perils of the last days, and you need to understand, every one, what you must do to be saved.

Be sure and bring the younger members of the family. You will never regret the expense or the trouble. It is seldom you will be favored, and perhaps never, with such an opportunity. May the Lord make you earnest and willing and glad to come up to this meeting. Come one and all, who can. You can and must come, Sister Brown. You need all the help and all the strength you can possibly gain to help you in your lifework.

God bless you and give you a heart to obey the prompting of His Holy Spirit is my earnest prayer.--Letter 74, 1893. (Written Nov. 28, 1893, at Wellington, New Zealand.)

The Camp Meeting Is a Success--Dear Bro. and Sister Smith: I send you in this envelope a letter written at odd times, as events occurred and purposing to copy it, but I send it as it is. With it I send a copy of a letter for a family with whom we labored most earnestly. Since coming to this meeting we are told that the husband has kept the two last Sabbaths. We thank the Lord for this. One of his sons was baptized the last Sabbath that we were in Gisborne. Still another son has taken his position since the father closed his shop on the Sabbath and one more son, fifteen years old, has decided to be a Christian. The father and mother and two daughters and three sons are in harmony in the truth. There is still another son, twenty-two years of age, at home who has not taken his stand. I shall address a letter to him sometime during this meeting.

Yesterday afternoon Elder Olsen arrived, looking well and feeling rested after his long trip on the water from Africa to New Zealand. You may be assured we were very much pleased to greet Elder Olsen. He spoke under the canvas meetinghouse last evening. All say they were much pleased and grateful to hear him. On Sunday, I had freedom in showing our colors on which were inscribed the commandments of God and the faith of Jesus. I told them that we were Seventh-day Adventists, and the reason of the name which distinguished us from other denominations. All listened with deepest interest. In the evening the tent was full and the grounds around the tent were full of people. They listened to a most solemn discourse from Elder Wilson. The camp meeting is a success. It is a marvel of wonders to Wellington. Meetings have been held for one week. This camp meeting will give character to our work, and do much to counteract the falsehoods that ministers have framed for others to repeat.

The camp looks nice. We have the reception tent furnished by Sister Tuxford as nice as we have in America. The tents are all new, some small and some large, made by the brethren in Australia. The weather has been beautiful, but today it rains. But the tents are nearly all erected. Some are coming whom they did not expect. The Lord is in the encampment. The Spirit of God is moving upon the hearts of believers and unbelievers. Visitors are pouring in to wonder over and admire the well-fitted-up tents which are to be the homes of those camping on the ground.

Well, I must close. I cannot write letters to America this week as I would be pleased to do. There are constantly arising matters which demand attention. Letters have to be written, and visiting has to be done, and much talking in meeting, much traveling, packing and unpacking beds and bedding, and I cannot tax my powers more than I have done. I must not get my mind in a worry, but keep it calm and peaceful. The Lord is helping and blessing me. I think of you and your family often, and do so hope every precious soul . . . will be united with the family who shall be prepared to see Jesus when He shall come.--Letter 75, 1893. (Written on Nov. 30, 1893, at Wellington, New Zealand.)

Reminiscences of the Wellington Camp Meeting--Dear Children: We are now on the deck of the Wairarapa, alongside the wharf. . . . Elder Olsen is to be shown now something of Auckland. We thought we would study economy. The same conveyance that will take us to ride will take us to the house of Edward Hare where we will be entertained, probably until we shall leave Auckland. We will have to leave Auckland harbor, I understand, Sabbath noon. We can hold meetings with the church this evening and tomorrow forenoon, then resume our position on the boat. The carriage takes us for our drive from the boat and saves us five shillings, going both trips in one. There are very fine drives about Auckland.

We were all just about used up when we came on board. Our meetings at Wellington were three weeks of solid labor, and I had spoken in Gisborne eleven times, in Napier once, and at Ormondville and Norsewood three times before this meeting in Wellington. We have not recovered from the strain yet. Elder Olsen was the main worker in Wellington. He was much liked by all who heard him. Dr. M. G. Kellogg was also much liked. He dwelt upon health questions and was a real help in the meetings.

I have told you how difficult it was to get any hearing in Wellington. The prejudice that has been created by false reports from the clergy has made congregations afraid of Seventh-day Adventists. An expensive effort was made to reach the people, but with little result. It was not thought it could be possible to have tent meetings and camp meetings in Wellington. The circus tried it with great loss. The winds are quite severe, coming up sometimes very, very tempestuous. Many of the circus tents were strung to ribbons soon after being pitched.

A very favorable place was secured, enclosed by a high fence, with a gate which was securely locked every night. This was a great protection from winds and from intruders. Nothing superfluous was arranged in the large tent. There were nature's own treasures of flowers and growing ferns --plenty of large choice bouquets. There was a reception tent, furnished by Sister Tuxford--mostly with her own furniture. She also furnished oilcloth for the floor. The book tent was in a portion of this tent. It was nicely prepared and very attractive. The tents were all newly made in Australia and transported to Wellington and are to be taken back for the Australian camp meeting.

We had much fear lest we would have a very slim attendance, but we were happily disappointed. From the first to the last there was a good appearance of congregation of the best class of our own people who fed on the bread of life during the meeting. Evenings there were good-sized congregations of outsiders. The camp meeting was such a marvel of wonders that everybody who could get to the campground came and visited it. All were delighted with the order and the thoroughly nice work which was manifested on the grounds.

The tents are floored and carpeted. Elder Israel's tent was a square, roomy tent. A section was reserved for my special benefit, then a center room was curtained off, then next there was a curtain beween Elder Israel's bedroom and the center room. Here I was perfectly at home. Besides this we rented two convenient rooms within two minutes' walk of the ground. We were well situated.

But the very best of all is that we have had good, large, respectful audiences and a very large number of people now understand what we do believe. The discourses have been close, plain, and thorough upon present truth, appropriate and applicable to our time. The people listened as if spellbound. The large tent had been spliced in the middle with new canvas, making the canvas to cover double the space of last year. The citizens were impressed with this meeting as nothing else could have transpired to impress them. When the winds blew strong there would be many looking with wonder to see every tent standing unharmed.

Brethren Wilson and Kellogg and your mother had the labor to perform the first week, but the Spirit of the Lord came into the meeting and hearts were moved. Outside attendance was excellent on Sunday and evenings. The most plain testimonies were borne from the first. I felt when speaking on Sabbath and Sunday afternoons that the trumpet must give no uncertain sound. I showed them plainly I had a message from the Lord that the Sabbath of the fourth commandment meant much to them and to us, in reference to the manner in which we treat it. To the obedient, it is a sign of their loyalty to God, not only for the Jews, but for all people, the whole posterity of Adam through all time.

At first the congregation could not be accommodated with seats, but plenty of seats were secured after the initial meetings and all seats were filled. Many were standing inside the tent and outside. Thus it has been evenings and Sundays. The third angel's message has been heard--proclaimed with a loud voice. Elder Wilson has done splendidly in his discourses and the people listened to the truth. It was the camp meeting which was a living notice to Wellington. One young man heard of the meeting by accident. He is about thirty years old. He has embraced the truth and has been baptized.

I think I wrote you about a family by the name of Brown whom I visited --a large family twenty miles from Wellington. I remained with them ten days and all who were at home pledged themselves to be Christians. One daughter has returned home. The mother, a very remarkable, pleasant woman, has been the mother of twenty children. Several are dead. She came the first part of the meeting. They rent a farm and the rent money comes quarterly, but for this once no rent money came in its season. I was very close in money matters, but I said, "This family, many of whom had never heard a discourse except from myself on that visit, should have the chance to attend this meeting. Well, the mother and three youngest members of the family came--Alex, sixteen years old, and the two girls, one fourteen and the youngest nine. I advanced two pounds for them to come to the meetings. These children remained with the mother, were baptized, and returned to their home and sent the older members--four grown daughters from seventeen years of age to thirty. These were all united with the Wellington church after their baptism. They have a church now at Long Point, Parramatta, numbering nine of their own household.

A very nice elderly lady has been living with them six years--a widow. She has a very nice house and a little farm, but rents it. She is a member of the State Church. She received the Sabbath and came to the meeting to be baptized. All were baptized and returned home happy in the truth. Twenty-two were baptized at this meeting.

I must stop writing for we now leave the boat.--Letter 121, 1893, pp. 1-4. (Written Dec. 15, 1893, at Auckland, New Zealand.)

White Estate
Washington, D. C.
April 28, 1981

ELLEN G. WHITE AND HER LAST FOUR BOOKS

I am thankful that I can remain at home for a time, where I can be close to my helpers. . . . I have been very fully employed in the preparation of matter for the Life of Paul. We are trying to bring out scriptural evidence of truth, and these, we believe, will be appreciated by our people.--Letter 4, 1911.

My workers are busy completing the work to be done on the new book, The Acts of the Apostles. This we expect to close up very shortly. . . . My workers are continually bringing in chapters for me to read; and I lay aside my other work to do this. . . . This morning I have already read several chapters on the Life of Paul.--Letter 60, 1911.

My work on the book The Acts of the Apostles is nearly completed.-- Letter 64, 1911.

My book The Acts of the Apostles has gone to the press. Soon it will be printed and ready for circulation.

I feel more thankful than I can express for the interest my workers have taken in the preparation of this book, that its truths might be presented in the clear and simple language which the Lord has charged me never to depart from in any of my writings.

The Lord has been good to me in sending me intelligent, understanding workers. I appreciate highly their interest, and the encouragement I have had in preparing this book for the people. I trust that it will have a large circulation. Our people need all the light that the Lord has been pleased to send, that they may be encouraged and strengthened for their labors in proclaiming the message of warning in these last days.--Letter 80, 1911.

There will be one more book--that dealing with the Old Testament history from the time of David to the time of Christ. The material for this book is written, and is on file, but is not yet put into shape. When this book is completed, I shall feel that my work is finished. Yet I can hold my pen as firmly today as I have done in years past.--Letter 4, 1912.

I must write you a short letter today. I have begun several letters to you, but have not succeeded in finishing any. I hope you will not cease to write to me, even though I do not write often. I am always interested in your work, and always glad to hear from you.

We are all very busy, doing our best to prepare the new book for publication. I want the light of truth to go to every place, that it may enlighten those who are now ignorant of the reasons for our faith.--Letter 28, 1912.

Just now, what strength I have is given mostly to bringing out in book form what I have written in past years on the Old Testament history from the time of Solomon to the time of Christ. Last year The Acts of the Apostles was put in print, and is being widely circulated; and now we are making good progress with this Old Testament history. We are advancing as fast as possible.

I have faithful and conscientious helpers, who are gathering together what I have written for the Review, Signs, and Watchman, and in manuscripts and letters, and arranging it in chapters for the book. Sometimes I examine several chapters in a day, and at other times I can read but little because my eyes become weary and I am dizzy. The chapters that I have been reading recently are very precious.--Letter 20, 1912.

I long to be personally engaged in earnest work in the field, and I should most assuredly be engaged in more public labor did I not believe that at my age it is not wise to presume on one's physical strength. I have a work to do in communicating to the church and to the world the light that has been entrusted to me from time to time all through the years during which the third angel's message has been proclaimed. . . .

During the past four years I have written comparatively few letters. What strength I have had has been given mostly to the completion of important book work.

Occasionally I have attended meetings, and have visited institutions in California, but the greater portion of the time since the last General Conference has been spent in manuscript work at my country home, "Elmshaven," near St. Helena.

I am thankful that the Lord is sparing my life to work a little longer on my books. Oh, that I had strength to do all that I see ought to be done! I pray that He may impart to me wisdom, that the truths our people so much need may be presented clearly and acceptably. I am encouraged to believe that God will enable me to do this.--Manuscript 4, 1913.

I have a company of faithful workers who are helping to prepare matter for the press. They are of good courage, and look on the bright side. We are doing our best to gather together the precious instruction that the people need.--Letter 9, 1913.

The past few months I have not done much letter writing; for I have wished to keep my strength for the reading of important matter in my book work. I have with me an excellent company of workers, men and women who are as true as steel to principle, and whose entire interests are bound up with this work. My faith has increased as I have tried to do my best to complete my writings.--Letter 11, 1913.

I am fairly well healthwise, not suffering much pain, but I realize that old age is reminding me that I am mortal. My book work is still taking my time, and I am trying to finish my work with joy and not with grief. I have not lost my courage.--Letter 13, 1913.

White Estate, Washington, D. C.
May 19, 1981

A CHARITABLE ATTITUDE TOWARD OTHERS

We shall have enough to praise God for in the future life. We shall thank God for every reproof which taught us our own weakness and our Saviour's power, patience, and love. Jesus' manner of working should be our manner.

I feel so grateful that the Lord is of tender pity, full of mercy. He deals not with us according to our sins, but is long-suffering. He sees our weakness. He knows our defects, our lack of faith and courage, and yet He bears with us still. The same divine sympathy, the same patient love, He shows to us who are so unworthy of His favors. I am not what I ought to be, or what Jesus would have me. I see that I must have more of the spirit of the Master.

I must not let one thought or one feeling arise in my heart against my brethren, for they may be in the sight of God more righteous than I. My feelings must not be stirred. We have battles to fight with ourselves, but we should continually encourage our brethren. We should lay no stumbling-blocks in their way and should cherish only the very kindest feelings toward them. Satan is willing and anxious to tear them down. Let us not unite our forces with his. They have their conflicts and trials. God forbid that we should add one trial to those they have to bear. . . .

Oh, I long for constant repose in God and not to have my mind in agitation in regard to minor matters. I constantly feel that my work upon the earth may not last long, and while it does last I want my thoughts and mind engaged in doing all I can to save perishing souls around me. I cannot and will not allow my mind to think unkindly of and misjudge my fellow laborers.

I will write out the testimonies of reproof for anyone and then my feelings shall not be exercised against them. I will look within. I will seek to make my ways in the strength of Jesus perfect before God. And when tempted to feel unkindly or to be suspicious and to find fault, I will put this out of my heart quickly, for the soul temple is surely being desecrated and defiled by Satan. The love that Jesus possessed, it is the duty of us both to welcome and cherish, and to have that charity that thinketh no evil; then our influence will be fragrant as sweet perfume.

The softening, subduing, refining, sanctifying influence of the Spirit of God must abide in us. If it is not there Christ is not enshrined in our hearts; for if He is abiding in us even our thoughts will be brought into captivity to Christ. The loins of the mind will be girded up.

I have been shown that unless we make most diligent work in purifying our own souls from all unkindness and bitterness, these traits will reveal themselves at times before we are aware of it, to do great harm to the cause we love. I have been shown that when we strictly heed the instructions God has given us in regard to cherishing pitying love, compassion, forgiveness, and kindness for others, and are forgetful of ourselves, we shall have a power of influence with our people such as no others can have. I was shown that it rests wholly with us whether we leave an influence behind us that is subduing, transforming and elevating --or to the contrary--whether we shall wound, injure, be dictatorial, overbearing, censuring, exalting and magnifying ourselves, and it be a relief to many who love and fear God when our voice shall be silent in the grave, our influence no longer felt.

I feel deeply, feel that we have erred in not manifesting greater love, forbearance, and pity for others. "The diseased have ye not strengthened" (Ezekiel 34:4), is the reproof given to unfaithful shepherds. Our feelings must not be a ruling power. We must walk in all humility of mind. The Lord loves His servants who are unselfishly engaged in the saving of souls. He will as readily guide them in judgment and teach them His will as He will teach us. We must believe that Jesus stands at the helm. He will be captain, and we may trust His own work in His all-powerful hands.

I know that God has conscientious, God-fearing men in the harvest field who will not spare themselves, who will, if required, sacrifice all for Jesus. Let us respect our brethren, give them credit for honesty of purpose and unselfish motives, as we wish they should do for us. We should treat all, rich and poor, high or lowly, exactly as we wish them to treat us. God is no respector of persons. The pure, those who are good and do good, are very near to Jesus. The disciple whom Jesus loved most was John, because he was the closest imitator of His character and was imbued with the spirit of love.

It was the joy of Christ's soul to do good to men. Many times He sighed in spirit and was very sorrowful. Many times His tears flowed, expressing His anguish of soul when He beheld the unbelief, the ingratitude, and felt the hatred of those He came to bless and save. Jesus in heaven looks with grief upon the insensibility of souls upon whom the richest of His favors have been poured without effect. He has made man, given him the wondrous faculties of the mind, the noble affections of the heart, and these gifts they use against the Giver. They despise obedience to Christ. Their ears are not inclined to hear His voice, their tongues speak not His praise. Oh, my soul is agonized at times that the hearts of even His professed followers who are daily receiving His mercies, should be empty of His praise.

Let us, dear husband, make melody to God in our hearts. Let us not be found accusers of our brethren, for this is the work Satan is engaged in. Let us talk of Jesus and His matchless love. I feel every day like deeply repenting before God for my hardness of heart, and because my life has not been more in accordance with the life of Christ. I weep over my own hardness of heart, my life which has not been a correct example to others. Let us bring ourselves into harmony with heaven and we will then be in harmony with our brethren and at peace among ourselves. Let us now, both of us, redeem the time.

Forgive me for any words of impatience that have escaped my lips, every seeming act of wrong in your sight. I mean to make straight paths for my feet and to have control over my own spirit, to keep my own heart in the love of God, and make sure work for eternity. Perils surround us; perplexities we must meet, and we cannot meet them aright unless we are fully consecrated to God and have self under the full control of His Spirit. May the Lord teach and lead and guide you is my prayer, and may nothing shake our hold on Him.--Letter 5, 1880, pp. 3-6. (Addressed to her husband, Elder James White, from Oakland, Calif. March 18, 1880.)

White Estate, Wash. D. C.
May 19, 1981

Manuscript Release #856

COUNSELS TO EDSON WHITE

You shall have all the means necessary for your tuition. But Edson, I hope you will not . . . let money, which is so important an item, slip through your hands without due and deliberate consideration. Live as plainly as we have taught and do not on any account become loose in regard to the principles of health reform. I need not tell you, Edson, that I have a thousand fears in regard to you. . . . Willie has been a great help to me. He is good and true, the best boy I ever knew.--Letter 4, 1866, pp. 1, 3. (To J. E. White, Sept. 22, 1866.)

I would say to you and your company [J. E. White and his helpers], as you go to your field of labor, go in the name of Jesus of Nazareth.--Letter 80, 1894, p. 7. (To J. E. White, Nov. 6, 1894.)

White Estate
Washington, D. C.
May 19, 1981

GOD'S WORD SUPPLIES SPIRITUAL POWER

The life of God, which gives life to the world, is in His word. It was by His word that Jesus healed disease and cast out demons. And by His word He stilled the sea and raised the dead: and the people bore witness that His word was with power. He spoke the word of God, as He had spoken it to all the prophets and teachers of the Old Testament. The whole Bible is a manifestation of Christ. It is our only source of power. Dc not rely upon any human agency for your wisdom. Take the Lord at His word, believing you do receive the things you ask of Him. [Matthew 28:18-28 quoted.]

As our physical life is sustained by food, so our spiritual life is sustained by the word of God. And every soul is to receive life from God's word for himself. As we must eat for ourselves in order to receive nourishment, so we must receive the word for ourselves. From the Scriptures there is the very instruction you need. "Search the Scriptures; for in them ye think ye have eternal life: and they are they which testify of Me" (John 5:39).

Yea, the word of God is the bread of life. Those who receive and assimilate this word, making it a part of every act, of every attribute of character, will grow strong in the strength of God. It gives immortal vigor to the soul, perfecting the experience, and bringing joys that will abide forever.--Letter 1, 1904, pp. 3-5. (To My Dear Brethren and Sisters, Dec. 31, 1903. Andrews University copy interlineations.)

White Estate, Washington, D.C.
May 30, 1981

ELLEN WHITE AND DOMESTICITY

I learn that Flora Merriam is dead. She was out at the camp meeting, but she now sleeps in Jesus. Her probation is ended. W. P. sickened and died suddenly. He professed to be a follower of Christ, but the attractions of the world ensnared him. When smitten by disease he was too sick to exercise his mind in repenting, and died, we fear, without expressing hope. Had he lived up to the light of health reform, he might not have died. I might relate several cases who have sickened and died suddenly without any time to prepare for their last change. I know not the facts in regard to Flora Merriam. She was an excellent girl--grave, sedate and retiring--more so than many who are older than she.--Letter 51a, 1874, p. 1. (To J. E. White and wife, Sept, 11, 1874.)

You are so fearful of incurring your husband's displeasure that you sin against God rather than to cross his will. You come far short of being a brave soldier for Jesus who gave His life for you. What greater love can be expressed for man than this? Jesus suffered for us. What are we willing to suffer for Him to save our souls from ruin? Your identity is submerged in your husband. His strong, imperious will, his overbearing and tyranny you stand in great dread of. You are aware he can make you very miserable and you dare not come into collision with him.

Great caution should be used by you that no strife shall be unnecessarily stirred up. And yet, when the question is raised between you in regard to the keeping of the Sabbath of the Lord, the turning point comes. Will you obey God or man? Whose authority and displeasure do you most fear? You are very much averse to discord and strife. You shrink from blame like the sensitive plant to the touch. You have allowed yourself to be placed in positions making it impossible to keep the Sabbath.--Letter 4a, 1880, p. 1. (To Sister Brigs, Feb. 8, 1880.)

Ever be true, open, sincere and frank. All affectation despise. Keep yourself aloof from young men. Let them know that there is one girl who will not be crazy and bewildered at their first notice and attentions. I want you to be prepared to travel with me and help me, if I want you.

You see those who have married cease their improvement and settle down to a dwarfed life. Be not afraid to tell me your whole mind and to seek counsel, and I will give you all the help I can. But above everything else preserve self-control, and a self-possession and womanly ways without appearing to know everything. Do not claim to know too much. Be modest in conversation, for people will be disgusted if a young girl talks as if she knew a great deal. You may evidence your wisdom by works, but do not do this by words and self-praise. Be cautious, discreet and humble.--Letter 28, 1885, p. 2. (To Addie Walling, Nov. 3, 1885.)

In the night season I am talking with ____ and once with Sister _____ cautioning her not to be too stiff, but to be sure and encourage tenderest sympathy and to bear in mind her own infirmities of body, and then put herself in the place where those are who are doing the work in the kitchen day after day, drudge, drudge, drudge, and encourage them and give them periods of rest. . . . There must be no rigid persistency to require more when the workers feel that they have done all they can safely do and preserve their health and patience.--Letter 130, 1893, p. 1. (To W. C. White, June 7, (1893.)

White Estate
Washington, D. C.
May 20, 1981

MISCELLANEOUS COUNSELS

[To A. T. Jones]--Dear brother, I am your friend, and I would stand in perfect harmony with you. I do not want those who have closed the door of their hearts to light to have any occasion to feel that they are right in criticizing you and Brother [E. J.] Waggoner and Brother [W. W.] Prescott. I have a great desire that you shall show Christlike wisdom in every move-ment.--Letter 35, 1895, p. 7. (To A. T. Jones, Nov. 21, 1895.)

[To S. N. Haskell]--I write a few lines to you this morning by lamp-light. Before receiving this, you will have met Professor Prescott. We would gladly have retained him in this country, but we dared not do this,for it would have savoured of selfishness. We hope he will do the brethren much good in South Africa, and that he will be received cordially, in brotherly love. He has the truth in the heart, as well as on the lips. God is with him, and will work by him if our brethren will receive him as one who bears to them a message from God. May it not be true of them, as of the people of Nazareth, that Jesus could not do many mighty works because of their un-belief. There is no virtue in refusing to receive the light which God shall send, and we need every ray of light from heaven. We should appreciate the love of God, who sends the light, and should accept the light joyfully.

Many need to learn that it is one thing to assent to truth, and another thing to receive the truth as the bread of God, of which, if a man eat, he shall live forever. Day by day we must feed upon the Living Bread that we may receive spiritual sustenance, as we partake of temporal food to give us physical strength. What is the Bread of Life? Jesus said, "Whoso eateth My flesh, and drinketh My blood, hath eternal life; and I will raise him up at the last day. For My flesh is meat indeed, and My blood is drink indeed. He that eateth My flesh, and drinketh My blood, dwelleth in Me, and I in him" (John 6:54-56). He does not leave us to misunderstand Him. He says, "It is the spirit that quickeneth, the flesh profiteth nothing: the words that I speak unto you, they are spirit, and they are life" (verse 63). The words of Christ are to be received with no half hearted, weak, hesitating faith. The Word gives light and assurance to all who educate their souls to believe. The heart needs the presence of the heavenly Guest--Christ abiding in the soul. We are to dwell in Christ, and Christ is to dwell in us by faith.

The largest promise that Christ could give to His disciples when He left them was the promise of the Holy Spirit. He was in search of the strongest consolation He could leave them, to do them good after His departure. Of all the subjects that were of the most importance to them, He chose that of the Holy Spirit. And what did He predict concerning the Spirit? "He shall teach you all things, and bring all things to your remembrance, whatsoever I have said unto you" (John 14:26). Truths been buried beneath the rubbish of misinterpretation--the maxims of men, the sayings of finite beings that had been exalted as being of more consequence than the word of the living God.

In our day the church has been to a great degree content with the surface truths of revelation, made so plain and easy to be understood that many
have thought these supplied all that was essential, and in accepting them
they have been content. But the Holy Spirit, working upon the mind, will
not allow it to rest in indolence. He awakens an earnest desire for truth
uncorrupted with error and false doctrines. Celestial truth will reward the
diligent seeker. The mind that is really desirous to know what is truth
cannot be content in indolence.

The kingdom of heaven is likened to treasure hid in a field, "the which
when a man hath found, he hideth, and for joy thereof goeth and selleth all
that he hath, and buyeth that field" (Matthew 13:44). He buys it that he
may work it, plow up every part of it, and take possession of its treasures.
It is the Holy Spirit's office to direct this search and to reward it. The
searcher, while digging the field, finds leads of precious ore of which he
seeks to estimate the value, and he sinks the shaft deeper for still more
valuable treasure. Thus many a rich lode is discovered. The gold fields of
the earth are not so interlaced with veins of precious ore as is the field
of revelation with leads that bring to view the unsearchable riches of
Christ.

The Lord would have every one of His believing children rich in faith;
and this is the fruit of the working of the Holy Spirit upon the heart. From
the heart the Spirit works outward, developing a character that God will approve. What a vast field of the treasures of truth did Christ add to the
domain of faith to be appropriated by His disciples! We need greater faith
if we would have better knowledge of the Word. The greatest hindrance to

our receiving the divine illumination is that we do not depend on the efficiency of the Holy Spirit. The Spirit is freely given us of God if we will
appreciate and accept it.   And what is it?--the representative of Jesus
Christ.   It is to be our constant helper.   It is through the Spirit that
Christ fulfills the promise. "I will never leave thee nor forsake thee."
"Verily, verily, I say unto you, He that believeth on me hath everlasting
life" (John 6:47). (The bell is sounding for morning worship. I must stop
here.)--Letter 38, 1896, pp. 1-4. (To S. N. Haskell, May 30, 1896.)

White Estate
Washington, D.C.
May 21, 1981

SPIRITUAL LESSONS FROM FARMING AND BUILDING

"Ye are God's husbandry." Will the students apply this lesson while they are working upon the land, tilling the soil, plowing and harrowing, putting all the skill they possess into the work of bringing the land into a condition where it will be fit for the planting of the seed, and the trees, preparatory for the harvest? Will they bear in mind that they are God's husbandry, a part of the Lord's farm, and that in this term of school there is a great deal of work to be done by those who are appointed to watch for souls as they that must give an account? There are hearts that need much more labor bestowed upon them because the soil has not been under the plow or the harrow. The hardened soil must be broken up and subdued, so that the Word of God, the gospel seed, may find favorable soil for the production of a harvest.

Let the students call all their faculties of discernment to bear upon this subject. Let their skills interpret the figures used. The earth has to be worked to bring out its varied properties favorable to the growth of the seed and fruit. But the harvest will reward the painstaking efforts made in a supply of food for the necessities of man. . . .

There must be an intelligent, harmonious cooperation of the divine and human. The working of the soil is a lesson book, which if read will be of the greatest benefit to every student in our school. They may understand that surface work, haphazard half-effort, will reveal itself in the harvest to be garnered. . . .

-37-

Preparations have been made to build a house for God. The word has come, "Arise and build a house for the Lord." The workmen have taken hold nobly and the angels of God, we testify, have been in their midst. This is the work the Lord would have done in Cooranbong, and let not one in our school work become discouraged.

This is a lesson to be applied to our spiritual building of character with solid timbers. The very best kind of timber was secured for the building of our church. We did not stint in measurement, for we wanted the presence of the people who needed to assemble to worship God, and we wanted the heavenly angels and Jesus Christ in our midst. Let us apply the figure, "Ye are God's building"--a temple prepared to be a home where God shall preside, a home where God's attributes shall be constantly shining forth in our characters, showing that we are living with God's presence. The inner sanctuary of the soul is consecrated to God and we are to keep the soul dedicated, cleansed, purified for the sacred repository of truth. . . .

We need to consider carefully our own spiritual interest. If we are abiding in Christ we shall not allow ambitious business transactions, even in our service for Him, to come before the spiritual fragrance that should characterize our association with our brethren, so that the crude elements in our characters shall break forth into action. In all the mechanical business our hands and minds shall undertake, let us be sure that we represent Christ's kindness, His long forbearance, His compassion, His goodness and love.

We cannot afford to become too absorbed in our business transactions, even in doing service to God. We must strive prayerfully to hold in check our overambition in any enterprise, lest we run ahead of Jesus and meet obstacles that test and provoke us. If we will walk in the companionship of Christ, He will prepare the way for us, for His righteousness goeth before us, and the glory of the Lord shall be our rereward. We are to follow where Christ leads the way. He makes no crooked paths for our feet to travel.

We are dishonoring the Lord Jesus if we claim to be following Him and then are in altogether too great a hurry to take time to pray, "Lead me, my Saviour, by Thy Spirit. Imbue me with Thy Holy Spirit that I may be pleasant in all my words, cheerful and thankful day by day, testifying that Thou leadest me."

As we listen to words of instruction that fell from His lips when He was instructing His disciples, we are to appropriate these words as if spoken directly to us, and He will purify us from vain ambition that has a desire to please and glorify self. Our individual selves must not get in the way. The Lord Jesus will purify our motives if we will let Him do this by working out our own salvation with fear and with trembling.--Manuscript 182, 1897, pp. 1-4. ("Ye Are God's Husbandry," Sept. 24, 1897.)

White Estate
Washington, D. C.
May 21, 1981

COUNSELS TO FREDERICK GRIGGS

The Need to Become Christlike--I was much pleased to receive a letter from you yesterday. I thank the Lord that He has enlightened you by His Holy Spirit, and I beg of you to walk circumspectly. The reason there is so great a dearth of means in Battle Creek at the present time is that the root of selfishness has been so long cherished that it has become a prevailing power to tarnish and corrupt the soul. There are occasional revivals, when the sword of truth, cutting both ways, cuts off the top of the plant of selfishness, but it is not taken out by the roots, and when anything is favorable for its growth, it springs up and flourishes, and thereby many are defiled.

This is the great evil which proves a curse to individuals, to families, to all our institutions, and to the church. We need not merely to talk about the Holy Spirit, but to open the door of our hearts and let Him come in. Then there will be a molding and fashioning of the character. Prayers are offered in the family circle, in the church, in the publishing house, and in our educational institutions, for the Lord to guide and direct, but when temptations come, the root of selfishness springs up, and the precious talents of reason and voice are placed on the enemy's side. . . .

The Lord has a controversy with parents, because they have permitted their children to follow their own pernicious ways, by which the way of truth is evil spoken of. Education should be commanded in the home at the dawn of reason, and is to be carried forward in the fear and love of God. The reason that children do not become godly is because they are allowed too much freedom. Their will and inclination is indulged. Parental neglect in restraining children is the cause of so much evil in the world today. Oh, what sad things the judgment will reveal. Many prodigal sons become such because of indulgence in the home, because their parents have not been doers of the Word. The mind and purpose are to be sustained by firm, undeviating, sanctified principles. Consistency and affection are to be enforced by a lovely and consistent example.

The Lord is watching the course of action of every youth and parent. Human nature is to be educated, disciplined, and characters are to become changed, elevated, ennobled, Christlike. The youth must be educated to respect themselves because they are bought with a price. . . .

We are to teach the youth to value themselves. We owe God obedience to the specifications of the moral law. We are to love God supremely and our neighbor as ourselves. The work must be wrought in God. This will impress the children who manifest opposition, stubborn unbelief, and a sullen will. Let cheerfulness, hope, and happiness be seen in the deportment of teachers. Try to please the students, but do not indulge them.--Letter 117, 1898, pp. 1, 4, 5. (To Frederick Griggs, Dec. 1, 1898.)

SDA Institutions Should Scatter Out, Not Centralize--I have received your letter of August 18. Yesterday I sent you a telegram, in which I told you to publish in the Review and Herald the article you have written regarding the reopening of the Battle Creek College. I felt that I could not but consent to the publication of this article. The light given me by the Lord --that our youth should not collect in Battle Creek to receive their education--has in no particular been changed. The fact that the sanitarium has been rebuilt in Battle Creek does not change the light. All that in the past made Battle Creek a place unsuitable for our youth exists today so far as influence is concerned.

Word has come to me that letters have been sent out to our churches in the different States offering our youth special inducements to connect with the Battle Creek Sanitarium. The leading men in our conferences are requested to send their most promising young men and young women to the Battle Creek Sanitarium to be educated and trained as nurses. This is an effort to counterwork the counsel of the Lord. Those who present these inducements are walking contrary to the will of the Lord.

Had the sanitarium been re-established in accordance with the Lord's design, it would not now be in Battle Creek. The Lord permitted the sanitarium to be destroyed by fire, to take away the objection raised to moving out of Battle Creek. It was His design, not that one large building should be erected, but that plants should be made in several places. These smaller sanitariums were to be established where they could have the benefit and advantage of land for agricultural purposes. It is God's plan that agriculture shall be carried on in connection with our sanitariums and schools. Our youth need the education to be gained from this line of work. It is well, and more than well--it is essential--that efforts be made to carry out the Lord's plan in this respect.

When the call came to move out of Battle Creek, the plea was made, "We are here, and all settled. It would be an impossibility to move without enormous expense."

The Lord permitted fire to consume the sanitarium building, and thus removed the greatest objection to fulfilling His purpose. Then a large building, different in design, but capable of accommodating as many patients, was erected on the same site as the old building. Since the opening of this institution a very large number of people have come to it. Some of these are patients, but some are merely tourists. But the large number at the sanitarium is no evidence that it is the will of God that such a condition of things should be. Our sanitariums were not designed to be boarding places for rich people of the world.

The care of the large number of guests at the sanitarium requires a large number of youth, and those in charge of our churches are asked to send in to our sanitarium the names of the most promising young men and young women in the church, that these youth may be communicated with by the manager of the sanitarium and invited to come to the sanitarium to take the nurses' course.

I would say, Be careful what moves are made. It is not God's design that our youth should be called to Battle Creek. Calling them to this place and associating them with worldly people of all grades, high and low, is like Lot taking his family into Sodom.

The Lord said, It is for the interest of our youth to be educated in some place other than Battle Creek. He declared it to be His will for the Battle Creek College to be removed to some place in the country.

At this time there was a heavy burden of debt on our schools. I prayed that some way might be opened whereby these debts could be lifted. Christ heard my prayers, and the prayers of many others, and a way was opened. I was instructed to give the manuscript of the book <u>Christ's Object Lessons</u> to our schools. Our publishing houses were to share in the gift by giving the work of printing and binding the book, and our people were to sell it and give their time.

The Lord has blessed the effort put forth to relieve our schools from debt, and I am told that three hundred thousand dollars have been raised toward lifting the debt. While engaged in selling <u>Christ's Object Lessons,</u> students and church members have obtained an excellent experience. As they have taken up this work disinterestedly, great blessing has come to them. Many have gained a knowledge of how to handle our large books. The Lord Himself has cooperated in this work.

It was about the time the light was given regarding <u>Christ's Object Lessons</u> that the Lord instructed me that the college in Battle Creek should be removed from that place and established in some other place. There were too many interests in Battle Creek. Smaller schools were to be established in different places away from the cities.

The establishment of the school at Berrien Springs had the commendation of God. Those in charge of the school at that place have much to encourage them.

Shall we now let the enemy manage for us? Because the sanitarium is where it should not be, shall the word of the Lord be of no account? Shall we allow the most intelligent of our youth in the churches throughout our conferences to be called to Battle Creek, to become servants to worldlings, to be spoiled and robbed of their simplicity by being brought in contact with men and women of all grades of society--men and women who have not the fear of God in their hearts? Such men and women will come in large numbers to the Battle Creek Sanitarium, and a large number of helpers will be needed. Shall those in charge of our conferences allow our youth, who in the schools away from Battle Creek could be fitted up for the Lord's work, to be drawn to Battle Creek, when for many years the Lord has been calling upon His people to move away from Battle Creek?

Human minds may not see the necessity for the call to families to leave Battle Creek and settle in places where they can do medical-missionary work. But the Lord has spoken. Shall we question His word?

Our youth are to be prepared to take charge of church schools in which the children in our churches will be taught the first principles of education. This is a very nice work, demanding the highest ability and the most careful study. Our young men and young women should be preparing to advance this line of work. Then shall we allow our most promising youth to be called into a work that is not fulfilling the specifications of God? . . .

I am instructed to say to those professing to be medical-missionary workers: Remember that the Lord has a very large vineyard which He designs shall be cultivated. He saw that the Battle Creek Sanitarium was too large. The work was not being accomplished by physicians that God desired should be accomplished. There was not seen that unselfish purity of principle that marks true medical-missionary work. Many things were done, many plans were made, by which the law of God was not honored. Plans were carried out, and

-45-

passed as medical-missionary work that God refused to acknowledge--plans that greatly dishonored God.

The truth of God is to regulate the life. But this it cannot do if left in the outer court. An occasional Christianity, an occasional generosity, an occasional doing of good deeds, is not the Christianity that will accomplish the work for which God calls. Truth planted in the heart brings man into harmony with God.

Letters of inquiry are coming to us asking, "Has Sister White changed? Does she now favor the re-establishment of a college in Battle Creek?" In the past I have given the word of the Lord in regard to the removal of the school from Battle Creek, and I have not changed. If anyone is determined to place himself in a position where he counterworks the work of God, we are to leave that one with the Lord. I am to have no controversy with him. But such a man must not be allowed to call the most promising young people away from positions that they can fill in the Lord's work, to a place from which the Lord has declared that His people are to move.

In connection with every one of our sanitariums there is to be provision for the training of the youth as medical missionaries so that our young men and women need not go to Battle Creek to receive an education in these lines. It is the intelligent and promising youth who are called for, to come to Battle Creek, and these are the very ones that are needed in other places, in our schools, in our sanitariums. These young men and young women will be needed to do the work that must be done in different parts of the Lord's vineyard. There are many lines of work to be carried forward, and many laborers are needed. We need one hundred laborers where now there is but one. Our forces are not to be centered in one place. They are to be scattered throughout the field. Plants are to be made in all parts of the Lord's vineyard. We protest, in the name of the Lord God of Israel, against the calling of our youth into a place to which the Lord has declared they should not go.--Letter 189, 1903, pp. 1-4, 7, 8. (To Frederick Griggs, August 26, 1903.)

White Estate
Washington, D. C.
May 28, 1981

A. F. BALLENGER AND THE SOUTHERN WORK

The plan of teaching agriculture to the colored people is a good one. . . . If you can secure a man who is fitted to become an intelligent director, such a school as you propose would be a great blessing to the colored race. . . . I shall be glad if by your counsel you can set in operation a work that needs to be done.

But to take hold of this work yourself would not be wise. You have not the necessary qualifications for a business man. You are not adapted for financiering. . . . To take an evangelist out of the field in order to bear the responsibility you speak of would not be wise. You would not be a success. . . .

Your work is appointed you by God. Ministry as an evangelist is your calling, and in no case should you trifle with your moral responsibilities. --Letter 90, 1899, p. 6, Andrews University copy. (To A. F. Ballenger, June 6, 1899.)

White Estate
Washington, D. C.
May 28, 1981

CHRISTIAN UNITY

God's chosen ones are to reveal to the world their union one with another. It is not possible for a few to walk to heaven alone because they can agree with no others. God's people are a unit. If some entertain ideas so peculiar that God's people cannot accept them, they should compare notes in a teachable spirit and be willing to learn. They should make the most strenuous efforts to be one, to come into the unity of the faith in the bonds of peace. [James 2:12-18 quoted.]

The Lord has called us to unity in the bonds of Christ and fellowship and love. In His prayer for His disciples, Christ said: [John 17:20-23 quoted.]

We see that which the Lord requires of us. Shall we not put our pride and our dignity where it shall not be so easily bruised and wounded? Shall we not lay it all at the feet of Christ? Shall we not allow our minds to be sharpened by the Holy Spirit, that we may not act like children in our association with one another, but as Christ's brave soldiers, going without the camp and bearing the reproach for His sake? "A new commandment I give unto you," Christ says, "That ye love one another; as I have loved you, that ye also love one another. By this shall all men know that ye are My disciples, if ye have love one to another" (John 13:34, 35). Shall we not, at the beginning of the year 1897, covenant with God that we will not be like the children of the wicked one, pettish, envious, jealous, and full of evil surmisings, but like the tree that is known by its good fruit? Then by our unity and love for one another all men will understand that we are Christians. Shall we not cherish love, rather than strife and malice and hatred? [John 15:7-14 and Ephesians 2:1-8 quoted.]

No provision has been made for Christians to draw apart from each other. By our unity and love we are to reveal the character of Christ. "Be ye therefore followers of God, as dear children; And walk in love, as Christ also hath loved us, and hath given Himself for us an offering and a sacrifice to God for a sweet-smelling savour" (Ephesians 5:1,2). There is a class named in this chapter that we are not to associate with. If we cannot lift them up, they will pull us down. We know the will of God. Shall we not practice His word? Shall we not love each other as brethren? [Colossians 3:12-17 quoted.]

The Word of God clearly points out our duty. We are to cultivate kindness and forbearance and love. We are to represent Christ in character. Evil speaking, accusing, and faultfinding, misrepresenting our brethren because our own individual ideas are not considered as of the highest value, can find no place in a Christian's life. By our conduct we show what our influence and the principles we hold are worth. If self is our center, self will be seen in all we do. If Christ is our center, we shall bear His likeness. [1 Thessalonians 5:9-15 quoted.]

Are we striving most earnestly to obey these words? Shall we not eat and practice them? Shall we not draw nigh to God, fearing to sin against Him by being unjust to our brethren? Then we shall fear to offend His children. We will not wound or bruise His heritage. If we hope in His mercy for sinners, we shall manifest the most tender interest for all for whom

Christ has died.   We shall not, because our ideas are not exalted and honored as we think they should be, handle the reputation of our brethren in a way that offends God, who loves them as He loves us, and who takes as much pleasure in them as He does in us.--Manuscript 157, 1897, pp. 3-7. ("Make Straight Paths for Your Feet," no date.)

White Estate
Washington, D. C.
May 28, 1981

FREQUENT REVIEW OF INSTITUTIONAL ACCOUNTS

In the case of church schools, men of financial wisdom should look over the accounts once, twice, or thrice a year, to ascertain the true standing of the school, and see that enormous expenses do not pile up.--Letter 166, 1899, p. 2. (To G. A. Irwin, Oct. 24, 1899.)

The light was given me eighteen years ago [1881] that there would be great losses because there was so little close, thorough instruction given to students in bookkeeping, keeping accounts. The Lord would have nothing go at haphazard, and the result show, as today, mountains of debt and no way to get out of them. If the advice had been followed that the Lord has given, to have bookkeeping taught and practiced, there would be at this time men of wisdom that could stand in the position to go from place to place, review all account books, and then instruct in the school, interest the scholars, and make this a portion of the students' lessons.-- Letter 166a, 1899, p. 1. (To G. A. Irwin, Oct. 24, 1899.)

White Estate
Washington, D. C.
May 28, 1981

ELLEN WHITE IN AUSTRALIA

On Sunday, Brother Lawrence took us in the trap* and we drove over a good share of the school ground. In some places, the roads were very rough, but I kept thinking, let the cart jolt, it is a change of exercise, it will do me good. I enjoyed the trip, and we were out roughing it nearly all day. We came home just at dark.--Letter 14, 1894, p. 2. (To Marian Davis, August 27, 1894.)

_____
*A horse-drawn conveyance.

White Estate
Washington, D. C.
May 29, 1981

CHRIST'S WORK IN THE SANCTUARY

Christ's Work in the Holy and the Most Holy Places--Then he [Moses] was carried down to the period of time when a view of the heavenly sanctuary should be given to God's people; when the veil would be parted, and by faith they would enter within the Holy of Holies. Moses knew something about the sanctuary in heaven. He understood the sacred ministrations connected with the holy place and the Most Holy. The significance of the typical service in the earthly sanctuary was made light and clear by the reflection of the Sun of Righteousness upon the types and symbols.

When Christ, the Mediator, burst the bands of the tomb, and ascended on high to minister for man, He first entered the holy place, where, by virtue of His own sacrifice, He made an offering for the sins of men. With inter-cession and pleadings He presented before God the prayers and repentance and faith of His people, purified by the incense of His own merits. He next entered the Most Holy Place, to make an atonement for the sins of the people, and cleanse the sanctuary. His work as high priest completes the divine plan of redemption by making the final atonement for sin.--Ms. 69, 1912, p. 13. ("The Sin and Death of Moses," copied Sept. 10, 1912.)

Cleansing the Heavenly Sanctuary and the Soul-Temple--Godliness, sobri-ety, and consistency will characterize the life and example of every true Christian. The work which Christ is doing in the sanctuary above will

engage the thoughts and be the burden of the conversation, because by faith
he has entered into the sanctuary. He is on earth, but his sympathies are
in harmony with the work that Christ is doing in heaven. Christ is cleansing the heavenly sanctuary from the sins of the people, and it is the work
of all who are laborers together with God to be cleansing the sanctuary of
the soul from everything that is offensive to Him. Everything like evil
surmising, envy, jealousy, enmity, and hatred, will be put away, for such
things grieve the Holy Spirit of God and put Christ to an open shame. Love
of self will not exist, nor will any engaged in this work be puffed up. The
example of Christ's life, the consistency of his character, will make his
influence far-reaching. He will be a living epistle, known and read of all
men.--Ms. 15, 1886, pp. 2, 3. ("Christian Integrity in the Ministry," n.d.)

White Estate
Washington, D. C.
July 9, 1981

Manuscript Release #868

WESTERN TRANSPORTATION IN THE TIMES OF ELLEN WHITE

Cheyenne, Wyoming, August 21, 1878--We are now in the hotel waiting the overland train from California. It is rather warm. We have had no sleep of any account yet. I left one package of "Sunshine Series" for that gentleman who attended to the sprained ankle. The package of hominy is in father's room on the shelf. We feel that we will get through all right. I feel that I am in the way of my duty, although I am very tired, and long for rest. The train comes to take us at half-past three. I hope you will all go over to the park and have a pleasant camping trip. You may never have as good a time again to make this trip.--Letter 45, 1878, p. 1. (Post card to Ellen White's family, who were vacationing at Rollinsville, Colorado.)

Council Bluffs, Iowa, August 22, 1878--We have made the change all right. Glad you were not on board today; hot, almost unendurable. We have a lower berth in drawing-room car. Well situated. Three dollars to Chicago. Cheap enough, I think. I am glad that so many of you are in the cool mountains. Stay there as long as you can. I think Emma would be rather oppressed with her woolen dress. I am glad she is not on board this train. The heat would wilt and exhaust her. At one time today it seemed as though I should faint away, but a cool breeze sprang up and we feel better. I think I am in the way of duty. It is fearfully oppressive, yet God will sustain.--Letter 45, 1878, pp. 1,2. (Post card to James White.)

Chicago (?), October 23, 1878--We left Battle Creek Wednesday, October 23. Found Brother Armstrong waiting for us. Took a streetcar after walking a quarter of a mile with our baggage. We rode about five miles to the home of Brother Armstrong. We found a cheerful fire in the sitting room. This was our sleeping room. After social conversation we had a season of prayer and retired feeling we were blessed indeed.--Ms. 5, 1878, p. 1. (Diary entry.)

Chicago, October 24, 1878--Thursday morning. Rested well through the night. Awakened with feelings of gratitude for the favors received and the blessings of God with which He has abundantly supplied us. My heart goes out to God in prayer for His guidance and His grace.

We met Elder Butler and Elder Andrews' mother in the Chicago depot. Elder Butler was on his way to Battle Creek. He assisted us in re-checking baggage and in moving baggage to sleeping car. Brother Armstrong's daughter was very attentive, accompanying us to depot and interesting herself in our being properly arranged in the car.--Ms. 5, 1878, p. 1. (Diary entry.)

Between Chicago and Richland, Kansas, October 25, 1878--On the cars. Rested well last night. We had our window open and gave our lungs food. The cars were very hot, and no ventilation was allowed from the ventilator above. This morning there is a great complaint of faintness and lanquor when no effort is made to give us fresh air. There are thirty who have passed the night in a closed car. Emanations from the bodies and exhalations from the lungs have poisoned the air, yet no windows except mine have been raised to let in the rich blessing heaven has provided in fresh, pure air. Must the health and life of travelers be imperiled by being left to the control of ignorant porters and one or two sick passengers? We will have air from outside. We will not endanger health and life because of the ignorance of porters.

We changed cars at Kansas City. The porter put us in the wrong car and we were obliged to pay six dollars for our passage over the road. When we arrived at Topeka we met Brother Miller, a stranger to us, but he had a printed notice pinned upon his coat--"Camp Meeting." We made ourselves acquainted and were soon preparing to step on board his carriage. In my great weariness and hurry I left my velvet sacque. The depot was crowded and I overlooked it. I did not discover my loss until we had gone about five miles. At first I was much troubled but I fought with my feelings until I had them under control and the conflict was ended and peace took the place of regret and unhappiness.

We rode twelve miles over the broad prairie. It was keen cold. We became thoroughly chilled, for we had not even a laprobe or buffalo robe to cover our feet and limbs. When we arrived on the ground [at Richland, Kansas] we found a small board tent made for us, furnished with bed, table, and stove, and having floor with carpet on it. We were made very comfortable. We felt thankful in our hearts to our dear friends for this thoughtful care and tenderness of us. A crock was brought with a very fine chrysanthemum in full bloom. We rested and slept well that night.--Ms. 5, 1878, pp. 1, 2. (Diary entry.)

Crossing the Red River, Texas, April 30, 1879--We left Denison April 25. Encamped two miles out of Denison, waiting for the ferry to be in a condition to cross. We remained until April 30 in a waiting position, for the sick to be able to travel and the ferry so that we could cross. We then started on our way with eight covered wagons and one covered spring wagon with two seats. Thirty composed our party.

About noon we crossed the ferry with special instructions to drive quickly as soon as off the boat because of danger through quicksands. We were all safely landed on the other side of Red River except Will Cornell, who did not come up in time. Moore and Farnsworth teams waited for them while our hack and three wagons went into camp some five miles on upon the open prairie.

We had a severe tempest strike us soon after our tent was pitched. My husband was trying to hold on the tent. It was a most serious downpour, and the tent not trenched. I think we will learn something on this journey--to trench the tent as soon as it is staked.--Ms. 4, 1879, p. 1. (Diary entry.)

In Oklahoma (Indian) Territory, Thursday, May 1, 1879--At noon we camped in a woods. It was not very pleasant. At night we did not reach any good camping ground and were obliged to stop by the bank of a river in a low spot of ground.

It seemed very lonesome journeying in the thick forest. We thought what might be if robbers or horse thieves--Indians or white men--should molest us, but we had a vigilant watch guarding the animals. We found ourselves in a better condition than we feared.--Ms. 4, 1879, pp. 1, 2. (Diary entry.)

Friday, May 2, 1879--After taking breakfast we were all hustling and hurrying, picking up, ready for another move. We crossed Blue Creek all safely.

Friday night we camped near Johnson's ranch. Here we found plenty of grass for horses, and at the farmhouse, good milk, butter, and eggs. We were having our first experience of overland journeying in transporting our sick and those too poor to pay car expenses, but the Lord cared for us.-- Ms. 4, 1879, p. 2. (Diary entry.)

In Eastern Kansas, May 19, 1879--We had some trouble last night finding a camping ground. We had to accept a poor spot, at least one mile from Humboldt. Our tent was no sooner arranged, staked, and thoroughly ditched-- as I determined it should be--than the storm struck us. It was a marked display of the power of God. The sun was shining in a portion of the sky and it was amber in the west. The other portions of the sky were black and threatening. The rain was pouring in torrents. Our tent proved a most welcome shelter.

We attempted to find a place in a hotel in Humboldt where we could be free from tempest and storm. We were shown our room--a small, very small, room with two beds in it. The air was close and stifling. We decided to take our chance in the tent and endure the storm rather than the close, stifling air of a small, ill-ventilated room. We returned through the storm to our tent. The wind blew fearfully. We feared the tent would not stand the tempest. As we rode through the town the air seemed to enclose us. It was hot, even while it was thundering, lightning was flashing, and rain at times pouring down. Our carriage had to be made a bedroom for some of our party, but there was no complaint. Last night our party of women washed their clothes in the trenches we had made.

It is a beautiful morning. The sun is shining and all in camp are astir for breakfast, while some are packing the wagons for another move.

We are on the way again, slowly making our way over the broad prairies of Kansas. At nine o'clock we turned out to let the horses feed on grass.

At noon we all drew up upon the broad prairie to take our dinner, within six miles of Neosho. Teams are now being prepared for another move, while Mary and I, Adelia and Etta, are gathering up, washing the dishes, and putting the food in baskets. The order comes, "Move on." In one hour and a half we shall be at Brother Glover's.

When within two miles of Brother Glover's, we sent forward Elder Corliss to learn the situation and inform Brother Glover of our coming. He returned with the information that many had not received the news of the change of appointment and had come on the ground. The meeting was in session and Brethren Glover and Ayers had moved on, journeying to the camp meeting. We decided to take the train for Emporia. We had three quarters of an hour to make the change. We took our two trunks, and without opportunity to change our apparel, we slept on board the train.

We arrived at Emporia about seven o'clock. We engaged an omnibus to take us to the campground, about two miles. Four powerful horses were put before the bus and we were carried speedily to camp. All seemed glad to meet us. We pitched our tent and one and another brought us a piece of bedding, so we had a passably comfortable bed.--Ms. 4, 1879, pp. 4, 5. (Diary entry.)

Swan Lake, Dakota Territory, July 17, 1879--It seemed to be duty to attend the first camp meeting held in Dakota. The conference has been organized and we hope good as been accomplished. Last Tuesday we rode in a hired carriage twenty-one miles to meet the cars at Beloit, Iowa. When we learned that there had been a bad slide and we could not take the cars before one or two days--and it may be a week before we can go on our way to Colorado--we hired a man to take his team and bring us twenty-eight miles to

Sister Anner's, where we are at the present time.--Letter 32, 1879, p. 1. (To Brother and Sister A. G. Daniells*.)

Near Cheyenne, Wyoming, February 26, 1880--Rested a portion of the night. Coal gas from the coal stove came into the car, affecting my lungs and heart. Have written two pages foolscap to send back to Battle Creek for Volume IV. Sent four pages to Mary Clough. We are having a hailstorm. It is now two. We entered Cheyenne quarter past one.

Passed Cheyenne about three o'clock. It is snowing and hailing. I feel like breathing out my heart's desire for the protecting care of God on this journey. When I think that this is the fifteenth time we have passed over this road without accident or harm, I feel grateful to God and trust Him still. He will be our guide and guard on this journey. My heart is grateful, very grateful, for the assurance I have of the presence of God. I love Him; I trust Him; I will praise Him.--Ms. 7, 1880, p. 1. (Diary entry.)

Arriving in California, Sunday, February 29, 1880--We had a beautiful sunrise. The sky was broadly striped with crimson, gold, and silver. What a picture of loveliness painted for us by the great Master Artist! Instinctively my heart was filled with gratitude to God. His wondrous love to fallen man, in giving His Son to shame, reproach, insult, mocking, and an ignominious death, seemed so deep, so rich, so broad, my heart throbbed with glad joy that I was privileged to be a child of God. In the night I found dear Mary resting upon her elbow viewing in the bright moonbeams the scenery

---

*Arthur Daniells was, at this time, a 21-year-old minister in Texas. Elder and Mrs. White spent the winter of 1878-79 in Texas with A. G. Daniells and his wife.

of nature. We passed Cape Horn in the night. Wild, grandly wild, was the scene. Arrived at Oakland about eleven o'clock. We were received heartily by our friends.--Ms. 7, 1880, p. 2. (Diary entry.)

Oakland, California, March 17, 1880--The trains have been delayed some-times nine hours and other days twelve hours in consequence of snows. It has been unusually cold here this month and some days we hear all talking of the disagreeable northers as in Texas.--Letter 13, 1880, p. 2. (To James White.)

Woodland, California, March 29, 1880--We have had a very pleasant season of labor here. We took a train two hours too early and had to wait at Davisville in a cold, disagreeable depot two hours. As there was no fire in the depot, I much desired to sit in the sun.

Elder Haskell tried to borrow a chair for me from the office connected with depot, but officials were not gentlemanly or courteous and refused me a chair although they were not occupying one, at least. I explained the matter in my mind as I saw these men continually smoking in this little office. They were enveloped in a cloud of smoke. Tobacco using benumbs the fine sensibilities and debases and degrades the user, we have marked, in very many cases.--Letter 17, 1880, p. 1. (To W. C. and Mary White.)

At the Camp Ground Between Hanford and Lemoore, California, April 23, 1880--Willie, Mary, Barbara Stickney and I left Oakland yesterday at four o'clock p.m. for Fresno. We arrived here this morning at 4:00 a.m. We feel not so bright this morning. We could not obtain berths on sleeper and had to change cars at 2:00 a.m. at Goshen. We had a pile of baggage, bedding, mattresses, satchels filled with books and baskets of provision. We shall return much lighter loaded. At Goshen we were directed to wrong cars and after getting well loaded were obliged to unload and change to cars on opposite track. We slept some in cars but my hip troubles me so that I cramped and could not sleep much.

We stopped at the ground. Brethren Haskell and Israel met us at the cars and took us to our tents. We had Elder Loughborough's tent, now the property of General Conference. It was furnished with floor, a strip of carpet, bedstead, stand, rocking chair, wash dish and good little stove. Barbara and I sleep in this tent. There is still another little tent for Will and Mary with bed in it; no wood floor nor stove. Very neat and comfortable.

There are forty tents upon the ground--a restaurant which is the best conducted of any I have seen at any of our camp meetings.--Letter 25, 1880, p. 1. (To James White.)

I am not sure when this may reach you, as the road has been blockaded by terrible snowstorms and avalanches have demolished freight trains. When we took the cars for this route there were fifty stout men waiting to take cars for the blockaded roads for the purpose of shoveling snow. It took six engines to drag the cars even a short distance. There had been no mails for two days, and they said it would take more than two days to remove the obstructions so that they could get through with mails.

Telegraph wires are down and general calamity seems to be on California. Levees are giving way and Sacramento is flooded. There is great damage done by these last rains. It has rained nearly all the time for three weeks. Most of the time it has poured. It is about the first rain they have had in this country.--Letter 26, 1880, p. 1. (To James White.)

Oakland, California, July 23, 1880--I have been waiting to know what to write definitely in regard to my plans. I have received three letters from Bro. Burrel and I wrote him that I could not attend any of the camp meetings east. The expense of crossing the plains would be no less than three hundred dollars if I returned for camp meetings here. A dispatch came yesterday with Burrel's and Farget's name signed urging me in no case to disappoint them--my expense should be met. I may come alone. Shall leave here Monday or Wednesday. Why these particular times? So as not to be under the necessity of changing cars on the Sabbath.--Letter 35, 1880, p. 1. (To James White.)

Humboldt, Wyoming County, Nevada, Wednesday, July 28, 1880--Dear Children: It is not yet two days since we left you and it seems one week. We have had a pleasant and comfortable time thus far. The train stopped six hours at Rockwell. We went out in search of our people. We were made welcome at Sister Prosser's. Her husband is not a believer but he gave us a hearty welcome. We took dinner with them. Was sorry I was not in a better visiting order, for I was so worn visiting was a tax. We prayed with them about two o'clock and then went to the train only a few rods from their house. We have not yet put up our bed. We, Sister Hall and myself, lie down and sleep much of the time. The more I sleep the more I want to sleep. I am not worth much.

Our car has been filling up until it is filled. Every seat is full and men lie and roost upon the upper berth, spread their lunch and make that their home. Upper berths mostly are taken. We retain ours as yet, but may have to give it up any time. As long as we can retain this, we will be as comfortable as on the palace car. We have slept a good share of the forenoon. While I write it is a little past two o'clock.

We have just passed Humboldt, not yet half way to Odgen, 385 miles to Ogden. We have come 335 miles. Our changes will be made Friday morning at eight o'clock. This relieves my mind. I shall be anxious to hear how Willie is. I hope he is improving. My head aches all the time. I can scarcely hold my eyes open. I feel grateful for the comfortable time we are having.

All the passengers are first class. No regular emigrants. We were pleased to find the rolls, but sorry that any of the oranges were left, for they will be the most expensive for us to buy. . . .

I found my credentials. Elder Haskell's name was on the envelope so I did not recognize it.

We just draw shawls about our berth and eat and sleep in our own room and no one to gaze upon us. We have a pleasant breeze today. Nothing today in scenery but alkali and sage brush. We have scarcely a bit of dirt. Conductors say that the emigrant cars are made so comfortable the first-class passengers are but few, but now all are crowded, first class, palace, and emigrant.

My heart says, God bless my dear children. Be of good courage. Jesus is the Captain of our salvation.--Letter 37, 1880, pp. 1, 2. (To W. C. and Mary White.)

Nearing Cheyenne, Wyoming, August 1, 1880--Dear Children Willie and Mary: We are nearing Cheyenne. We have had not one moment's regret coming this route on emigrant ticket. I have had nervous headache nearly all the way since leaving Oakland. We have had a full car all the way. Every seat was full and upper berths taken and was rather of a comical sight to see men sitting on edge of upper berths with feet dangling over the heads of ladies in under berth, eating their lunch and some playing cards.

We had no reason to complain as we had both lower and upper berths to ourselves. Sister Hall and I have had the very best chance to rest. We kept our bed made up for use nearly all the time, curtains about it, making a bedroom for ourselves.

Friday at 9:00 a.m. we changed cars at Ogden without much difficulty. Sister Hall made for the car, secured seats. I handed smaller parcels in at the window. A lady kindly put through the car window all our large bundles and a gentleman volunteered to put them in the car. So we are again moved, but there was some disagreeable contention about position in the cars, but after a time our camp was settled and angry contention at an end.

The two ladies sitting opposite us, rather prepossessing in appearance, were not very dignified in their deportment. They condescended to the most boisterous laughter and joking away into the night, until I suggested we remember what time of night it was. But they kept on the same screaming and laughing with forward men and a base conductor, until I was thoroughly indignant. These women professed to be _____. One was a mother of young men. She was as old as myself. Her hair was nearly white and yet she was jesting and joking with young men of questionable morals. I finally spoke out and told them we had had quite enough of this extravagant mirth and constant joking and thoughtless talk and laughter and that more thinking and praying would be far better. They quit then and let us have a little peace.

Sabbath we shut ourselves up to ourselves and as I was sick, we lay in our berth all day nearly. It was very hot. We had, we found to our sorrow, the sunny side of the car. Last night till ten o'clock the same gassing and boisterous laughter was kept up. I spoke again, "Friends, please let us have quiet and rest. Last night we were kept awake for many hours. We need

-67-

our rest. This is our right." Everything hushed down after a while and we had a peaceful rest.

We feel better today. It is a most beautiful morning. We shall be in Cheyenne tonight at five o'clock. We shall not reach Omaha until Monday night or Tuesday morning and will have to wait over twelve hours there, be attached to express train for Chicago. We have very scrimped time. Shall shift off if we see we shall be too late for appointment at Alma. We can but just make it at the best. We feel the need of that Sunday we spent in Oakland ever so much. We shall want to hear from you all. I have not written anything. I dread even the exertion of writing letters. We want to hear from you as soon as possible, for I worry about Willie.--Letter 38, 1880, pp. 1, 2. (To W. C. and Mary White.)

Near Laramie, Wyoming, August 15, 1883--Dear Children: We have had another good night's rest. We are near Laramie. The journey thus far has been the most pleasant of any we have had in crossing the plains. In the last car the seat opposite us was occupied by only one man. We used it a good share of the time. Yesterday we changed at Ogden and there was no one in the opposite section. We had the entire command of our own section and the one opposite us, so we have not been crowded at all. We have an excellent sleeping-car conductor and on both trains good accommodating porters.

The weather has been rather hot in midday, but it might be worse. We feel deeply grateful for the protection we are assured we have from God. I feel cheerful and happy. I have a good time to think and to pray. I am stronger than when I left Oakland. I feel the need of special help from God, for I know we are indeed exposed to Satan's temptations and to his malice. We need the guardianship of angels day by day, hour by hour.

We need your prayers daily that the Lord would prepare me to do His work and give me largely of His Spirit, for without this grace and His special assistance I cannot do anything. Oh, I long, I thirst for salvation, for special help from God, to know for myself that my life is hid with Christ in God. I do know that there is nothing on earth I desire beside Him. He is the crown of my rejoicing. Separated from Jesus I should be indeed miserable.

I am seated next to that large man, a Frenchman, who was in the depot when we entered it. He is a theater manager. He has a little woman with short cut hair--an actress. We have become quite well acquainted. . . .

This party are very kind and courteous, but the raid they make upon bottles of champagne and wines is to me a marvel. The lady takes her glass with as much ease as the gentleman. I have been courteously invited to join them, but frankly told them I never in my life tasted the article and had no need for anything of the kind. They opened their eyes with astonishment.

I see every gentleman on the train has his liquor flask and the eyes of some testify that they drink brandy and considerable of it; but I find the lemon you kindly provided for us fully meets all my wants as far as drinking is concerned. I treat the different parties with my precious fruit and they try hard to make some exchange but fail. I have all of the kind of food that I would at all accept from them. They feel disturbed to think they are in my debt.

There is a family from India on their way to England, soldiers. They complain of the heat here--worse, they say, than in India. They were in the healthful part of the country. They have a nurse for the little boy. She is a native, curiously dressed and curious in appearance. Her hands are tattooed completely. She wears a pink calico dress nearly straight as a bag, with a short sacque of the same, then a pink figured calico mantle which crosses before, fastened behind. She . . . is really a good nurse.

Yesterday while the cars stopped at a small station a young man came into the cars. Said he had eaten nothing for twenty-four hours. Sara gave him provision to supply present wants. He was about eighteen years old. Said he had no money to buy anything to eat.

We have just finished breakfast. It is now five minutes past eight o'clock. We are about ten miles from Laramie. We shall not be able to make way with our provisions. Sara bought a bottle of milk and some warm water this morning. I put ginger in it and it went well.--Letter 22, 1883, pp. 1-3. (To W. C. and Mary White.)

East Portland, Oregon, June 27, 1884--Sunday I had great freedom in speaking upon temperance. The power of the subject was never seen and felt by me as upon this occasion. The people from the city listened attentively. Several unbelievers who have used tobacco since their youth have left it off and say they will not touch it more.

We left the ground, ten o'clock p.m., stepped on board the train and were on our way for East Portland. Tuesday morning the cars stopped at Multnomah Falls for twenty minutes, that all the passengers who chose might ascend to have a clear view. I undertook to go and I would not go back. It was very steep. There were steps made, then quite a distance zigzag, then more steps. This was repeated many times until we stood upon a bridge made to bridge a chasm above the first fall. This is the Bridal Veil.

The water pours from the top of a mountain about 900 feet high and as the water descends, it breaks upon the jutting rocks, scattering off in beautiful spray. Here was the most beautiful sight to look upon. I would have enjoyed it could I have spent an entire day viewing this scene, but we were grateful for the few moments, although it cost laborious climbing.

. . .

Eight hundred feet above us the water rolled from the mountaintops, dashing upon the cliffs and rocks, throwing the water like a veil on every side. Below us this water accumulating from the flow above dashed in a larger fall over the rocks. This was the work of the great Master Artist, and we could but exclaim, How wonderful are are Thy works, Lord God Almighty. We feel subdued and awed in the presence of such manifestations of the great God.--Letter 20, 1884, pp. 3, 4. (To Uriah Smith.)

White Estate
Washington, D. C.
July 15, 1981

NO ABSOLUTE RULE IN THE TRAINING OF MINISTERS

I have been shown that our conferences have been overburdened with resolutions. One tenth as many would be of far greater value than a larger
number. I stated these things clearly, but still you urged that the resolution should be carried into effect. You made it evident that if God was
leading me, He was certainly not leading you. Your resistance to my words,
and the manifestation of so much feeling expressed in your lowering countenance and your determined words impressed me very unfavorably.

Another resolution was passed that might have been laid upon the table,
i.e., the one in reference to training all licentiates before permitting
them to enter the ministry. This was to be an absolute rule, and notwithstanding all I had to say against this resolution it was carried. It was
not right for the conference to pass it. It was not in God's order, and
this resolution will fall powerless to the ground. I shall not sustain it,
for I would not be found working against God. This is not God's way of
working, and I will not give it countenance for a moment.--Letter 22, 1889,
pp 10, 11. (February 12, 1889.)

White Estate
Washington, D. C.
July 13, 1981

KEEPING THE SABBATH IN OUR SANITARIUMS

[Matthew 5:17-19 quoted.]

It is our work to give this message. We are to teach men and women not to regard lightly one principle of the law of God. By precept and example we are to explain the nature of God's holy requirements. Thus we shall be in the world a savor of life unto life.

Physicians are inclined to feel justified in doing many things on the Sabbath which they should refrain from doing. The needs of suffering humanity are never to be neglected. But as far as possible, all work should be laid aside on the Sabbath. At this time we should do all in our power to let light shine to a benighted world; for Satan is doing his utmost to cast his hellish shadow across the pathway of every soul.

Please read Ex. 31:12-18. Could anything be more positive than this? The Sabbath of the fourth commandment is not to be hidden under a bushel. In all our sanitariums the light on this question is to shine forth. By our methods of work we are to exalt God's memorial. We are ever to acknowledge the binding claims of the Sabbath command. This, God declares, is a sign between Him and us throughout our generations forever.

Let us remember that it means much to the educators and those being educated in our sanitariums to keep the Sabbath aright. This should be regarded as much more important and essential than it has been in the past. Testing truth is to be given to the world. Men are to be taught that the seventh day is God's memorial of Creation. Yet this truth is not to be

presented in such a way as to render it offensive. The light is to shine

forth in such a way that it will illuminate the minds of all.--Letter 14,

1901, pp. 7,8.   (To Dr. S. Rand, Hamilton, Newcastle, NSW, Australia,

January 22, 1901.)

White Estate
Washington, D. C.
July 13, 1981

ELLEN WHITE'S HEAVY BURDENS IN 1906

I am now carrying a very heavy burden for those who are lost in the mysteries of false science. I have had physical suffering of the heart; therefore I could not quickly answer the questions that you [Dr. David Paulson] and Elder Sadler have presented to me. A severe cold has been upon me ever since the Loma Linda meeting. I assure you it is not because I do not respect you, Brethren Paulson and Sadler, that I do not answer your questions now. Pray for me, and I will pray for you; and as soon as I can I will clear up, if possible, the misunderstandings regarding the work God has given me to do. Certainly a very great work is before us. I must now watch and pray and wait.--Letter 172, 1906, p. 3. (To Dr. David Paulson and Elder W. S. Sadler, June 14, 1906.)

White Estate
Washington, D. C.
July 20, 1981

THE NEED FOR DECENTRALIZATION

A New Order Urged for the General Conference in 1901--God forbid, brethren, that this Conference [1901 General Conference session] should close as our conferences have closed in the past, with the same management, the same tone, the same order. The Lord wants those who have a knowledge of the truth to come to their senses. He wants them to arouse. It is time for us to arise and shine because our light has come, and the glory of the Lord has risen upon us. . . .

From the light God has given me, everything connected with this conference is to be regarded as most sacred. Why? Because at this time the work is to be placed upon a proper basis. Wrong principles have been followed. For the last fifteen years wrong decisions have been made; and now God calls for a change.--Ms. 43, 1901, pp. 3, 4. (A Talk in the Battle Creek Library, April 1, 1901.)

Cooperation Urged for the Advancement of SDA Work in Europe--Now I was shown in America that there must be here [Europe] the very same growing in the work as there was there; that all should feel that they are under obligation to God to help in the work. Then these individuals will feel that the cause of God is a part of them. I was shown that there should be additional laborers in the field to carry forward the work. Brother Matteson has had upon him a tremendous load. He has not only been laboring in the

field, but has been doing a great amount of writing. Now Brother Olsen has
come here to your conference and he can take hold with Brother Matteson, and
Brother Matteson with him. They can thus help each other in carrying forward this work.

A few of our brethren who have taken hold of the truth have no idea what
it will accomplish. What is needed is a more thorough conversion to the
truth of God. There needs to be an education of the people up to the standard. They need organized, systematic effort for every church. If everyone
here feels that it is the great and solemn work of God, and that they are
individually to be a light that is to be reflected to the world, then we
shall see that the cause and work of God will advance more rapidly than it
has in the past.--Ms. 6, 1886, p. 2. ("Beginnings of Work in Scandinavia,"
June 23, 1886.)

Church Urged to Adopt Correct Business Principles--It is essential that
correct principles in business lines should be laid before the whole body of
Seventh-day Adventists. I am instructed that this should have been done
years ago. Our brethren and sisters are not to be led on blindfolded, not
knowing what movements will next take place. If we are not in earnest in
remedying this evil at the heart of the work, we shall give occasion to
those who have been agitating the danger of organization, to justify themselves in their position.--Ms. 11, 1895, p. 12. ("Publishing Houses," April
10, 1895.)

Local Conference Presidents to Bear Their Share of Responsibilities--The
men who act as presidents of State conferences should be carefully selected.

Then let these men bear the responsibilities of the conference in a most thorough, earnest, God-fearing manner. If they are not qualified to do the work thoroughly and successfully, do not keep them in that position.

A mass of matter is laid before the General Conference. Every burden is carried to Battle Creek. This makes the presidents of the State conferences very irresponsible. Many are not growing in aptitude and in judgment. . . .

Let the presidents of State conferences walk humbly with God, and they will not have occasion to write to the president of the General Conference to leave his work to settle little matters for them. Even many large matters may be carried to God, and God will give counsel in every State conference. The Lord can be approached by all. He is much more accessible than the president of the General Conference. Let the president of the General Conference educate the presidents of State conferences to take care of their portion of the moral vineyard where they are situated wisely, without laying their burdens upon him.--Ms. 17, 1896, pp. 4, 10, 11. (Untitled Manuscript, May 13, 1896.)

Management Responsibilities to Be Delegated--The management of the business interests of the sanitarium should not rest upon the doctor [J. H. Kellogg] as it has done. Others must attend to such matters. A multitude of cares may thus be removed from him. He should make every exertion on his part to qualify men to engage with him in the work, and should give them an opportunity to share his responsibilities. This would be a mercy to himself and a great blessing to them. Unless he does make efforts to save himself, he will become, unexpectedly to himself, a complete wreck, when with proper exercise of his powers, restraining inclination, he might be able to do a good work, enduring as eternity.

This advice and warning was given to me to give to my husband, and has been given to many others. They were urged to unload, and not break under the continual strain and burden. . . .

Elder D might have lived had he encouraged and educated others to share the burdens with which he loaded himself down. He deprived them of an education they might have had, because he did so much himself and allowed them to rely upon his brain instead of doing their own thinking. Every man can be a man, a whole man. By patient, thoughtful effort, put forth with zeal and energy, all may overcome cowardice and ignorance and inefficiency. . . .

The Lord has said, "No one man's mind or judgment is sufficent to exert a controlling influence in any of our institutions." Therefore it is neces- sary that councils be held, that plans be considered by men of different stamp of character. Then if there are defects, they will be discovered and removed.--Letter 1, 1885, pp. 5, 6, 8, 9. (To Sanitarium Directors, October [probably November] 3, 1885.)

Let Others Develop Their Talents and Bear Responsibilities--You are not the only men whom God will use. Give the Lord room to use the talents He has entrusted to men in order that the cause may grow. Give the Lord a chance to use men's minds. We are losing much by our narrow ideas and plans. Do not stand in the way of the advancement of the work, but let the Lord work by whom He will. Educate, encourage young men to think and act, to devise and plan, in order that we may have a multitude of wise counse- lors. . . .

This same character of spirit [centralization of power] is found here in Europe. For years Elder D held the work back from advancing, because he feared to entrust it to others lest they should not carry out his precise plans. He would never allow anything to come into existence that did not originate with him. Elder E also held everything in his grasp while he was in California and England, and as a result the work is years behind in England. . . .

The children of this world are wiser in their generation than the children of light. Jesus said this, and we see that the world works on a different plan in these matters. Weighty responsibilities connected with the business of the world are not placed wholly upon one man. In large business enterprises responsible men choose others to share their burdens and lift their responsibilities so that in case one should fail there is someone ready to step into his place. Someone should feel a burden over these matters, and a decided change should take place in the manner of our work.-- Letter 12, 1885, pp. 3-5. (To G. I. Butler and S. N. Haskell, October 28, 1885.)

What Might Have Been Accomplished If Selfishness Had Been Eradicated-- It is not wise to open up more fields than can be thoroughly worked. If selfishness from the first had been eradicated from the hearts of the laborers; if the love of Jesus and the love of souls for whom Christ died had controlled the workers, what a strong company might have been raised up. Jealousies, evil surmisings, envyings have built up barriers between you and God, making it impossible for the Lord to do His work, His precious work of bringing souls to the knowledge of truth. If many had been converted, who would have been able to care for these lambs, these newly come to the faith? What lessons they would have learned of envy, jealousy, and evil surmisings. Wherein would inquiring souls find the right kind of instruction? Who would educate and train them for the work of the Master?--Letter 3, 1892, p. 15. (To W. D. Curtis, Jan. 16, 1892.)

Decentralization of Power Urged--The matter in regard to centralizing all the power in one body in Battle Creek, has become serious. From the light given me, I see that this administration is embracing altogether too much, and is trying to carry burdens and interests which it has not strength or wisdom from heaven to bear, or to conduct successfully. The Lord is just as willing to impart wisdom and ability to men in distant fields as He is to impart wisdom and ability to the men in Battle Creek. . . .

Distant conferences should not be compelled to depend upon Battle Creek to manage for them. In every country men should be appointed to assist the presidents of the different conferences. The carrying forward of the message should be entrusted to willing men--men who, in the fear of God, will minister in His service. As these men do their best, according to their ability, working with a deep, earnest love for the souls for whom Christ has died, God will help them.--Letter 88, 1896, pp. 1, 2. (To W. W. Prescott and Wife, Sept. 1, 1896.)

White Estate
Washington, D. C.
July 20, 1981

CHRISTIAN INTEGRITY IN THE MINISTRY

I have been shown that in times past men have made grievous mistakes. Some who have stood in positions of sacred trust have sullied their integrity. They have not, in their individual responsibility, stood in moral power before God. Those who were not worthy have been flattered, while those who have stood fast for truth and for righteousness, because their ideas did not agree with those of their brethren, have been denounced, discredited, and misjudged. Evil has been imagined against them.

Greatness without goodness is valueless. It is as a tinkling cymbal. The man who does not gather about him the rays of light that God has let shine upon his pathway will surely surround himself with the shadows of darkness. God designs that His people shall press closer and still closer to the light. Then they will go forward and upward.

"Light is sown for the righteous, and truth for the upright in heart." There is altogether too little searching, with painstaking effort, for the truth as for hidden treasure. With hearts softened and subdued by the grace of God, the conscience quickened by habitual prayer and searching of the Scriptures, the whole soul may become familiar with heavenly truth. Such will stand firmly for the right because it is right. Pure and undefiled religion will be interwoven with the life-practice. They will honor God, and God will honor them.

I have been shown that there is a fault with us. We honor and flatter human beings, accepting their ideas and their judgment as the voice of God.

We advocate their cause. But they are not always safe to follow. Their judgment is erring.

God would have us ever refuse to plead against the truth. His frown is upon all that is false or unfair. This should be the position of everyone who stands to minister in the service of his Master. For if one to whom God has entrusted holy responsibilities allows envy, evil surmising, prejudice, and jealousies to find place in the heart, he is guilty of breaking the law of God. And his words, his ideas, and his errors will extend just as far as his sphere of influence extends.

God says to every man to whom He entrusts responsibilities, "Put not your trust in man, neither make flesh your arm." Look to God. Trust in His infallible wisdom.   Regard as a sin the practice so common, even among Seventh-day Adventists, of becoming the echo of any man, however lofty his position. Listen to the voice of the great Shepherd, and you will never be led astray. Search the Scriptures for yourself and be braced for duty and for trial by the truth of God's Word.

Let no friendship, no influence, no entreaty, let not the smiles, the confidence, or the rewards of any man, induce you to swerve from the path in which the Lord would lead you. Let Christlike integrity and consistency control the actions of your life. The man who sits most at the feet of Jesus, and is taught by the Saviour's spirit, will be ready to cry out, "I am weak and unworthy, but Christ is my strength and my righteousness."

Godliness, sobriety, and consistency will characterize the life and example of every true Christian. The work which Christ is doing in the sanctuary above will engage the thoughts, and be the burden of the conversation, because by faith he has entered into the sanctuary. He is on earth, but his sympathies are in harmony with the work that Christ is doing in heaven. Christ is cleansing the heavenly sanctuary from the sins of the people, and it is the work of all who are laborers together with God to be cleansing the sanctuary of the soul from everything that is offensive to Him. Everything like evil surmising, envy, jealousy, enmity, and hatred, will be put away, for such things grieve the Holy Spirit of God, and put Christ to an open shame. Love of self will not exist, nor will any engaged in this work be puffed up. The example of Christ's life, the consistency of his character, will make his influence far-reaching. He will be a living epistle, known and read of all men.

[1 Peter 3:8-12 quoted.]

It is not safe for us to open our minds and hearts to envy and evil speaking. The fruits of God's Spirit are plainly specified, so that we need not entertain or cherish those attributes that proceed from the enemy of God and man. The false tongue beguiles the unwary, and makes an easy conquest of those who are not strengthened, stablished, and settled, having root in themselves. The atonement of Christ is to be the anchor of our hope, and the Word of God a lamp to our feet, and a light to our path. Then our words will not be of self, but of Christ and of the all-essential work for this time.

With many there is but a very limited perusal of the Holy Scriptures. The truth is not dwelt upon, and the result is that it is not made the theme of conversation. It is made evident that Christ is not abiding in the heart. Our tongues should speak more of the matchless love of Jesus.

[Romans 11:17-22 quoted.]

The Lord has shown me that as a people we must have a purer morality. There is among us a flippant reproduction of arguments that are the product of other brains than ours, while the man who first uttered them has not spent hours of earnest study each day in order to know the truth. In his self-sufficiency he has turned away from the truth unto fables. He has not poured out before God his earnest prayer that he might know the hidden mysteries of God's Word, that he might present to the people things new and old, which by painstaking effort he has dug from the mine of truth.

Mysteries which have been hidden for ages are to be revealed in these last days to a humble people, who lean upon the arm of infinite power. Truth will be opened to the humble seeker, whose life is hid with Christ in God.

God calls upon His people to be Christians in thought, in word, and in deed. Luther made the statement that religion is never so much in danger as among reverend men. I can say that many who handle the truth are not sanctified through the truth. They have not the faith that works by love, and purifies the soul. They become accustomed to handling sacred things, and because of this, many handle the Word of God irreverently. They have not walked in the light, but have closed their eyes to light.

This is an age of signal rejection of the grace God has purposed to bestow upon His people, that in the perils of the last days they may not be overcome by the prevailing iniquity, and unite with the hostility of the world against God's remnant people. Under the cloak of Christianity and sanctification, far-spreading and manifest ungodliness will prevail to a terrible degree and will continue until Christ comes to be glorified in all them that believe. In the very courts of the temple scenes will be enacted that few realize. God's people will be proved and tested, that He may discern "between him that serveth God, and him that serveth Him not."

Vengeance will be executed against those who sit in the gate, deciding what the people should have, and what they should not have. These take away the key of knowledge. They refuse to enter in themselves, and those that would enter, they hinder. These bear not the seal of the living God. All who now occupy responsible positions should be solemnly and terribly afraid lest in this time they shall be found as unfaithful stewards.

Satan has come down with great power, knowing that his time is short. The continued apostasy, the abounding iniquity, which chills the faith and constancy of many, should call the faithful ones to the front. Straight, clear, decided testimonies, freighted with light for the time, will be given. Truth, undimmed by the furnace, will shine brighter and brighter until the perfect day. The Spirit and power of the coming One will be imparted in large measure to those who are preparing to stand in the day of God, who are hastening the second advent of our Lord and Saviour Jesus Christ. To these faithful ones Christ gives special communications. He talks with them as He talked with His disciples before leaving them. The Spirit of truth will guide them into all truth. God has lines of communication with the world today. Through His appointed agencies, He speaks to the people He is purifying, warning and encouraging them.

There are those who listen with open ears and quickened understanding for the words of reproof and encouragement addressed to them. But Satan is ever on the alert to make these words of counsel of none effect. He seeks to close every avenue through which people receive truth. Unto those that have shall more be given, but from those that have not, shall be taken away even that which they have.

If the ears are dull of hearing, if the eyes are closed to the light which God flashes into the pathway, the light previously received is so mingled with supposition, uncertainty, and darkness, that light cannot be distinguished from darkness.   There are those whom we have loved in the faith who have turned from it, and given heed to seducing spirits.   "They went out from us, but they were not of us; for if they had been of us, they would no doubt have continued with us: but they went out, that they might be made manifest that they were not all of us" (1 John 2:19).

The love, the tender compassion, the marvelous condescension of Christ for His disciples is without a parallel. He made them the depositaries of sacred truth, as they could comprehend it. But He said to them, I have many things to say unto you, but ye cannot bear them now. Although Christ was with them, as their instructor, yet their former teaching had so molded their ideas and opinions that should Christ unfold the many things He longed to communicate, they would have misinterpreted His words.

While He was with them, He sought to impress upon them the knowledge there was for them in the mysteries of the kingdom of God. He would have them see that it was an evidence of His love for Him to lift the veil of the future, and make them the depositaries of knowledge concerning events to come. But much He had told them had been dimly comprehended, and much would be forgotten. He told them that after His crucifixion and ascension the Holy Spirit would open many things to them, and give them a better understanding of what He had tried to tell them. He would still continue to reveal sacred truth to them, and His Spirit would more fully impart truth to them.

While Christ unfolded the iniquity and sorrow that must come to His disciples, the persecutions, and the trials they must bear, and the rejection of their testimony, He did not design that they should cloud their lives by looking on the dark side. He assured them that they would not be left alone, but be sustained by His Holy Spirit, which would guide them into all truth. "The Comforter, which is the Holy Ghost," He said, "whom the Father will send in My name, He shall teach you all things, and bring all things to your remembrance, whatsoever I have said unto you" (John 14:26). "I have yet many things to say unto you, but ye cannot bear them now. Howbeit when He, the Spirit of truth, is come, He will guide you into all truth: for He shall not speak of Himself, but whatsoever He shall hear, that shall He speak: and He will shew you things to come" (John 16:12, 13).

Here is a precious promise--the purposes and plans of God are to be opened to His disciples. What is a disciple? A learner, ever learning. Coming events of a solemn character are opening before us, and God would not have any one of us think that in these last days there is no more that we need to know. This is a continual snare of Satan. He [God] would not have us meet coming events without that special preparation which is essential to guide us through every difficulty. He would not have all stumbling their way along in ignorance, making self-conceit, self-esteem, self-confidence, take the place of true knowledge.

The more satisfied anyone is with himself and his present knowledge, the less earnestly and humbly will he seek to be guided into all truth. The less of the Holy Spirit of God he has, the more self-satisfied and complacent he will feel. He will not search earnestly and with the deepest interest to know more of truth. But unless he keeps pace with the Leader, who is guiding into all truth, he will be left behind, belated, blinded, confused, because he is not walking in the light.

All who follow Christ will walk in the light as He is in the light. They will not then regard light with indifference, nor will they misapply the light, or stumble over it as did the Jews.

A spurious light will be accepted in the place of truth by some who feel called upon to be expositors of the Scriptures, because of their calling or position. Extravagance, dishonesty, fraud, licentiousness, are mingled with sacred things, until no difference is made between the sacred and the common. Many who claim to preach the Word contemplate some portions of Scripture truth, but do not apply it to the heart and character. They expatiate upon the plan of redemption and upon the law of God and become enthusiastic upon some of these glorious themes, but they take no personal interest in the matter. Christ is not brought into their lives.

Can we then be surprised to hear of ministers falling under temptation and sin, disgracing the cause they were professedly advocating? Can we wonder that there are apostasies when men who urge conversion upon others are not themselves converted; when they commend to others the love of Christ which does not glow in their own souls, preaching repentance which they themselves have not practiced, and faith which they have no experimental knowledge of, telling of a Saviour whom they have never known except by rumor? They are self-deceived men, not far from destruction. Pitiful indeed is their situation. All may seem peaceful to them, because the palsy of death is upon them. We are fully aware that dishonest men, immoral men, who preach the Word, are not always reproved and warned. They are not unmasked. They learn to hold the truth in unrighteousness, and can tamper with it without a trembling of heart and rebuke of conscience. Oh, that with pen and voice we might lead the people who claim to be the depositaries of sacred and eternal truth to feel the necessity of enthroning the Word of God in their heart, and bringing every thought, word, and action into subjection to Jesus Christ. It is a fearful responsibility to be in daily connection with the truth of God, telling others of eternal truth and yet be unsanctified through the truth.

It is not safe to place men in the position God should occupy, for men cannot be trusted. If they do not constantly live as in the presence of God, if they do not walk humbly before God and their brethren, they will diverge almost imperceptibly, and by slight degrees, from the straight line of God's work. Trusting to their own wisdom, they will deceive themselves and their fellow men. Their ideas become so confused that they offer strange fire before the Lord.

The Word of God is to be the man of our counsel. With pen and voice I proclaim to all who bear credentials, to all licentiates, to all colporteurs, and all canvassers, that the Bible, and the Bible only, studied on your knees, laid up in your heart, and practiced in your life, attended by the Holy Spirit's power, can be your safeguard. It alone can make you righteous and holy, and keep you thus. Every human influence is weak and varying unless the truth of God's Word is brought home to the soul, and placed upon the throne. Not till this is done will the heart be sanctified, purified, and made holy, a fountain out of which are the issues of life.

Discourses that have little of Christ and His righteousness in them are given in the desk. They are Christless sermons. To preach in the demonstration of the Spirit is completely beyond the power of those who are without Christ. They are feeble, empty and without nourishment. They have no Christ to carry with them in private life. They are full of boasting, of pride, of self-esteem, speaking evil of things of which they have no real knowledge. They manifest an impatience of everything that does not follow in their line. They will even scoff and mock at sacred things, because they do not see that spiritual things are spiritually discerned. They degrade themselves by perverting and falsifying truth.

By His Holy Spirit the Lord will demonstrate that His word is the only thing that can make men right and keep them right. I have been shown that God's revealed truth alone can keep men in the path of humble obedience. Standard bearers are falling around us, not only through death, but through the deceptions of Satan. All heaven is looking upon the remnant people of God, to see if they will make truth alone their shield and buckler. Unless the truth is presented as it is in Jesus, and is planted in the heart by the power of the Spirit of God, even ministers will be found drifting away from Christ, away from piety, away from religious principle. They will become blind leaders of the blind.

Our faith cannot be vested in any man. We need Christ's righteousness. We need Jesus ever by our side. He is our Rock. It is by His might that we conquer, and by His righteousness that we are saved. When I see men exalted and praised, extolled as almost infallible, I know that there must come a terrible shaking. When God's lamp of life shines into the heart with clear and steady ray, darkness will instantly be dispelled. Every idol will be dethroned, and the peace of God which passeth all understanding will reign in the heart. Truth, precious truth, will be seen, appreciated, and obeyed. The standard will be elevated, and many will rally round it.--Ms. 15, 1886. (Written at Basle, Switzerland.)

White Estate, Wash. D.C.
July 21, 1981

THE POCOCK FAMILY MOVES TO COORANBONG

Brother Pocock and his family came to Cooranbong yesterday. He has given up the home he selected several years ago. This place is among the rocks, on the side of a mountain, in a place which cannot be reached with a horse and carriage. He has five very pretty children. The eldest, I learned last night, is ten years old. Last week he came by request to paint on the school buildings. We learned that the necessities of his family were very great, and we borrowed three pounds, put it in his hands, and sent him back for his family. Meanwhile we are trying to find a house for him.

The house by the long bridge on the way to Dora Creek was all that we could find, but Mr. Walmsley, the owner, asked three [shillings] and six-pence a week for it, and it is not fit for habitation. So we passed by that offer, and made inquiry of Mr. Hughes, who has recently built himself a nice cottage. He at once offered Brother Pocock a home in the two-roomed cottage they had left when they moved into their new home. He said that he would not charge them any rent. This was gratefully accepted, and last evening Sara established Brother Pocock and his family in their cottage, furnishing them with provision and bedding until their meager stock shall come.

The whole family were obliged to walk three miles in the hot sun, and the heat of the sun soon cut down the little boy of four years, who is next to the youngest child. Sara had to begin her work for the two younger

-92-

children, who were both sick, when they came here, but more favorable symptoms appeared.

Now we must secure for this family a spot of land, and put them in a way to get a little house on the land. This is missionary soil. Brother Pocock is one of the most conscientious, self-denying, self-sacrificing, uncomplaining men I have ever seen. He is just such a man as will do credit to the truth.

We should keep the land reserved for such ones as, without help to obtain a situation, cannot possibly provide a home and support their families. Now Brother Pocock will have a chance to help himself. He is a hard worker, but circumstances he could not control have kept him in poverty. We must help such ones.--Letter 61, 1899, pp. 2,3. (To Elder and Mrs. S. N. Haskell, April 2, 1899.)

Sister McEnterfer has been just called away, at one o'clock at night, in the greatest storm we have had since we came to Cooranbong. I have not seen her since last evening. A sweet little child is very ill, and we fear dying. There are five children in the family, which was once in good circumstances.

The father, Brother Pocock, is a coachmaker by trade, and he is also a carpenter, but unfortunately he was thrown out of work, and observing the Sabbath has kept him out of work. In appearance he is a refined gentleman, but for several years he has been living with his family in a house on the side of a mountain, two miles from the nearest neighbor. He had to carry the material of which his house is built up the mountain on his back. The land is covered with rocks, so that it cannot be cultivated.

We knew that Brother Pocock was out of work, and we sent for him to come and paint on the school building. He came a week ago last Sunday, but when we learned from Brother and Sister Starr the situation of his family, their deep poverty and their lack of nourishing food, we advised him to return and bring his family to Cooranbong.

Brother Pocock has been the means of bringing three families into the truth. Brother Starr was sent to baptize these people, and by this means we learned of Brother Pocock's necessity. We borrowed money and loaned it to him to enable him to bring his family up, and told him to let his shanty go. Come he must. He arrived yesterday. We had secured for them a house of two small rooms from Mr. Hughes, who said that he would charge them no rent. They are now situated where they will be comfortable. We will not see them want.

All were glad to get here, but two of the children were sick, the youngest, a baby in its mother's arms, and a four-year-old boy. The whole family had to walk three miles on a very hot day in order to reach the cars, and we think this boy was sunstruck. We settled them in their house yesterday, and until evening Sara gave the sick child treatment. She was called up again in the night to go to see him, and I have not seen her since. We fear the child will not live. But I am glad they are not in that terrible place among the rocks in this fearful storm.

Brother and Sister Pocock have nothing. For three years we have supplied them with clothing. They have bought nothing, they say, for they had no money. We shall now do our best to get them a little home on the school ground, and will help them by giving him work. He has two good trades at his command and will be able to amply support his family. Their experience has indeed been trying, but they have never murmured, never complained. If they had told us anything of their situation, we should have urged them to leave that place three years ago.--Letter 63, 1899, pp. 3-5. (To Brother and Sister John Wessells, April 4, 1899.)

Several weeks ago Brother Pocock was sent for to help in the painting of the building. He is a coachmaker and a painter and builder. We had been calling for him for some time, but he was reluctant to leave his wife and little ones. We have from our family sent them clothing from time to time, and the clothing you left will help them.

We made most searching inquiries in regard to the situation of his wife and children, for we had been informed by Brother and Sister Starr of their extreme poverty. We learned that he could not live where he was and provide for his family. We sent him right back with word to bring his family to Cooranbong without fail. When they reached here the two youngest children were very sick. The whole family had had to walk three miles in the hot sun to reach the train, and they thought the little boy had been sunstruck. He is four years old, a pretty child and very intelligent.

They came to our house from the train, and after dinner they were taken by their earnest wish to the cottage of two rooms which Brother Hughes of Cooranbong has in the liberality of his heart granted them. Mr. Hughes and his family have done everything they could do in their kindness of heart for Brother and Sister Pocock. This family must be saved if possible.

Sara immediately began giving the little boy treatment. We soon saw that his symptoms were those of acute poisoning. He was not well when he left his home. After walking three miles he drank a lot of water. The day before leaving, the father and mother sent the children to the grandparents, while they slept in their shanty for the last time. The grandparents are not believers, and they had cooked a parakeet,* of which the boy ate very heartily. He was tired and hungry, and this used him up. Afterwards nothing could be given him which he could retain on his stomach, but the discharges continued nearly constantly.

Sara was with him night and day, and Sister Rodd was sent for to share the burden with her. We knew that it would be a battle for his life, and everything was done that it was possible to do. But the boy died on Sabbath about 11:00 a.m.--Letter 70, 1899, pp. 2, 3. (To Elder and Mrs. S. N. Haskell, April 14, 1899.)

A few acres are now being secured for our much-esteemed Brother Pocock. He is the pattern of a Christian gentleman. I tell the school board that I will consent to trust him and let him pay as he can. In our family all who are able will unite in helping him to put up a house, which will be built cheaply, costing about forty pounds. He has suffered much poverty. He has a good trade and is an excellent workman.

We encouraged him to leave his little house among the rocks on a high mountain. No carriage could reach this place. He carried up on his back to

---

*A large jungle parrot.

this place all the lumber needed to build a little shanty. But the family
were often hungry. Once or twice a year our family sent them a box of
clothing, and this is all they have had.

One of the little children died a week after they moved to this place.
He was poisoned by eating a cooked parakeet. Everything was done for him
that could be done. Sara was with him day and night, but the poison had
taken hold too deeply. The night before they left their home the parents
sent the children to their grandparents while their goods were carried to
the boat to be brought to this place.--Letter 75, 1899, p. 3. (To Dr. J. H.
Kellogg, April 20, 1899.)

White Estate
Washington, D. C.
July 21, 1981

APPEAL FOR SPIRITUAL MINISTERS

I am assured again and again that the Lord has a great work to be done in this country. He has laid upon me a burden that I dare not refuse to carry. We have greatly needed a sanitarium in this country. The medical-missionary work is to be as the hand and arm of the gospel message to be borne in this new world. We needed a sanitarium to give influence and character to the work, to accomplish the reforms so much needed! The ministry of the word and medical—missionary work, properly combined, would have exerted a much greater influence for good than working alone.

Never was there a place where medical missionary work would have told with more power than in Australia. But in our efforts to do this work we have been handicapped for want of means. The money we should have had to invest in a sanitarium has been used in erecting sanitariums in places where they were not so much needed. The Lord Jesus Christ was the greatest physician this world has ever known. We cannot in the full sense of the word call him a medical missionary. He was the divine Healer. He was imbued with power to heal all manner of diseases without resorting to drugs.

Daniel's experience is of great value to all who would be Christians. When Daniel was brought in before Belshazzar, as the king and his nobles sat at their sacrilegious feast, he plainly told the king that the calamity to come upon Babylon was the result of a disregard of heaven-sent light. He disregarded the light given to Nebuchadnezzar, and thereby lost the benefits he might have received had he been obedient to the light. God gives His people lessons to instruct them and lead them to reform. If they do not receive and practice these lessons, their neglect will surely bring judgments upon them.

We read again in Daniel: [Daniel 10:12,13 quoted].

By this we see that heavenly agencies have to contend with hindrances before the purpose of God is fulfilled in its time. The king of Persia was controlled by the highest of all evil angels. He refused, as did Pharaoh, to obey the word of the Lord. Gabriel declared, He withstood me twenty-one days by his representations against the Jews. But Michael came to his help, and then he remained with the kings of Persia, holding the powers in check, giving right counsel against evil counsel.

Good and evil angels are taking a part in the planning of God in His earthly kingdom. It is God's purpose to carry forward His work in correct lines, in ways that will advance His glory. But Satan is ever trying to counterwork God's purpose. Only by humbling themselves before God can God's servants advance His work. Never are they to depend on their own efforts or on outward display for success.

I call upon those who believe the truth for this time to reform, to purify the heart and humble self. Sincere belief of the truth and earnest prayer are our weapons of warfare. The exercise of all the musical talent among us will not change the hearts of the church members or increase their spirituality.

Humiliation, confession and most earnest prayer will bring about that which all the devising of men, be they high or low, cannot accomplish. Let us remember that it is Satan's purpose to set at work forces which will obscure the testing message for this time. If ever there was a time when self-sacrifice must be made, when earnest sincere prayer must be offered, when diligent work must be done, it is now. Satan has come down with great power to work with all deceivableness of unrighteousness in them that perish.

God looks with contempt upon the large assemblies at the Battle Creek Tabernacle, while the hearts of those present are lifted up unto vanity. Their numbers displease Him. Is there not a world to be warned? Why then are there those assembled in the Tabernacle whose hearts well with vanity because of their large assembly and their music. Let there be a humiliation of soul before God, that He may remove the discipline He has placed upon His people because they have departed from God.

The simplicity and integrity that God requires His people to show is the line of demarcation between those who serve God and those who serve Him not. At the very heart of the work there is necessity for sincere, true humiliation, which has not yet been seen. God will vindicate every message He has given to His people. He will justify all His dealings with them. They have departed out of the way, and the only course that can bring relief and hope and success in bearing the solemn message for this time is for them to humble themselves under the mighty hand of God.

There is a careless, venturesome spirit which needs to be guarded. It is humiliating for us to acknowledge that we have done wrong, but this is often necessary. The effectual fervent prayer of a righteous man availeth much. Prayer will draw down from heaven great blessings when those who claim to believe the truth shall come down from their stilts of self-exaltation and afflict their souls, even as Daniel afflicted his soul.

The Lord is not pleased with the spirit or the principles that have a controlling power in the Review and Herald office. The strong spirit of man rules; not the spirit of God. God will not work with their devising. When men get out of the Lord's way, and let Him work upon hearts and minds, blessings will come to them. The fervent prayers, the sincere humiliation, the self-denial and self-sacrifice which blends with the supplications made, will bring down rich blessings.

Through His chosen agencies God will graciously make known His purposes. Then the grand work of redemption will go forward. Men will learn of the reconciliation for iniquity and of the everlasting righteousness which the Messiah has brought in through His sacrifice. The cross of Calvary is the great center. This truth acted upon will make Christ's sacrifice effectual. This is that which Gabriel revealed to Daniel in answer to fervent prayer. It was of this that Moses and Elijah and Christ talked at His transfiguration. By the humiliation of the cross He was to bring everlasting deliverance to all who would walk after Him, giving positive evidence that they are separated from the world.

All who will endure to the end will be saved. All who will hold the beginning of their confidence firm unto the end will have eternal righteousness. But those who depart from the principles which give character to the truth need converting as verily as does the hardened sinner.

[Ephesians 2:1-10, 6:10-13 quoted.]

God is represented as weighing the characters, actions, and motives of men. Christ said to Nicodemus, "Ye must be born again" (John 3:7). He is speaking the same words to those who know not the spirit that moves them to action. Under the inspiration of the Holy Spirit, Hannah, the mother of Samuel, said, "The Lord is a God of knowledge, and by Him actions are weighed" (1 Samuel 2:3). David says, "Men of low degree are vanity, and men of high degree are a lie; to be laid in the balance, they are altogether lighter than vanity" (Psalm 62:9). Isaiah declares, "Thou, most upright, dost weigh the path of the just" (Isaiah 26:7). And Solomon writes, "All the ways of a man are clean in his own eyes; but the Lord weigheth the spirits" (Proverbs 16:2).

There is not a motive in the heart that the Lord does not read. He reads every purpose, every thought of the heart. It is not an increase of light that is needed; it is the surrendering of the soul to God, that by the power of His grace He may make the light He has caused to shine into the heart a living principle of action. When a man who has had great light, who is supposed to be led and taught by God, turns out of the way because of self-confidence, he makes false paths for his feet. He follows crooked practices, and many who have admired the supposed nobility and integrity of his character, follow his example, thinking that the Lord is leading him. The false step he took resulted in thousands of false steps.

The great worker of evil is on the track of every soul. Unfair dealings, the misappropriation of the Lord's funds, the investing of money in worldly projects, is holding back work which the Lord designs shall be done.

Thus Satan inspires men to block the way of the advancement of God's king-dom. God sees every deed done, and He sees also the outcome of that deed. Those who have done deeds which have hedged up the way of the work of salva-tion are weighed in the balances and found wanting.

We have before us in the Word of God instances of heavenly agencies working on the minds of kings and rulers, while at the same time Satanic agencies were also at work on their minds. No human eloquence, in strongly-set-forth human opinions, can change the working of Satanic agencies. Satan seeks continually to block the way so that the truth shall be bound about by human devising; and those who have light and knowledge are in the greatest danger unless they constantly consecrate themselves to God, humiliating self, and realizing the peril of the times.

Heavenly beings are appointed to answer the prayers of those who are working unselfishly for the interests of the cause of God. The very highest angels in the heavenly courts are appointed to work out the prayers which ascend to God for the advancement of the cause of God. Each angel has his particular post of duty, which he is not permitted to leave for any other place. If he should leave, the powers of darkness would gain an advantage.

In the record of Daniel's experience we read: [Daniel 10:16-21 quoted].

Day by day the conflict between good and evil is going on. Why is it that those who have had many opportunities and advantages do not realize the intensity of this work? They should be intelligent in regard to this. God is the Ruler. By His supreme power He holds in check and controls earthly potentates. Through His agencies He does the work which was ordained before the foundation of the world.

As a people we do not understand as we should the great conflict going on between invisible agencies, the controversy between loyal and disloyal angels. Evil angels are constantly at work, planning their line of attack, controlling as commanders, kings, and rulers, the disloyal human forces.

I call upon you who are not ready for the last great controversy to wake up. You are not watching for that which is soon coming upon the earth. Human instrumentalities under the control of fallen angels, are seeking to gather in their harvest. Those who would find themselves under the protection of the angels of God must live wholly for God's glory, prepared to stand in their lot and in their place. They are to be faithful and true, even as Daniel was, a man called by the Lord, "greatly beloved," a man who felt the need of praying and confessing his sins. Those who do as Daniel did are not asleep, but are keenly alive to their exposure to the enemy's malignant devices. They see that their only safety is in keeping the commandments of God. They pray as Daniel prayed, confessing their sins and finding pardon.

Over every man good and evil angels strive. It is the man himself who determines which shall win. I call upon the ministers of Christ to press home upon the understanding of all who come within the reach of their voice, the truth of the ministration of angels. Do not indulge in fanciful speculations. The written Word is our only safety. We must pray as did Daniel, that we may be guarded by heavenly intelligences. As ministering spirits angels are sent forth to minister to those who shall be heirs of salvation. Pray, my brethren, pray as you have never prayed before. We are not prepared for the Lord's coming. We need to make thorough work for eternity.--
Letter 201, 1899. (Addressed "To Our Ministering Brethren.")

White Estate, Wash. D. C.
July 22, 1981

Work for the Jews

A great work is to be done for the Jewish nation, and there will be men whom God has appointed who will give the message God has for them to bear, and Gentiles will be converted, for the Lord Christ is the power that is going before His people. . . .

Jews and Gentiles are to be converted.--Letter 354, 1905, pp. 6, 9. (To Brother Vincent, June 11, 1905.)

White Estate
Washington, D. C.
August 20, 1981

ELLEN WHITE LETTERS TO RELATIVES AND FAMILY MEMBERS

Speaking at Open-Air Meetings--My health failed me two months since. I have labored earnestly without rest since last December. I attended two grove meetings, speaking to an interested audience of people. In the last of these meetings the wind blew in the pine and oak trees, making it very difficult for the speaker. My turn came upon the afternoon of first day, when the wind was blowing so strong it was almost impossible to make the voice heard by all the people assembled. I spoke one hour and a half, clear and loud; every word was heard distinctly. Outsiders said there could not be found one man in a thousand that could be heard as distinctly as I was heard. I think the effort was too much. That week I began to fail. (It is the turn of life with me.) I was attacked with palpitation and fainting. Could not stand five minutes upon my feet.--Letter 5, 1867, p. 1. (To Stephen and Sarah Belden, September 24, 1867.)

We arise this morning in good spirits. The great day of the meeting is over. Yesterday Brother [Uriah] Smith spoke upon the Sabbath question. In the afternoon I spoke one hour and a half upon temperance. About six thousand were on the ground. Many could obtain no seats but stood during the two hours' service. I never yet witnessed such perfect attention. Those standing were as motionless as though they were riveted to the ground. There was no leaving the congregation or scattering upon the ground.

Many seemed to feel deeply while I was speaking. I had great freedom and left the stand with throat and lungs free from pain and with more strength than I have had since I left home.

This morning I awake with freedom from pain, of good courage in the Lord, cheerful and hopeful.

Father [James White] is improving all the time. He needs to be held up, encouraged, and cheerful words spoken to him. The Lord lives and reigns. He is our strength and deliverer.

There are forty tents on the ground. It is a beautiful encampment. All is neatness and order. Those who come to the grounds have much to say in praise of the arrangement and order--and the meetings they are delighted with.

After I ceased speaking, the first men of the place came into our tent and stated that that discourse was the greatest that had been given in this country. The whole world should have heard it. This is the general feeling. I was solicited to speak at Stow to the temperance club. It is a place of great resort in the summer. The largest church in this place was secured for me, but Father was fearful that I should do too much, so I withdrew my appointment.

There were one thousand teams upon the ground Sunday. We may leave tonight for the New York camp meeting.--Letter 17, 1877. (To "Dear Children," September 10, 1877.)

My dear boy [W. C. White], we trust you will yet be a blessing to others. Oh, Willie, I do want that you should glorify God in your life. This world, this life, is of but little account; the better life, the better world, live for this, my precious boy, and you will never regret it. No, never. I can never express the love I feel for you, my boy, yet I had rather bury you as much as I love you, rather than to have you forget God. Heaven, heaven, nothing is sure but heaven. Pray to your heavenly Father for strength and health of body and mind.--Letter 12, 1870, p. 2. (To W. C. White, September 6, 1870.)

Correct Conceptions Necessary--It will be essential to have correct conceptions of Christ's life, Christ's habits, that His principles may be reproduced in us who would be Christlike. A half service, loving the world, loving self, loving frivolous amusements, makes a timid, cowardly servant. Such follow Christ a great way off.--Ms. 1, 1867. ("Our Late Experience," n.d.)

White Estate
Washington, D. C.
August 22, 1981

ELLEN WHITE'S WORK WITH W. W. PRESCOTT

Questions Asked Led Ellen White to Present What She Might Not Otherwise Have Presented--I had a long talk with Professor [W. W.] Prescott last Thursday or Friday in regard to school education. This will come out soon. I have a great work to do and must have the Holy Spirit's guidance. Professor Prescott drew me out as your father [James White] used to do, and many things I could say and did say that I otherwise might not have spoken. Then he said I must write it.--Letter 144, 1896, pp. 1, 2. (To "Children," February 16, 1896.)

Thoughts on Christian Education--Battle Creek, November 22, 1889. At about half past eleven o'clock a.m. Brother Prescott called. He is the president of our school and we have had many precious seasons of communion together in regard to the best plans to uplift the students religiously. We believe Brother Prescott is a man fitted for the work in which he is engaged. The question is constantly arising and has to be met and treated with great wisdom: Are we, as Seventh-day Adventists, doing what we should do in combining religious education--which is science--with the education of science in our schools?

We conversed together upon this matter and could not arrive at any other conclusion than that our former position on this question is correct. We cannot go back upon this important subject of keeping the education of every faculty equal. Each is to be improved by all the advantages within our reach, always making the most of our opportunities, that all the powers of our being may be consecrated wholly to the service of God. The teachers in our colleges may do a high, noble, holy work in educating the youth that they may reach the highest standard in intellectual acquirements. There is no danger of their soaring too high, if balanced by the sanctification of the Holy Spirit.

The fear and knowledge of God are to be combined with all their education. The knowledge of God, the understanding of His will in His Word as far as finite minds may grasp it, incorporated into the thoughts, interwoven in the character, will make efficient men. The study of the Word of God will give knowledge as to how to do the work of God intelligently and acceptably. The mind will become sanctified through watchfulness and prayer and will be enriched, enlarged, and broadened in comprehension. There will be constant self-improvement, constant going forward and upward to meet the highest standard, because they are seeking to be made partakers of the divine nature.

Daniel was closely connected with the Source of all wisdom, and this knowledge was to him more precious than the gold of Ophir. He kept his religious training equal with the advantages which were within his reach of becoming a wise and learned man in the sciences. Daniel worked with his entrusted capital of talent. He was aroused by the situation in which he found himself, in the king's court of Babylon. He cooperated with God to use every power God had given him, that he should not be second in anything. And we read, "As for these four children, God gave them knowledge and skill in all learning and wisdom: and Daniel had understanding in all visions and dreams" (Dan. 1:17). Because Daniel was connected with God, the secrets of the Lord were opened to him, for they are "with them that fear Him" (Ps. 25: 14).

[Dan. 1:19,20 quoted.]

If the Lord God of heaven and earth will become the teacher of men, will they not have the very best kind of knowledge for this world, as well as for the next? This world is our preparatory school.

Continual growth in religious wisdom and intelligence did not in any sense disqualify these youth for the faithful, intelligent discharge of the important duties assigned them in the business transactions pertaining to the kingdom of Babylon.

The schools, the colleges, and the seminaries for the educating and developing of the mind are essential for the formation of character. Natural and mental resources come alone from a knowledge of the laws which God has established in nature and in our own human structure, and obedience to these laws must be observed, or our lives will prove a failure.

Under the controlling influence of Jesus Christ, the human intellect can achieve wonderful things. If ten righteous persons would have saved ancient Sodom from destruction, of what value is righteousness for every nation! The cultivation of the intellect alone, disconnected from moral and religious education and training, would have a baleful influence.

Christ came to our world to destroy nothing but the works of the devil. In this age the Lord can better impress His children in forest homes and in the wilderness, to do service for Him, than in the bustle and confusion of city life. The Lord understood all about the settlement of America, and He moved upon the oppressed Pilgrim Fathers to make that land their retreat from religious persecution. In the wilderness in this strange land the exiles found want, deprivation, and terrors by day and night.

Battle Creek, Michigan, November 23, 1889--It is the holy Sabbath. I arose in the early hours of the morning and presented my humble request to my heavenly Father for the grace and Spirit of God which I so much needed today. I then put my heart in a trusting frame, believing I find peace and quietude in committing my soul to God as unto a faithful Creator. I must be a wholehearted, decided Christian in all things. I must be persevering. I must not trust in myself alone as capable of perfecting a Christian charac- ter. If I do, I shall certainly fail. While it is my privilege and duty to grasp and improve as a blessing every gracious opportunity, every means pos- sible for the improvement of my mind and the strengthening of my soul, I look alone to Jesus who is the true source of all power to mold my character after the divine pattern. While I will look to Jesus, who is the author and finisher of my faith, catching the divine rays of light from heaven, I am daily pressing forward toward the mark for the prize, believing that what grace has begun glory shall crown in the kingdom of God.

Friday, November 22, Elder Prescott, who is the principal of our col- lege, made request for me to meet with them Sabbath afternoon in their social meeting in the college. I had been suffering with infirmities and thought it not prudent to do this. But my heart turned toward the students and my great interest and desire for the welfare of their souls made me earnest to go. We found a large number of the students assembled. It was not only a precious occasion but a blessed sight to see the attentive, earnest, intelligent countenances.

Professor Prescott spoke most appropriate words in regard to the lesson of Christ in the figure of the vine and the branches--appropriate words indeed and so applicable to the individual cases of all present.

I then spoke for about thirty minutes in regard to the importance of Bible and religious education combined with the education in all the sciences. I tried to present the importance of a living connection with God as essential for all their education. The elevation of man is because of the cultivation of the superior faculties with which God has endowed him.-- Ms. 23, 1889, pp. 10-14. (Diary, November 22, 23, 1889.)

Thursday, February 13, 1896--In the afternoon Professor Prescott and wife again visited me in my room. We had a long talk in regard to the management of school matters. As questions were asked the Holy Spirit revived many things in my mind, and I could tell them the way many matters concerning our educational interest had been presented to me. We are to lay the situation of dearth of means before the whole school and then make known the Lord's plan as presented to me. In place of devoting time to inventing amusements to use their muscles, they can strengthen nerves and muscles to good advantage in the work that needs to be done on the school grounds. If we shall be compelled to hire the work done, the price of tuition must be increased. Every student may consider it to be his privilege to have a part in saving means they would pay for hiring work done, that themselves can do. Earning their expenses is to be considered a part of their education. Every student is to exercise brain and bone and muscle. Here is the education of the whole man, right on the ground--an education essential for all, for there is work for all to do. . . .

Friday, February 14, 1896--Professor Prescott came to see me and read several letters to me in regard to the highest education--education in our schools. One was from Professor [Frederick] Griggs. We had some important matters to consider.--Ms. 62, 1896, pp. 3,4. (Diary, Feb. 13, 14, 1896.)

White Estate
Washington, D. C.
August 22, 1981

GEOGRAPHICAL DESCRIPTIONS AND TRAVEL IN THE WESTERN U.S. IN 19TH CENTURY

The Mountains of Colorado, 1872--Here I am at Mr. Fair's, husband to your cousin, Addie Clough Fair, looking out and upward upon mountains of perpendicular rocks estimated at five hundred feet high. From the foot of these mountains to the top, upon ledges of solid rocks, slight excavations have been made and houses built in every spot that could be made available by stone foundations. Directly in front of me are several tiers of houses, rising one above another. Never did I behold such a scene as this. There is scarcely a sign of vegetation, no trees, but abrupt, barren rocks.

Some of these houses are very nice and expensive. Just before me is a large, fine house, built high on the top of the mountain. A wall of masonry several feet high bears up the front of the house, while the back of the house rests upon the solid ledge drilled and chiseled out for the builders. A very nicely furnished barn is built in the same manner. In stepping out of the house there is not a level place for the feet to stand upon unless built up like a platform.

There are but a very few natural yards and these are lower down the mountain and are only one or two feet in width. They build up a yard several feet high, draw dirt and place upon the top of the stone and then have but a few feet to just step out of the doorway. It is only the most wealthy who can afford this extravagance. The [homes of the] poorer class, and even some very nice homes, have not one foot of level land around them. The banker's wife's mother stepped out in one of these high, made yards to hang out clothes. She was sixty years old. She made a misstep, fell from the wall and broke her neck.

The streets are exceedingly dusty. Black Hawk is an incorporated city which runs into Central, another incorporated city. Both have eight thousand inhabitants, including Nevada. The mining enterprise keeps the country alive, but they say business is very dull now in the mining region.

Mr. Walling took us up, up, up the mountains. We feared sometimes that we should never reach the top. We had a commanding view of the country. We could look down upon Black Hawk and Central, and see all there was of both cities. It looked fearful so high, and below was a fearful precipice of rocks. If the horses had stepped over to one side we should have fallen hundreds of feet. We had a commanding view of the mountains. They were on every side of us. We could distinctly see the high mountains covered with large patches of snow. These banks of snow are estimated to be from fifteen to fifty feet deep. Some of them are perpetual. Frequently the air coming from these snow banks was so chilly, although the sun was shining very warm in the valley, [that] we were obliged to put on extra garments in the mountains.

Black Hawk and Central are a rough, seamed, scarred country. Heaps of rocks and dirt that have been cast out from the mining mills and from which the precious ore has been taken, were lying everywhere. We went into one of these, called stamp mills, in Nevada, and saw the machinery at work to separate the ore from the rubbish. It was quite a tedious process, and it was very interesting to see the working of the machinery. We obtained some fine specimens of quartz. The view upon the top of the mountain was most interesting, but words cannot present the picture before your mind in its reality.--Letter 12, 1872, pp. 1-2. (To Edson and Emma White, July 31, 1872.)

Landscape and Travel in the Mountains of Colorado, 1872--We have been slowly climbing the ascent with two engines drawing the train. We are upon the summit. One engine has been run off. We are now descending. We are eight thousand feet above the level of the sea. We are one hundred and thirty-some miles from Denver. The scenery is not charming. No farms or cultivated lands from Denver to Cheyenne. It was plains with nothing to relieve the monotony but large herds of cattle, two thousand or more in a herd.

Since we left Cheyenne the land is undulating at first, becoming more uneven and the land broken. There are scattering evergreens, scraggy and stunted, apparently growing out of the crevices of the rock. There are large boulders; they seem as regular as if they had been laid by the hand of a mason workman. We have passed five deep cuts covered with a roof that travelers shall not become snowbound. The soil is gravelly sand. Rocks seem to be congealed sand and gravel of a red cast. We have just passed a small house down among the rocks. Among the rocks are little patches of cultivated land.

Rocks, rocks everywhere, bearing the appearance of great age. Rocks cast up like fortifications seem as though placed by a workman. I see at this moment immense rocks of singular shape composed of sand and coarse gravel. We are just viewing a shanty. The chimney is topped with a barrel. The door is open and the white heads of four small children are brought to view. No sign of cultivation anywhere in this view.

We now leave the rocks and hills behind. The land is more like a plain. In some places four rows of fences are built to protect the roads from drifting snows.

Half past four: It is now snowing slowly. It has been quite pleasant all day, not uncomfortably warm or cold. We are now at Red Buttes; elevation 7,336 feet. Castles of rocks and pyramids of rocks of every conceivable shape.

A train just passed with two engines, one with six drive wheels, the other with eight.

Tuesday morning, September 24, 1872, on the cars: We all are accommodated with berths on the sleeping cars and we rested very well. Took our breakfast this morning with good appetites. A lady named Hafenway spoke to me in the sleeping cars. I think she had heard me, also your father, speak at the Health Institute. She was there when Mrs. Baker left for her home. We had an interesting interview. She is going to California for her health. Her sister is in a precarious condition. She has had hemorrhage of the lungs. Mrs. Hafenway is a banker's wife in Nebraska. She says she was benefited at the Health Institute, but home cares, the charge of three children, keep her debilitated. She says she shall live out of doors the most

of the time this winter when not too cold. The climate of Nebraska is varying and changeable.

We have just passed a mud village, houses made of mud smoothed so nicely they really looked nice, so nice. We thought them now in process of
building, but we learned it was an old settlement left to decay. The village was moved to another section of this barren waste country. We have now
passed a village of houses composed of mud, wood, and cloth. Many roofs are
covered with cloth and mud placed on the top of cloth. No trees are to be
seen anywhere, no cultivated lands. In these villages the railroad men
reside. Nothing can be raised here.--Letter 26, 1872, pp. 1-2. (To Edson
and Emma White, Sept. 23, 1872.)

Traveling by Train From San Francisco to Battle Creek, 1873--Thursday,
Feb. 27, 1873: Left San Francisco at 7:00 a.m. We arose at five o'clock to
get our breakfast, finish our packing, and get to the boat which took us to
Oakland. The people were unwilling to let us leave them, but as there was
no one to accompany my husband we felt that it must be right for us to go
with him. We took seats in the cars at Oakland at 8:00 a.m. We had a
stateroom, retired if we chose to be [apart] from the passengers. I was
sick in consequence of passengers being allowed to smoke on the cars. I
could not eat; lay down much of the time. We passed much beautiful scenery.
Passed Cape Horn, a most romantic and fearful spot, about dark. We felt to
lift our hearts to God for His care and protection on the journey, especially in passing such dangerous places.

(En route to Battle Creek) Friday, Feb. 28, 1873--It is a beautiful day. We all rested well during the night. I became very sick--headache, stomach sickness. Ate but little through the day. We had pleasant company on the train. My husband felt unusually well. Sister Hall was troubled with pain in her limbs. We saw snow, the first we had seen during the winter.--Ms. 4, 1873, p. 13. (Diary, February 27, 28, 1873.)

Saturday, March 1, 1873--We have had a beautiful day. We passed this holy Sabbath upon the cars. We kept by ourselves. We changed cars at Ogden. I was very sick all day; could not eat anything. The strong, aromatic smell of cigars affected me seriously. My head was full of sharp pain, my stomach sick. I would break out in profuse perspiration, then become deathly faint and sick. I struggled hard against it. I prayed for help from God. I fainted quite away. Smoking was banished from the car when the conductor learned its effect upon me. My husband, Sister Hall, and myself prayed earnestly, silently, for help from above. How precious was Jesus to me in my pain and perplexity. Our prayers were answered; relief came. From this time I improved.

Sunday, March 2, 1873--We had another lovely day. I felt quite well, except for weakness and loss of appetite. We slept well during the night. We passed over the most dreary desert--nothing interesting to be seen but snow and bunches of sagebrush.

Monday, March 3, 1873--We have had a beautiful day. We have had no hindrance on account of snow. We passed through many snow sheds. I conversed with a young man who is dying with consumption. He is an infidel I cannot reach. He says when he dies it is the last of him. He has led a dissolute life and dies as the beast dieth. It made the Christian life look so bright in contrast with the gloomy prospects of this poor sinner who could not comfort himself with any bright picture when he should live again. His brightest hope is in no existence beyond the grave. I gave him lemons and tried to make him as comfortable as possible, but sad, sad is the thought of this man's future. A just God he must meet.

Tuesday, March 4, 1873--We are still blessed with beautiful weather. My rest was not as good last night. We have a beautiful car, heated with steam pipes. We have lived out of our basket the entire journey with the exception of expending thirty-five cents for sundries. We are losing our appetites. Our friends go out to meals. They frequently expend one dollar each for a hasty meal, and lie down at night restless and cannot sleep because of eating so heartily. We have rested well nearly every night. We took our last meal at one o'clock p.m. Changed cars at Chicago. Arrived at Battle Creek at half past ten p.m. Brother Abbey was waiting with sleigh for us. We came to our own home. Got to rest at (?) o'clock a.m.--Ms. 5, 1873, pp. 1-2. (Diary, March 1-4, 1873.)

Home in Battle Creek--Dear Children: We have received two letters from Edson and I think three from Willie. We should have written you immediately, but I thought Father would write and he thought I would write, so between us both you were neglected.

We had a very pleasant journey home with the exception of smoking on board the cars, which made me very sick. For three days I could eat scarcely anything. I could not understand my feelings. I learned that smoking was allowed in the palace car. We paid nearly forty dollars extra for the conveniences of the palace sleeping car. I decided to endure the smoking so as not to be called a fusser.

The third day when the aromatic odor of the cigars came to me I became stomach-sick. The most intense pain pierced my eyeballs and back of the eyeballs in my head. It seemed that the top of my head was crashing like broken glass. My distress became very great. I thought I was going into a fit. Large drops of perspiration stood upon my face and my entire body broke out in profuse perspiration. Then came a confused noise in my head and I became blind and fainted entirely away. In half an hour I revived by lemon juice being pressed in my mouth. I knew as soon as I revived that it was the smoking of cigars which had thus affected me. All in the cars were alarmed and smoking was banished from the car. I have not fully recovered from the effects of this illness.

In regard to the journey, it could not have been better for us in July. We made close connections and arrived at Battle Creek Tuesday, ten o'clock p.m. Brother Abbey was waiting for us with sleigh. We telegraphed him soon after leaving Chicago to meet us at 10:05 p.m. It seems very nice to rest in our own home on our own good bed after an absence of nine months.--Letter 24, 1873, pp. 1-2. (To Edson and W. C. White, [March] 1873.)

Travel by Train Westward to Colorado, 1873--Wednesday, June 25, 1873: My husband and myself occupied the stateroom. Sister Hall and Willie kept the seats in the car and rested very well. We had no dust. We could not have had a more favorable time for traveling. At Cheyenne we changed cars for Denver. The heat on this last one hundred miles was almost beyond endurance. The blood rushed to my head and my face felt burned. The very air seemed hot, and seemed to burn our flesh. It seemed some like the time that will scorch men with heat. We were one hour behind time. We did not get to Denver till about thirty minutes past seven o'clock. We hired an express wagon and were taken to my niece, Louise Walling's. We were well received and we were very weary and glad to get to rest.

(Denver, Colorado) Thursday, June 26, 1873--We have all rested well. It has been a cool night. It is a beautiful morning. We walked out to purchase some things, but did not expend anything.

(Denver) Friday, June 27, 1873-Another beautiful day. We walked one mile and back from the city stores three times. We ordered mattresses made of white hair and a couple of pillows. We have much confusion among the children. Cannot write. We purchased cloth and batting for comforts; linen for Willie a coat.

(Denver) Sabbath, June 28, 1873--We have another beautiful day, but quite warm. We took our writing and walked quite a distance to the shade of a tree to find a quiet place to write. We enjoyed the quiet, but the shade was not sufficient to prevent our being burned by the sun. My husband corrected a sermon which has been reported to be put in Review. We took our simple lunch under the tree. About noon we saw a covered carriage coming towards us. It was Mr. Walling. We decided to start after sundown that night for the mountains. We did not get away from the city until past eight o'clock. We traveled to Golden City and put up at a hotel. We did not get to rest before one o'clock.

(Colorado) Sunday, June 29, 1873--We all rested the few hours of the
night after we retired. We were on our way about half past seven. We rode
about three miles and stopped for breakfast. We purchased milk and had a
very good breakfast. The scenery is very grand. Large mountains of rocks
stretching toward heaven, tower one above another. My husband endured the
journey well. We took dinner and enjoyed eating in the open air. My husband has been wonderfully preserved.--Ms. 8, 1873, pp. 9, 10. (Diary, June
25-29, 1873.)

Travel by Train From Denver to Battle Creek, 1873--(Denver, Colorado)
Thursday, November 6, 1873: We are at Denver. We are preparing to leave on
the train at six o'clock tonight. Mrs. Walling [Ellen White's niece] is in
a very troubled state of mind. She has pursued her course of fretting and
scolding her husband and children [Addie and May] until she has weaned his
affections from her. He insists that the children shall go with us to California. The mother reluctantly consented. Little May had a little frettish
turn, but I was firm and yet gentle with her before her father and mother,
and it passed over very well. The mother feels bad. May God show her the
error of her ways before it shall be too late. Mr. Walling attended us to
the cars and parted with us and his children. The children are perfectly
happy with us.

(En route to Battle Creek) Friday, November 7, 1873--We had a portion
of night's rest. The Legislature sits in Cheyenne, which fills the hotels.
No room for us to have a bed until two o'clock; then some beds were vacated.
We had a good rest when we did retire. My husband felt his mind turned to

Battle Creek. We consulted together and decided to go to Battle Creek and send Sister Hall on with the little children. To this she agreed cheerfully. We arranged our trunks and parted, Sister Hall going to California and we turning our course to Battle Creek.--Ms. 13, 1873, p. 1. (Diary, Nov. 6, 7, 1873.)

Travel by Train From Omaha to Oakland, 1873--Dear Children, Edson and Emma: We are seated in the cars at Omaha en route to California. We have made our transfer all right. Now we have only one more change to make before we shall reach Oakland, California. This is appreciated by us who have so great an amount of baggage. We slept excellently well last night. Your father is feeling quite well for him. He is cheerful. We have seen but little snow thus far. The weather is mild indeed for this season. In two days we shall reach the summit, then we may be sensible of a change and experience cold weather.--Letter 23, 1873, p. 1. (To Edson and Emma White, Dec. 24, 1873.)

Travel by Train From Odgen to Sacramento--Dear Children Edson and Emma: We have been passing over the plains through a very barren, desolate-looking country. Nothing of special interest to be seen but a few herds of buffalo in the distance and an antelope now and then.

The scenery over the plains has been uninteresting. Our curiosity is excited somewhat in seeing mud cabins, adobe houses and sagebrush in abundance. But on we go. From Cheyenne the engines toiled up, up the summit against the most fearful wind. The iron horses are slowly dragging the cars

-125-

up the mountain to Sherman. Fears are expressed of danger, because of the wind, in crossing the Dale Creek bridge--650 feet long and 126 feet high---spanning Dale creek from bluff to bluff. This trestle bridge looks like a light, frail thing to bear so great weight. But fears are not expressed because of the frail appearance of the bridge, but in regard to the tempest of wind, so fierce that we fear the cars may be blown from the track. In the providence of God the wind decreased. Its terrible wail is subdued to pitiful sobs and sighs, and we passed safely over the dreaded bridge. We reached the summit. The extra engine was removed. We are upon an elevation of 7,857 feet. No steam is required at this point to forward the train, for the down grade is sufficient for us to glide swiftly along.

As we pass on down an embankment we see the ruins of a freight car that had been thrown from the track. Men were actively at work upon the shattered cars. We are told that the freight train broke through the bridge one week ago. Two hours behind this unfortunate train came the passenger cars. Had this accident happened to them, many lives must have been lost.

As we near Ogden the scenery becomes more interesting than the sagebrush, dugouts, and mud cabins. There are grand, high mountains towering toward heaven, while these are interspersed with mountains of less size. As far as the eye can see them mountaintops rise above mountains, peak above peak, ridge on ridge, intermingled, while the snow-capped heights glitter under the rays of sunlight, looking surpassingly lovely. As we looked at the varying beauty of this Rocky Mountain scenery, we were deeply impressed with the greatness and majesty of God. We long to have a little time to view at leisure the grand and sublime scenery which speaks to our senses of the power of God, who made the world and all things that are therein. But a glance only at the majesty around us is all we can enjoy.

Between Ogden and Sacramento the eye is constantly delighted with the wonderful scenery. Mountains of every conceivable form and dimension appear. Some are smooth and regular in shape, while others are rough, huge granite mountains, their peaks stretching heavenward as though pointing upward to the God of nature. There are blocks of smooth, timeworn rock, piled one above another, looking as though squared and chiseled by instruments in skillful hands. There are high overhanging cliffs, gray old crags and gorges clad with pines, continually presenting to our senses scenery of new interest. We come to the Devil's Slide. There are flat rocks set up like gravestones of nearly equal depth running from the river up the mountainside far above us a quarter of a mile, which mountain is covered with grass and shrubs. The stones are from fifty to two hundred feet high, standing upon their edge as though malletted into the rocky mountain. There are two stone walls, about ten feet apart, of this masonry. The space between is covered with green foliage. It is a most interesting and wonderful sight.--Letter 18, 1873, pp. 1-2. (To Edson and Emma White, Dec. 27, 1873.)

Dear Children Edson and Emma: We have been passing over the plains, through a very barren, desolate-looking country. Nothing of special interest, but a few herds of buffalo, occasionally an antelope.

The scenery is uninteresting. Mud cabins, adobe houses, sagebrush in abundance of a very strong flavor. But on we go and the engine toils up, up, up against the most fearful wind we ever experienced. It is all the two

iron horses can do to drag the train slowly up the mountain. Fears are expressed that there is danger of crossing the bridge which spans Dale Creek
from bluff to bluff. It is 650 feet long and 126 feet high. In the providence of God the wind decreased its fearful wail to a piteous sob and sigh
and we went safely over. The summit is gained and now we pass through a
tunnel excavated through the rocky mountain. We stop a short time for the
second engine to be removed and then we pass along very pleasantly. We
cross another bridge and down the embankment we see the shattered ruins of a
freight train. We are told it broke through the bridge the week before. It
was two hours in advance of the passenger cars. If the passenger cars had
met with this disaster many lives might have been lost.

As we near Ogden we have a change of scenery--something more grand than
sagebrush, mud cabins, and dugouts. There are grand mountains and wonderful, towering mountains of masonry, filling our hearts with awe and wonder.
Gladly would we linger and view more definitely and fully the different
wonderful, varying scenes presented to the senses, but on, on steadily moves
the iron horse giving us but a glance at the wonderful works of God in
nature.

I hesitate whether to place my pen upon paper to give you even the
faintest, slightest description of the wild, romantic scenery of the Rocky
Mountains. Immense mountaintops rise above mountains. Some mountains of
lesser dimensions are wavy and appear smooth and regular in shape. Mountains of masonry have the appearance of being hewed, squared, chiseled, and
polished by art and piled one above another in grand towers, stretching upward toward heaven as though directing the minds of all who look upon them
to God.

Then we see abrupt bluffs and singular shaped rocks of every form, huge and without comeliness, having the appearance as though thrown together in most beautiful disorder. We come to a wall of rocks, flat and broad as though chiseled from the quarry and arranged by art one flat stone overlapping another, two walls almost exactly similar about ten feet apart running straight up the steep sides of the Rocky Mountains for one quarter of a mile. This strange piece of masonry is called the Devil's Slide.

But I become discouraged at the poor efforts I have made in describing the scenery of nature.

Some of the mountains are interspersed with dwarfed and stunted evergreens.--Letter 19, 1874, pp. 1-2. (To Edson and Emma White, Dec. 27, 1873.)

Travel by Horse-drawn Wagon in Northern California, 1874--Stretching to the right and left before us was still a rapid-running, deep, broad river. We were in a quandary what to do. Your father and I unhitched the horses again. He mounted Kit's back while I had all that I could do to keep restless Bill from breaking away from me and following his mate. Your father crossed and recrossed the river twice to make sure the way of safety for the carriage. The water came above his boots. We marked the course he took by a mountain on the opposite side. We hitched our horses to the wagon the second time, at nine o'clock at night, and passed over to the other side. The water came up to the body of the wagon. We felt to thank God and to take courage. . . .

Santa Rosa: We are now at home. Brother [D. M.] Canright is here. He is certain that Cloverdale is the wrong place for the tent. Cloverdale is a most romantic place, surrounded by mountains, but the inhabitants are a drinking class. It is the terminus of the railroad. It is not surrounded by a farming community.

I am satisfied our duty is upon this coast this summer. We will write you again soon.--Letter 67, 1874, pp. 1, 2. (To W. C. White, April, 1874.)

Travel by Train by Herself From Oakland to Newton, Iowa, 1874--June 4, 1874: Left Oakland this morning for Omaha, for the purpose of attending the camp meeting at Newton, Iowa. I cannot obtain a sleeping berth and must ride day and night in the car, and then attend the meeting and labor hard. May God help me to do my duty.

We have resided at Oakland about four weeks. I have spoken at Oakland and Brooklyn about six times under the tent. There has been a great excitement there upon the local-option question. The leaders of this temperance movement are women, aided by men. The large tent was granted them and they held their meetings in it for one week. Oakland gained the day upon temperance. There was a majority of 260 votes in favor of no license. The excitement is now changed to Brooklyn.

June 6, 1874: We left Ogden about eight o'clock a.m. We shall arrive at Omaha Monday morning. Mountains are surrounding us, covered with snow. It is indeed a most grand sight. We have passed the Devil's Slide--a strange looking sight indeed. The wonderful sights we pass are very interesting.

June 8, 1874: We arrived at Omaha at two o'clock p.m. Here I re-
checked my trunk. This was new to me. The day was oppressively hot, but we
were at last all ready to go on our way. We traveled until twelve o'clock
at night. We stepped off the car at Newton [Iowa], found Brother Hart waiting for me. We rode half a mile through the mud to the campground. We
quietly entered Brother [G.I.] Butler's tent and I rested my weary body upon
a hard straw bed with a straw pillow. It rained powerfully.--Ms. 4, 1874,
p. 1. (Diary, June 4-8, 1874.)

Journey From Chicago to California, 1875--Dear Willie: We are now on
board the palace car. Have good berths secured in the center of the car.

We all found good lodgings at Wilbur's. They are usually well.

Father heard some men talking in regard to the fare to California, that
they got tickets from Boston cheaper for signing a paper that they had a
time ticket, that is, do not stop off. We got our tickets for California
for $106 from Chicago. We are all feeling quite well this morning.

There are some things we will think and talk of in regard to on the
cars and write our decision. Mary is cheerful and feeling all right.

We hope that you and Lucinda will not overdo, for we want Anna and
Lucinda and Willie to enjoy the trip when you come.--Letter 2, 1875, p. 1.
(To W. C. White, Jan. 28, 1875.)

Dear Willie: We are in good spirits and all are well. Weather is
pleasant but cold. We are free from dust and cinders also, for we have to
keep the windows closed. We are anxious to hear from you all and hope to
have a letter from you soon after reaching Oakland.

Our walnuts are just splendid. Willie, put in the box those you do not use. You must prepare some for yourself on the way. I want Lucinda to be sure and make every preparation to come to California.

At two o'clock we are at Pulpit Rock. There is a wildcat and small mountain lion.

We are delayed. It is now half past two. The passengers got no break-fast before two o'clock. They were an uneasy, hungry set. We have enough to eat and are cheerful and feeling tolerably well.--Letter 5a, 1875, p. 1. (To W. C. White, Jan. 31 (?), 1875.)

On the Train, Nearing Chicago, 1875--I left Oakland none too soon. We have had the most favorable, pleasant trip across the plains this time that we ever had. There has been no dust or cinders. Our companion travelers have been, with scarcely an exception, agreeable, very courteous. We have not been crowded any of the way. Some have kept their berths made up all day. We have had an entire section to ourselves. I am rested on this journey and shall step off the car with improved health.--Letter 15, 1875, pp. 1-2. (To Edson and Willie White, May 4, 1875.)

On the Train, Near Sparta, Wisconsin, 1875--Dear Children, Edson and Emma: The lamps are being lighted. We shall soon pass through a tunnel. We have passed through three tunnels; the last was the longest. I inquired of the conductor its dimensions. He told it me was 3,812 feet long and 266 feet under ground.

The conductor tells us there is beautiful scenery before us. We find it even so--granite rocks, beautiful trees, green fields, and cultivated lands. Here is revealed indeed a beautiful picture of nature's loveliness. The air is pure. Nature seems fresh-robed in her natural lovely dress of green. The waving grain and cultivated soil, the lofty trees with their bright green foliage, make even this world very beautiful. God has given to us tokens of His love. We may read His love in the book of nature. Every tree, every shrub and bud and blooming flower tells us God is love. We look up through the things of nature which God has hung before our senses in His created works, and we adore the Giver.

The train is delayed a short time. There has been a washout. But the conductor thinks the train will not be long delayed. We are again moving, passing slowly over the dangerous road.

We shall get to the campground tonight. No rest. Just time to get from meeting to meeting.

At the Jewel Hotel in Wyoming, about three o'clock: We are disappointed in getting through tonight. We learned about one hour since that there were several breaks in the road and no means of transfer. One washout is forty rods long. We have secured a room in a hotel until tomorrow at eleven o'clock when we shall, if Providence favors, go on to the camp meeting. We deeply regret this delay, but make it a point to be surprised at nothing that may occur and not to become impatient or faultfinding. This place presents a very attractive appearance and the surrounding scenery is lovely. There are low bluffs covered with trees and verdure.--Letter 19a, 1875, pp. 3-4. (To Edson and Emma White, June 24, 1875.)

Near Eagle Lake, Minn., 1875--I send you [W. C. White] manuscript for paper, written mostly while the cars were in motion, in depots, and in almost every inconvenient position. We are now in the midst of camp meeting. Everything is wet in consequence of two days of rain.

We were hindered on the road. At Wyoming we were told there was a washout and the cars would not pass over the road until next day. We tarried at Jewel Hotel, hired a room, and engaged in writing. Next day we took the cars, rode about sixteen miles, then came to a sudden standstill. The freight cars had, in passing over the break in the road, broken through; so we waited in the cars from two o'clock until eight before the break could be repaired. I improved this time in writing. We did not reach Eagle Lake [Minnesota] until three o'clock in the morning. While waiting on the track for breakage to be repaired, the heavens gathered blackness. We had a severe storm of thunder and lightning, rain and blow. We learned this storm had spent its force before it reached us.--Letter 21a, 1875, p. 1. (To W. C. White, June 27, 1875.)

On the Train Between Ogden and Sacramento--Dear Children: We have had a trying day today. We are on the plains and the whole surface of the ground is nearly as white as snow, encrusted with alkali. We have been on the road since Sunday morning at two o'clock, five days and four nights. Everything has thus far been very favorable.

We have been, until today, remarkably free from dust. It has been cool and very pleasant. We have rested some and written considerable; this, with

the care of our children, Addie and May,* has taxed me considerably. Not
that the children have been unusual and unmanageable. They are good children. They are universally cheerful and happy and willing to obey our expressed wishes, cheerfully. This has lightened my burden of care wonderfully. Were these children as unruly and boisterous as many children in
this car, I should be indeed worn out before this time, but their innocent
ways and happy laughs are contagious. We cannot be otherwise than cheerful.

On this train, in this car, are many wealthy families traveling with
their children. One family, residents of Oakland, California, have four
children, bold, quarrelsome, impolite, and generally disagreeable.--Letter
33, 1875, p. 1. (To Dear Children, Sept. 22, 1876.)

Near Laramie Plains, Wyoming, 1876--Dear Children: We rested well last
night. Our quarters are not nearly as good as in the stateroom when we left
Oakland. But we are making the best of the situation and are therefore
quite comfortable. Our comfortable condition is made by the tone of our
feelings within. None can but be happy, if they take the happy with them.
If we are connected with heaven, the content and peace and happiness of
heaven will be ours. Our slights, our neglects, our sorrows and griefs,
will not, cannot, depress the heart that is borrowing its strength and
serenity from heaven. I have enjoyed my breakfast this morning. Food good.
Love the brown bread; brown turnovers turned out their inward treasury in

---
*Addie and May Walling, Ellen White's nieces, whom she reared as her
own daughters.

the oven, leaving nothing but crust for us. But we have plenty that is good
beside this.

I feel that I am right. Praise the Lord for the evidence we have of
His care and protection on this journey. Mary does all the   caretaking and
generals matters through excellently. She is very thoughtful of my comfort,
kind and attentive.

Yesterday while waiting for a train, we got off and were looking for a
stone or something as a memento. A lady said she had picked up some specimens which she would give me. She gave me freely specimens of moss agate,
petrified wood and bits of petrified sage. She said she had come to visit
her sister who lived at the station, and she would stay a week and could get
all she wished. I thought it was certainly very kind and liberal of her to
thus accommodate a stranger.--Letter 28a, 1876, p. 1 (To Dear Children, May
24, 1875.)

From Omaha to Kansas City, 1876--Dear Children, Willie and Mary: We
arrived at Omaha about 3:30 p.m. We were immediately put on the sleeping
car for Kansas City. Had good accommodations; rested well until four. We
were then obliged to leave the train. We are waiting at a hotel close by
depot to take the train at ten o'clock for nearest station to Melvern, which
is Barbondale Avenue. We know not how far the station will leave us from
the campground, but we may find definite directions there. We have endured
the journey well. I have a headache this morning, but this is nothing
strange, being on the road so long. I have eaten the first warm meal this
morning. Mary has eaten twice on the road. We have not taken the nearest

route, but the best we could take, because tickets were not sold through. Others came the same route we have taken because it was the best and cheapest, so we have come the best way. I thought you would be relieved to hear this. We will write you as soon as we can after we get on the ground. We will not write much more now, but will get off another today.--Letter 29, 1876, p. 1. (To Willie and Mary White, May 25, 1876.)

On the Cars En route to Council Bluffs, Iowa, 1876--Now in Iowa: In two hours shall be at Council Bluffs. Tomorrow shall take the cars for Marshalltown, Iowa. Must travel all day tomorrow.

Dear Children, Willie and Mary, I thought as my letter written day before yesterday has not yet been mailed I would write a word more on the cars.

Yesterday we arose early and rode through miles over rough road to see the train move grandly out of the depot, leaving us behind. We then went to Brother O'Brien's and waited till next morning. This was the most distressing day to us we have passed for a long time. We were all three debilitated. I very much so.

It is cooler today and we all feel better. We arose very early, rode to the depot six miles and took the cars at half past six and have been riding all day. It is now 5:00 p.m.

I find when the entire burden of labor rests on your father and myself, we do not find time and have not strength to write even letters. But Brother [Uriah] Smith will join us in Iowa so that we shall be better able to write we hope.

We have had very good meetings in Kansas and Missouri, but the best was in Kansas.--Letter 31a, 1876, p. 1. (To Willie and Mary White, June 7, 1876.)

On Board the Train En Route for California, 1877--Dear Children: All well as usual. Father slept more than he has done for many nights. He also slept over one hour through the day yesterday. It was a clear, cold night. No fire in the cars. We depended on a foot stone till we had no fire to warm it; then by much exertion we obtained our tin can of hot water. They would not let us or the porter have any hot water at Omaha. Sister Clemens went to the restaurant, the depot and two private homes. All said they had none. Rum and liquor of all kinds could be obtained readily, but not a drop of hot water. Mary went to a hotel and obtained warm water, but no hot. This she had to heat herself and dared not wait longer for fear of being left. She then started out with a determination and went to a private house and succeeded in getting our can filled. This was fortunate for father's feet were almost freezing cold. The porter filled the can at night and it remained warm all night. He was comfortable. Today he is comfortable. All are crying out now at the prairie fires. Mary has cooked father's breakfast over the little stove and we have all had hot drink. She has just heated water to fill father's can. It is made hot and it will retain its heat a long time. Tell the tinner it is a complete success--size just right.-- Letter 21, 1877, p. 1. (To Dear Children, Oct. 11, 1877.)

Dear Children: All well as usual. Father slept splendidly last night. We all rested well. Father enjoyed his breakfast this morning. He ate quite heartily. Mary obtained some nice graham flour at Cheyenne. And we have now warm gruel at our meals. Father is cheerful and we think much better, if we can judge by appearances, than when he left home. We get to Odgen tonight at half past six o'clock. We have plenty to eat. We get hot water to fill the tin can and it keeps warm all night. Filled in the morning it keeps warm all day. Mary is an excellent general on such a trip. She manages splendidly.

I am getting rested. No fire in car. We feel inconvenienced from cold for some hours in the morning. Then we are comfortable all day. Not much danger of catching heat in this car. It is altogether better for us all. It is so good to be supplied with warm clothing to make us comfortable. He has his warm can of water, warm blankets and his warm egg every morning-- just as he had it at home. We all strive our best to gratify every wish.

We are looking forward with pleasure to our arrival at Oakland. We shall be better off there than at any other place this cold winter.

May God preserve you my children and bless you and Aunt Mary. Cling to the Mighty One, hold fast to the promises. They will never, never fail. Bear your whole weight upon them and test them. Live in God. Our hours of probation are short at best. Work in God, put self out of sight, but let Jesus appear as the chiefest among ten thousand and the One altogether lovely.

Much love to the entire household, especially to my little girls [Addie and May Walling]. I hope that they will learn to come and serve God early.

They are none too young to give their hearts to God.--Letter 22, 1877, p. 1. (To Dear Children, Oct. 12, 1877.)

Dear Children: We have just had a nice walk for twenty minutes at Carlin. Father walked all the time. We rested well last night. Father is cheerful and happy, although our provision is getting stale and dry. Only three meals more. We have splendid gruel equal to custard cooked by Mary upon our little stove.

This car is well warmed, but it was very cold this morning even in the car. We could write our names on the frosted windows. The scenery now is alkali and sagebrush. We meet plenty of Indians at Carlisle Station. There is one Indian on the train in irons who was engaged in the last massacre. He is to be taken to the reservation for trial.

We are all doing well and are looking forward to the time when we shall arrive at our Oakland home. The cars jostle so I cannot write more.--Letter 23, 1877, p. 1. (To Dear Children, Oct. 13, 1877.)

From Sioux Falls, SD, to Colorado, 1879--We are anxious to get to Colorado where it is cooler. We take the stage tomorrow, ride twenty-five miles, then take the cars and ride sixty-five miles, then change and ride seventy-five miles; then stop over, and next day ride twenty-five miles to Omaha.--Letter 22a, 1879, p. 1. (To Addie and May Walling, July 14, 1879.)

On the Train En Route for California--Dear Sister Lizzie:*   After I left you Monday, I was very sick.   Tuesday, nervous and suffering with headache,
      *Probably Ellen White's sister, Elizabeth Bangs.

-140-

unable to sit up. Tuesday night we arrived at Council Bluffs. There we stopped off to visit Sister Milner. After walking about half a mile we found her not at home. I had not tasted food through the day and was still suffering with nervous headache. We walked back to a hotel, the nearest one we could find. It was not very promising. We were shown to our rooms--two very small rooms above the kitchen. In the rooms were only small windows, one in each room.

The scent of cooking had full access to these rooms with no current of air to take away the nauseating smell of ham, pork, onions, cabbage, and all kinds of scents. If I had not heretofore been most thoroughly disgusted with pork, I should have been [so] now. I could scarcely refrain from vomiting. I became sick and faint, but my good daughter Mary opened the window as far as possible and moved our bed so that the head of it was close by the window, the bed being quite nice. We slept well and felt refreshed in the morning, notwithstanding unpleasant odors.

We took the transfer car to Omaha. We enjoyed our breakfast very much. There came into the depot a woman about forty years old, followed by a large flock of children. One boy about ten years old went out on the platform. His mother went after him and came dragging him in, he resisting at every step. She pushed him with violence into the seat bringing his head with considerable force against the back of the seat, really hurting the lad. Then came screech after screech, equalled only by the screaming engine. His mother threatened him, but to no purpose. He was in for regular war-cry. When he became tired out, he lowered his voice to the monotonous long-drawn-out drawling cry just for the purpose of being persevering and

-141-

revengeful. Here the mother, I judge, was as much to blame as her boy. The
boy was stubborn, she was passionate. . . .

We purchased our sleeping-car tickets--sixteen dollars--to Ogden. We
should be two days and a half and two nights reaching there. We obtained
two lower berths and were told that if we had applied the day before we
could not have been accommodated. But the travel was light from Omaha that
day, which was much in our favor.

On leaving Omaha we found ourselves--and numerous baskets and satchels
--well disposed of in an elegant palace sleeper, only seventeen passengers
in our car, no babies to cry, no invalids to exclaim, "Please close the
ventilators. Will you shut down that window!" We are at perfect liberty to
open and close windows for our convenience. There was nothing special to
engage our attention Wednesday night but the prairie fires. These looked
grand and awful. In the distance while the train is slowly moving onward,
we see the long belts of lurid flame stretching for miles across the prairie. As the wind rises the flame rises higher and becomes more brilliant,
brightening the desolate plains with their awful brightness. We see farther
on, haystacks and settlers' homes guarded with furrows broken by the plow to
protect their little homes. We saw dark objects in the distance guarding
their homes from the fire fiend by throwing up embankments.

Thursday morning we arose from our berths refreshed with sleep.   At
eight o'clock we took a portion of the pressed chicken furnished us by the
matron of the Sanitarium, put the same in a two-quart pail and placed it on
the stove and thus we had good hot chicken broth. The morning was very cold
and this hot dish was very palatable. I limited myself to only one meal

each day during the entire journey. When the cars stopped at stations any
length of time we improved the opportunity by taking a brisk walk. Generally in approaching Cheyenne and Sherman I have difficulty in breathing.

Thursday noon we were at Cheyenne and it was snowing and cold; could
not walk much that day. "All aboard" was sounded about half past three and
again we were moving onward. Nearing Cheyenne we were interested by the
view of the Rocky Mountains. Dark clouds obstructed our view. As we neared
Laramie we were having a hailstorm. Occasionally the sunlight would break
through the clouds, striking full upon the mountaintops, but night drew on
and we were all huddled together while preparations were being made for us
to occupy our berths. This night the wind blew the coal gas into the windows, nearly suffocating me. I was afraid to sleep. This night was the
only disagreeable one upon the route. In the morning after we had taken our
breakfast from our well-filled dinner baskets, we felt much refreshed. I
wrote several pages back to Battle Creek. Here we began to come to scenery
worth our attention.

The cars move slowly and smoothly along giving the passengers a fair
chance to view the scenery. An additional engine is added to help draw the
train up the summit of Sherman. We reached Sherman about six o'clock and
had no inconvenience in breathing. The elevation between Cheyenne [and
Sherman] is two-thousand-and-one feet, the distance nearly thirty-three
miles. The ascending grade averages from Cheyenne sixty-seven feet per
mile. The two engines puff and blow as if requiring a powerful effort to
breathe. At length the summit is reached and the descent begins two miles
west of Sherman. We cross Dale Creek bridge. It looks frail, as if incapa-

ble of sustaining the ponderous train, but it is built of iron and very sub-
stantial. A beautiful narrow, silvery stream is winding its way in the
depths below. The bridge is 650 feet long, 126 feet high, and is considered
a wonderful affair in this route.

We look in the valley below and the settlements look like pigeon
houses. We pass rapidly down the grade through the snow sheds and granite
cuts. We have now as we pass on a full view of the Diamond Peaks of the
Medicine Row Range. They are with their sharp-pointed summits pointing
heavenward, while their sides and the rugged hills around them are covered
with timber. When the atmosphere is [clear] the snowy range can be distinctly seen clothed in the robes of perpetual snow. A chilliness creeps
over you as you look upon them so cold, so cheerless, and yet there is an
indescribable grandeur about these everlasting mountains and perpetual
snows.

But night draws her sable curtains around us and we are preparing to
occupy our berths for the night. The wind was blowing strong against us,
sending the smoke of our heating stove into every opening and crevice in the
car. I slept, but awoke with a suffocating scream. I found myself laboring
hard for breath. The coal gas was so stifling I could not sleep for hours--
dared not sleep. This was the most disagreeable night that I had on the
journey. In the morning I felt better than I expected. We again prepared
our breakfast, making a nice hot broth. Our two tables were prepared, one
in each seat, and we ate our nice breakfast with thankful hearts. The porter, well-filled with silver donations, was very accommodating, bringing
lunch baskets, making room, and depositing our baggage with all pleasant-
ness.

We are known on the train. One says, "I heard Mrs. White speak at such a meeting." The book agent, a fine young man from Colorado, says he heard Mrs. White speak in the large mammoth tent in Boulder City. He was a resident of Denver. We have agreeable chats with one and another. As we move on slowly over the great American desert, with no objects in sight except sagebrush and distant mountain peaks, we seem more like a ship at sea. The massive train headed by our faithful steam horse, moving along so grandly, seems like a thing of life. You look occasionally back from the rear of the cars upon the straight track hundreds of miles with scarcely a curve, while wilderness and desolation meet you whichever way you may look. Passing Cheyenne, we soon entered snow sheds constantly varying from light to darkness and from darkness to light--the only change for miles.

I had been growing stronger as I neared Colorado. We were telegraphed to Ogden soon after leaving Omaha for seats in the car for California, and our seats were assigned us just as we were located in the car. We leave therefore. It is always best to secure good seats when you take the palace car from Omaha for that secures you good seats all the trip. Now the tickets have to be purchased at the ticket office before the baggage can be taken into the car. We are all settled some time before the sun has passed out of sight beyond the mountains.--Letter 6a, 1880, pp. 1-7. (To Lizzie [Bangs?], Feb. 6, 1880. Portion printed in RH, June 17, 1880.)

Near Kansas City, Missouri, 1884--We had a very pleasant season with our brethren, then were taken in the hack back to depot. From this point we had a dusty time; could not sleep well. The smoke from the engine was blown

back and it was very strong and throat and lungs were severely affected with
this coal smoke. But all this is over. We are at Edson's. He is pleasantly situated in a location separate from other houses and standing high and
dry. The location is every way better than the one they had before. I cannot write all I would be pleased to write, for I am not feeling [as if I
had] much life and energy. I had a severe pain in my heart yesterday. Today my hip troubles me considerably.--Letter 49, 1884, p. 2. (To Children,
August 10, 1884.)

On Eastbound Train, Nearing Reno, 1884--To Willie and Mary. Nearing
Reno: Will be at Reno in one half an hour. We had a very good night's
rest. After you left us, we were told our position was in the next car and
thither we went, seated ourselves, and found it was filled with men. We
were the only women in the car. At night we had two other women. We had
tobacco effluvia creeping into our car, which made my heart very active and
my throat and lungs sore, but I may not be troubled as much today. My head
aches some, but I feel of good courage.

We have no checks for trunks. Probably you have discovered this, as
well as we. We reasoned [that] the checks will be forwarded to Kansas City.
We learned there was a washout at Truckee. The train coming west was delayed, I think, one day and a half. This is all the news I have to write.

Willie, I wish Elder Waggoner and yourself would, in connection with
those in St. Helena, put Sister Ings in officially as matron of the institution there. This will give character to her work. We have not yet taken
lunch, so I cannot speak understandingly of our liberal outfit, but will

tell you in our next [letter] how this suits us. I am not as debilitated as
last year and think I will do well. My trust is in God. Will write again
today when I may have something to write.

P.S. Nearing Elko Station; about six o'clock. We have had a very
pleasant day. A number of men stopped at Reno. Brother Balborn and wife
called upon us while the passengers were taking breakfast. We had quite a
pleasant visit. Besides us, there are only three men in the car. The porter has been an old hand on the train, kind as kind can be. We have had a
little dust, and a small spurt of a shower.

A telegram was received in regard to our trunks and the conductor insisted on my telegraphing back to you, while he would telegraph to the parties in San Francisco. I knew it was not the least use to telegraph [you],
for you must know the trunks were not on the train. He insisted on our going into the baggage car. They got a chair and we climbed up and found no
trunks of ours. Then he telegraphed. The agent said he must punch my tickets or baggage would not be sent; the conductor said I must not get my tickets punched until the telegraph should notify us the trunks were on the way.
But the agent said he was mistaken, so my tickets are punched. We have
plenty of room, good food and plenty of it. Sister McComber scalded up the
chicken. Will scald the meat tomorrow morning. We arrive at Ogden at seven
tomorrow. I wish you had told me just how far you had paid for a sleeper;
sleeping car conductor says [it was] only [paid] to Ogden, so we must go
through that process of securing tickets in the Ogden depot. I shall get
the porter to do this for me.

We are doing real well. I am feeling well. We are having a pleasant trip. Feel very thankful to the Lord for His mercies and blessings.--Letter 63, 1884, pp. 1-2. (To Willie and Mary White, Autumn, 1884.)

En Route to Europe, 1885--(En route east) July 13, 1885: We left Oakland. There were twelve in our party. We were well accommodated. About twelve more occupied one end of the car until we reached Mojave. Then we changed cars, Wednesday noon. There were only three men in our car besides our party. The heat was very great, but we had no dust. We passed over heavy sand. We passed over a very large body of sand which was like a lake almost as white as snow.

July 14, 1885--We have very good accommodations. The weather is excessively hot--thermometer 125 degrees in the shade. I endure the heat much better than I had any reason to expect I could. I tell our party the best way to endure the heat is not to think about it or talk about it. As we came to Fresno, Brother [Moses] Church and son came on the cars bringing a box of peaches, a large box of grapes, and a very large watermelon.

July 15, 1885--As the rough class are no longer in our car we commenced religious services--singing and prayer. There was one of the workers on the train that looked as though he did not know whether to laugh or to cry. He afterward told Brother Lunt it was the first prayer he had heard for five years. His father and mother were praying people. He left home and had been in rough company, but the prayer he had listened to touched his heart and he felt a desire to be better than he was then. . . .

July 17, 1885--Friday. We had services in the morning and at the commencement of the Sabbath. I spoke to our people in regard to keeping the

Sabbath on the cars. I told them there should be every effort made--yes, extra effort--on our part to keep our minds reflecting upon proper subjects and our words select. There should be a determined purpose to honor the God of the Sabbath by keeping it holy. We did not want to lay aside our religion because we were on the cars. We did not want to backslide on the train, but to be in that spirit of devotion that we could keep our lips from uttering perverse things, and that we should be pure and holy, not light and jovial and trifling, but have our words seasoned with grace. The conductor seated himself in our little circle and remained until I had ceased speaking. . . .

July 20, 1885--I could not sleep much during the night for my pain was great in my hip. I was thankful for the light of day. We arrived at Chicago. Took cars at one for Battle Creek, Michigan. Arrived at Battle Creek about half past eight p.m. Met Brother Sawyer, who urged us to go to sanitarium. Edson was waiting for us and we took lunch at his house. W. C. White did not come with us on this last stage of the journey. He had business to transact in Chicago. The weather was excessively hot, not favorable for sleeping.--Ms. 16a, 1885, pp. 2-3. (Diary, July 13-20, 1885.)

Between Reno and Oakland, 1888--Dear Nephew: I received your letter and was glad to hear from you. But I have not received one line from Addie.

I have just written to her that I shall be in Reno, which is a station one day and night's journey from Oakland on the way east. I shall take no attendant with me, and shall depend upon her meeting me and rendering me the service I shall need at the camp meeting. If she cannot get there before the first of June, or if she will meet me to accompany me on the cars from

Reno to Sacramento and thence to Fresno and forty miles by private conveyance up into the mountains to Burrough Valley, where we intend to remain until the last of July, I can get along. I must be where so many people will not visit me, for I am much worn with constant labor.

This will save Addie some twenty dollars, save me some forty dollars, for I would have to take an attendant from here if I did not have her to return with me. I can have company to the meeting, but not from the meeting, as they intend going to Oregon camp meetings. So you can see the plan I have in view. The meeting commences the 24th of May and continues until the 5th of June.

I am hoping to meet Addie at that time. I write you this that you may know my plans. I want this to go this morning so cannot write more now.-- Letter 1a, 1888, p. 1. (To Dear Nephew, May 20, 1888.)

From Denver to California, 1889--Denver, Sunday, Sept. 15, 1889: The storm that had come down in steady rain Sabbath, the 14th, had passed and the weather was pleasant.

I spoke to a crowded tent upon the subject of temperance. "To him that overcometh will I grant to sit with Me in My throne, even as I also overcame, and am set down with My Father in His throne" (Rev. 3:21). I had freedom in speaking. Many outsiders were present and listened with apparent earnest interest.

We parted from our friends and dear Mary Sunday evening, to take the train en route for California the same night, leaving Denver at five minutes past nine o'clock.

En route to California, September 16, 1889--We have excellent accommodations. There are but two parties besides ourselves in the car, and we have plenty of room. I am so weary I must keep my berth made, for it seems as though it would be very difficult to sit up. I usually do some knitting, but I have no strength even for this. I am asking my heavenly Father for the strength required that I may do His will. I have a message to bear to the people, and although struggling against infirmities I am not comfortless. I have the blessed assurance, "Lo, I am with you alway, even unto the end of the world." The peace of Christ is of highest value.

We reached Ogden September 16, at 9:45 p.m.--twenty-four hours from Denver. Although we had a first-class ticket and could have the privilege of the palace sleeping car, we decided the four in our party could save twenty dollars by putting up with some inconveniences on the emigrant train. Money at this time is an important article, for there are missions to be established, missionaries to be sent, and the truth to be carried to all nations, tongues, and peoples. This will require means, and this is ever before me. Save, save all you can save.

My own expenses are very large, to keep my many workers employed and pay them their wages, amounting to $150 per month, for rooms, board, and wages.

At Ogden the car was filled with passengers. Some had been waiting over to take this train. They were obliged to wait hours on account of washed-out bridges.

September 17, 1889--The effects of the rain are not seen; it is dry and dusty. We eat and drink dust. Last night I was much afflicted for want of breath. I longed to breathe sweet pure air that was not filled with dust

and alkali and tobacco. All we can do is to exercise patience and look

forward with joy to the time when the sagebrush plains are behind us.-- Ms.

21, 1889, pp. 17-18. (Diary, September 15-17, 1889.)

White Estate
Washington, D. C.
August 22, 1981

STEADFASTNESS ON OUR SANCTUARY DOCTRINE

It is your privilege to know what is truth, because for more than half a century we have been guided step by step by the counsels of the Spirit of God. At this time many efforts will be made to unsettle our faith in the sanctuary question, but we must not waver. Not a pin is to be moved from the foundations of our faith. Truth is still truth. Those who become uncertain will drift into erroneous theories and will finally find themselves infidel in regard to the past evidence we have had of what is truth. The old waymarks must be preserved, that we lose not our bearings.--Letter 395, 1906, p. 4. (To S. M. Cobb, Dec. 25, 1906.)

White Estate
Washington, D. C.
August 22, 1981

PRINCIPLES OF TRUE EDUCATION

Levity Among Students Harmful to Character Development--It is the spirit of the age to despise restraint, to desire to follow inclination, to jest and joke and be jolly in amusement with young ladies; and the result has been wrecks of character, encouragement to impurity, licentiousness, immorality, and marriages which have ruined the usefulness and efficiency of men and women who had ability and talents, but who have been unable to rise to any noble heights after their unwise marriages. . . .

Separation of the Sexes--They [certain school administrators] cannot see any harm in the young people's being in one another's society, paying attention to each other, flirting, courting, marrying and giving in marriage. This is the main engrossment of this time with the worldlings, and genuine Christians will not follow their example, but will come out from all these things and be separate.

In our sanitarium, our college, our offices of publication, and in every mission, the strictest rules must be enforced. Nothing can so effectually demoralize these institutions, and our missions, as the want of prudence and watchful reserve in the association of young men and young women. --Ms. 4a, 1885, pp. 30, 33. ("Counsel to Physicians and Medical Students," July 27, 1885.)

The Place of Bible Study in SDA Schools--All the teachers in this school [South Lancaster Academy] should be men and women of principle and connected with God. We do not live in this world merely to please ourselves, but it is our duty, every one of us, to make the most of our God-given ability in order that we may uplift humanity that is around us. I have felt so interested in the education of the youth that I have said to individuals, "If you will go to our schools I will see that your expenses are met," but I cannot feel at ease to do nothing in this matter.

We know that there is a question whether the Bible should be brought in as one branch of the education. Why, it should be the main branch. We think that the Bible contains a knowledge of the very highest and loftiest science, and why should we not make it, as we are making it, a speciality in educating the children. We know skepticism and infidelity are dwelling in our land and we want to bring up the youth that they will become acquainted with history and there is nothing that can elevate the mind and understanding like the opening of their minds to the Scriptures.--Ms. 19, 1887, pp. 1, 2. (A sermon on "A Practical Education," August 18, 1887.)

Schools and Sanitariums Should Be Established in Many Rural Locations-- True missionary workers will not colonize. God's people are to be pilgrims and strangers on the earth. The investment of large sums of money in the building up of the work in one place is not in the order of God. Plants are to be made in many places. Schools and sanitariums are to be established in places where there is now nothing to represent the truth. These interests are not to be established for the purpose of making money, but for the purpose of spreading the truth. Land should be secured at a distance from the cities, on which schools can be built up, and where the youth can be instructed in agricultural and mechanical lines of work. . . .

What can I say to our people that will lead them to follow the course that will be for the present and future good? Will not those in Battle Creek heed the light given them by God? Will they not deny self, lift the cross, and follow Jesus? Will they not obey the call of their Leader to leave Battle Creek and build up interests in other places? Will they not go to the dark places of the earth to tell the story of the love of Christ, trusting in God to give them success?

It is not the Lord's plan, but human devising, for our people to crowd into Battle Creek.--Ms. 12, 1889, pp. 1, 2. ("Establish the Work in Many Places," 1889.)

Establish Schools Like the Schools of the Prophets--There are schools that may be established, not in the elaborate way of Union College or of Battle Creek College, but after a more simple style, with humble buildings, and then there should be teachers who will conduct them after God's plan as nearly as they can understand, after the school of the prophets.--Ms. 14a, 1897, p. 2. ("Work for the Fallen," Feb. 14, 1897.)

Mischievous Students Receive No Benefit From School, and Hinder Others-
Nothing is to be tolerated in the school that will counterwork the very object for which the school was established. In believing and receiving the truth, we may be doers of the word of Christ. Thus day by day we receive

grace sufficient for the duties and trials of the day. But no students should be allowed to remain connected with the school who allow their own mischievous, cheap, common, practices to control their whole mind. They themselves receive no good, and others are hindered from receiving good. Satan takes possession of them, and works through them to bring, not only their own souls into captivity, but the souls of other youth, who have not moral power sufficient to say, "We have had enough of this malarious atmosphere which poisons our thoughts." By their words students can confess or deny Christ.--Ms. 81, 1897, pp. 5, 6. ("Counsels to Students," July 7, 1897.)

Focus Attention on the Cross of Christ--Educators who will not work in these lines [Christian education] are not worthy of the name they bear. Teachers, turn from the examples of the world; cease to extol the professedly great men; turn the minds of your students from the glory of everything save the cross of Christ. That cross is to be bravely and manfully borne. Christ declares, "Whosoever will come after Me, let him deny himself, and take up his cross, and follow me" (Mark 8:34). And to all who will lift it and bear it after Christ, the cross is to them a pledge of the crown of immortality which they shall receive, which can never fade away.-- Ms. 11, 1898, p. 6. ("Word of God as a Study Book," Feb. 4, 1898.)

Students to Impart as They Have Received--Every soul is to obtain an education with the object in view of imparting his knowledge to others. The powers of the mind are God's gift, and we are to use them to benefit and

bless the members of the human family. As the mind is enlarged by true
knowledge, the heart will be softened and subdued into humility, kindness,
and true love. We are to gather all the knowledge possible for the purpose
of communicating the same that it may become the property of others.--Ms.
54, 1898, pp. 3, 4. ("Our School," May 2, 1898.)

Bible Teaching in SDA Schools Not to Be Restricted to One Man--In our
schools the work of opening the Scriptures to the students is not to be left
to only one teacher. This would not be wisdom. Other minds should be
brought in. One man may seem well able to present the truth, and yet this
is not evidence that he should teach the students from the Word of God term
after term. Others should aid in this work, for it is a great work.-- Ms.
158, 1898, pp. 3, 4. ("The Gift of the Holy Spirit," Dec. 7, 1898.)

The Benefits of Schools in the Country--It seems strange to everybody
that we should be located in the woods. But we do not want our students to
be near the city. We know that even though we bring them into the country
we cannot escape from all evil. We have a public house [saloon] here, and
not long ago a man left this public house drunk. As he was crossing a
bridge he fell from his horse and was killed. But in the country the youth
are away from the sights and the sounds of the city. We desire to take the
students away from the foul atmosphere of the city. Not that Satan is not
here. He is here, but we are trying to do all we can to place the students
in the very best circumstance in order that they may fasten their eyes on
Christ. . . .

Some parents, because their children say, "I am tired of the Bible," try in every way to manage so that they will not have so much Bible. I say, Give children and youth the Bible as their study book. God will work with children and youth who give themselves to Him. Samuel was educated for the Lord in his youth, and God passed by the hoary-headed Eli and conversed with the child Samuel.--Ms. 99, 1899, pp. 7, 8, 10. (Talk given on July 20, 1899.)

The Danger of Presenting to Students Things That Make God's Word of None Effect--Those who present the truth should be men of solid minds, who will not lead their hearers into a field of thistles, as it were, and there leave them. What is the chaff to the wheat? There are those teaching others who need that one teach them how to labor for the present and eternal good of those they instruct. Some readily catch up trivial theories, calling them truth, and neglecting for them the immortal principles which must be interwoven with the life-experience of him who is saved. They are ready to open the mind to any fallacy that is presented. These are in danger of bringing in vain things which make of none effect the important truths of God's Word. This Word is the Lord's revealed will, given for the instruction of His people. Let no one bring dishonor to the precious truth by mingling with it theories which have no foundation in the Word of God.-- Ms. 70, 1901, pp. 8, 9. ("What Is the Chaff to the Wheat?" July 20, 1901.)

The ABC's of True Education--All who are engaged in teaching the youth in our schools must have as the foundation of their knowledge the fear of

God, for this is the beginning of wisdom. They may have had years of train-

ing, and yet [may] not have touched the very beginning, the ABC of spirit-

uality, the ABC of devotion, the ABC of self-sacrifice. The science of

education is to love God, and to keep His commandments. Study the Word of

God intelligently. It is the foundation of all education.-- Ms. 84, 1901,

pp. 1, 2. ("Teachers to Have a Living Experience," August 20, 1901.)

The Bible to Be the Foundation of Education in SDA Schools--In many

places we have established our educational institutions. Our schools and

our sanitariums are to reach a high standard. The Bible is to be made the

great educational book. It is the Book of books, that gives us a knowledge

of Him whom to know aright is life eternal. It is to be made the foundation

of all true education.--Ms. 49, 1908, p. 6. ("Lessons From the Experiences

of Pentecost," May 9, 1908.)

Flesh Foods and Other Unhealthful Preparations Not to Be Served in SDA

Schools--I have been instructed that the students in our schools are not to

be served with flesh foods or with food preparations that are known to be

unhealthful.--Ms. 37, 1909, p. 4. ("Faithfulness in Health Reform" May 30,

1909.)

Demoralizing Effect of Games on Students Contrasted With Benefits of

Physical Labor--The Healdsburg College has been presented to me as being de-

moralized by disgraceful games. Games have been allowed such as God dis-

approves. It was to prevent this kind of thing that the Lord gave counsel

to the effect that students should learn useful trades. . . .

Where were these watchmen when these unseemly games and athletic sports, these trials of animal strength and exhibition of physical skill were in progress? Students could have had this class of education at home. . . .

Labor should be connected with study, and through following a course of this kind an all-sided, well-balanced education will be the result. This is the rational method through which souls may be barricaded against evil influences. In this way the mind may be preserved in its soundness, and the nervous energies may be regulated. Combining manual labor with the study of the sciences will preserve the living machinery in excellent condition, and by taking proper exercise, the mind may be taxed and yet not sustain injury in any degree.

But do not substitute play, pugilistic boxing, football, matched games, and animal exercises, for manual training. All of this stripe and type should be vigilantly prohibited from the school grounds.--Letter 27, 1895, pp. 1-3. (To F. Howe, May 21, 1895.)

Do Not Enlarge Battle Creek College; Scatter Out--Large gatherings in Battle Creek are a great mistake. Do you think the Lord can be well pleased to have still larger preparations made to accommodate a larger number of students when such definite light has been given upon this subject, and instead of distributing the light into many places of the earth it is concentrated at Battle Creek, and many do not appreciate or improve the light that is given them?--Letter 61, 1895, p. 7. (To O. A. Olsen, Feb. 2, 1895.)

Schools Not to Run in Debt--In regard to the school's running in debt:

The tuition has been altogether too low in America. Cannot those who con-

duct the schools in America understand that this is the only way out? Why

do they keep the price so low? An increase in price of educational advan-

tages would stop that increasing debt. The students are to be fed and they

need good, nourishing food. They should not be stinted in the wholesome

fruit and vegetarian diet; but cut off everything like the desserts. Let

abundance of fruit be eaten with the meals, but custards and pastries are of

no manner of use, all unnecessary.

Now when the wise heads officiating in our schools study to run the

school upon a sum wholly insufficient, year after year, they are engaged in

a work that will bring debts. It cannot be prevented. They have begun this

policy at Cooranbong [Avondale College], and the very same results will

follow. There is no justice, or requirement of God, for them to make such

loose calculations. They make it necessary to practice the closest economy

and it is not always wise to bring down the diet as a means of avoiding

debts. Economy must be practiced in every line to keep afloat and not be

drowned with debts; but there is to be an increase in the sum paid for

tuition.-- Letter 137, 1898, p. 11. (To Brethren Irwin, Evans, Smith, and

Jones, April 21, 1898.)

"Reformatory" Schools Needed Because of Parental Failure--Our school

[Avondale College] is not what is usually termed a "reformatory" school, yet

it is so in fact; and every child and youth is to be brought under strict

discipline, for many parents have failed in understanding their accountabil-

ity as parents.--Letter 97, 1899, p. 2. (To Mrs. Chick, June 26, 1899.)

Schools to Operate on a Sound Financial Basis--Altogether too large sums of money have been invested in the school building at Battle Creek, and too little wisdom and brain power has been brought into the practical methods to stop the increasing indebtedness of each year. It would have been far better to have closed the school until it should become a science how to conduct the schools in different localities on a paying system. . . .

The Lord is not pleased, for it reveals a lack of judgment with the kind of management that has been revealed in the past. Let teachers take less wages, and let the students' fees be raised. Let the strictest economy be practiced in the provisions made for the table. Let the one who has charge of the cooking gather up the fragments, that nothing be lost.--Letter 104, 1899. (To S. N. Haskell, August 1, 1899.)

Students to Avoid Food That Taxes the Body and Dulls the Mind--From this we see what an important part a simple diet acts in preparing students to hold positions of trust. Students should cooperate with God by abstaining from all food which will tax the physical powers and becloud the mental faculties.--Letter 34, 1900, pp. 2, 3. (To Brethren and Sisters in Australia, Feb. 24, 1900.)

Care in the Handling of School Money--Who is your bookkeeper? Who is your treasurer? Who is your business manager? Are they careful and competent? Look to this. It is possible for thousands of dollars to be misappropriated, apparently without anyone understanding how, and the school be losing continually. Those in charge may feel this keenly, supposing they

have done their best. But why do debts accumulate? Let those in charge of
a school find out each month the true financial standing of the school.--
Letter 187, 1903, p. 9. (To W. C. White, August 17, 1903.)

Do Not Sell School Land; Raise Crops on It--Instruction was given me
that a mistake was being made in selling so much of the school land. The
land should have been kept by the school, to be utilized in raising crops
that would have done much to sustain the school. I have said that if some
of the land that was sold could be purchased back, it would be well.--Letter
61, 1905, p. 1. (To A. J. Breed, Feb. 5, 1905.)

Build More, Smaller Schools--I am very glad that you and many others
are seeking earnestly to establish schools for our youth. Let not the
buildings erected be large, but plan for smaller schools in several places.
Fewer students in each school will be more favorable to its proper management to the one end that in the school here below they shall learn the meaning of obedience to the Lord's requirements. . . .

Distance of Schools to Cities--The Lord has designated that distance
from the cities affords the most favorable situation for our institutions.
You ask if 25 miles is far enough from the city to establish a school. I
think it is; and if nearer places can be found where there is good land for
cultivation, let it be nearer. But if such places are not obtainable, let
not the distance of a few miles be a hindrance to the establishment of the
school.--Letter 156, 1906, pp. 2, 3. (To N. D. Faulkhead, May 29, 1906.)

Madison School to Be Helped--The Madison School needs our help just as truly as help was needed for the sanitarium. The brethren connected with that school have done an excellent work. In their efforts to combine manual labor with other school work, all have gained a valuable experience. The Lord has not been pleased with your indifference toward the school.

The Madison School is in the very place to which we were directed by the Lord, in order that it might have an influence, and make a right impression upon the people.--Letter 156, 1907, p. 2. (To J. A. Washburn, April 18, 1907.)

SDA Schools and Degrees--In view of all this, our schools should have little to say now of "degrees," and of long courses of study. The work of preparation for the service of God is to be done speedily. Let the work be carried forward in strictly Bible lines. Let every soul remember that the judgments of God are in the land. Let "degrees" be little spoken of.-- Letter 382, 1908, p. 4. (To G. A. Irwin, Dec. 23, 1908.)

Care in Establishing Self-supporting Schools--At this time money is scarce, and very hard to obtain. There must be exercised great caution and good judgment in the establishment of self-supporting schools. If you have capabilities to do a good work as a teacher, I would encourage you to unite with others in school work.--Letter 122, 1909, p. 1. (To Brother Spaulding, August 13, 1909.)

Areas of Special Instruction in SDA Schools--Thorough instruction will be given in Bible study, physiology, the history of our message; and special instruction will be given regarding the cultivation of the land. It is hoped that many of these students will eventually connect with schools in various places in the South. In connection with these schools there will be land that will be cultivated by teachers and students, and the proceeds from this work will be used for the support of the schools.--Letter 215, 1904, p. 10. (To Miss M. A. Davis, June 30, 1904.)

Care in Selection of Textbooks for SDA Schools--Certain books which have been brought into our schools as textbooks, because teachers deemed these essential to a complete education, are to be exchanged for those books that will educate the students in lines that will fit them to graduate to the higher school of the courts above, where Christ will lead His people and instruct them in a deeper knowledge of His Word.--Letter 28, 1909, p. 4. (To Anna Rasmussen, Jan. 15, 1909.)

Sanitariums and Schools to Be Located Near Each Other--I wish to speak of some things presented before me concerning the establishment of the school and the sanitarium that is to be established near Nashville [Madison institutions]. Careful attention is to be given to the advantage that may be gained in locating these institutions near each other. In regard to the institutions to be established in Takoma Park [Washington Adventist Hospital and Columbia Union College], I was shown that the Lord would certainly be honored were these institutions placed near enough one another to be a help and a blessing to one another.

The students who will attend the Nashville school will be helpful to the sanitarium, and the sanitarium will be a blessing to the school. . . .

On the school farm the patients will have abundance of room in which to roam about in the open air. The beauty of the scenery will attract them, and the truth will take hold upon their minds.

Let these two lines of work be carried on in close proximity with each other, yet as far distant from each other as the judgment and wisdom of those in charge shall determine. One institution will give influence and strength to the other. Money will be saved, for both institutions can share the advantages that they will both need.--Letter 369, 1904, pp. 1, 2. (To Brethren Hayward and Hansen, Sept. 21, 1904.)

Physical Work Combined With Book Study--There has been some delay in getting the title to the Buena Vista property [Sonoma, California]. We are looking forward to having the matter settled soon. This is an excellent site for a school. As soon as I saw it, I was sure that it would make an ideal place for the carrying on of our educational work, for we can combine physical work on the farm with the study of books. Here the students can be taught to build and to engage in many useful lines of labor, as the students at Madison are being taught to do. There should also be sanitarium facilities in connection with the school, for I have been shown that where we have a training school we should have a sanitarium where the students can receive instruction in caring for the sick and suffering.--Letter 18, 1909, p. 2. (To J. E. White and wife, Jan. 13, 1909.)

Establish Sanitariums in Connection With Training Schools--Health institutions will need to be established in many places. And in this work we
are to remember that it is well to establish small sanitariums in connection
with our training schools.--Letter 390, 1907, p. 4. (To G. I. Butler, Nov.
29, 1907.)

Cautions Regarding the Establishment of SDA Schools--I have been warned
that the teachers in our younger schools should not travel over the same
ground that many of the teachers in the Battle Creek College have traveled
over. Popular amusements for the students were brought into Battle Creek
school under a deceptive garb. . . .

The Lord has thought it essential to give reproof, correction, and instruction in righteousness on many points regarding the management of
schools among Seventh-day Adventists. All the light that has thus been
given must be carefully heeded. No one should be connected with our schools
as a teacher who has not had an experience in obeying the Word of God. The
instruction which the Lord has given our schools should be strictly regarded, and if the education given is not of a different character from that
which has been given at the Battle Creek College, we need not go to the expense of purchasing land and erecting buildings. . . .

The students coming to our schools have had an abundance of amusement
which serves merely to please and gratify self. They are now to be given a
different kind of education, that they may go forth from the school prepared
for any service.--Ms. 172, 1898, pp. 1-3. ("The Character and Work of Avondale School," Dec. 20, 1898.)

White Estate
Wash. D. C., Aug. 22, 1981

ALL-ROUND CHRISTIAN EDUCATION

Distrust of Self Is Essential--In His Word the Lord enumerates the gifts and graces that are indispensable for all who connect with His work. He does not teach us to ignore learning, or to despise education, for when controlled by the love and fear of God, intellectual culture is a blessing; yet this is not presented as the most important qualification for the service of God. Jesus passed by the wise men of His time, the men of education and position, because they were so proud and self-sufficient in their boasted superiority, that they could not sympathize with suffering humanity and become co-laborers with the Man of Nazareth. In their bigotry they scorned to be taught by Christ.

The Lord Jesus would have men connected with His work who appreciate that work as sacred; then they can cooperate with God. They will be unobstructed channels through which His grace can flow. The attributes of the character of Christ can be imparted to those only who distrust themselves. The highest scientific education cannot in itself develop a Christlike character. The fruits of true wisdom come from Christ alone.--Ms. 14, 1896, p. 1. ("Qualifications Essential for the Work of God," April 28, 1896.)

The Bible to Be Studied--In our school [Avondale College] the Word of God is to be our main study. We are to learn not only to read the Word, but to study it as the book which we must understand in order to be complete in Christ. . . .

The human agent must cooperate with the Divine. Your thoughts will become pure and heavenly as you diligently peruse the lessons of the Old and New Testaments. The Word of inspiration should be your daily food. It alone is the tree of life.--Ms. 54, 1898, pp. 1, 2. ("Our School," May 2, 1898.)

Lessons From Nature, and the Importance of the Bible in SDA Schools--By a study of natural things, they [Christian teachers] may exemplify spiritual things. The Lord has given the open book of nature in material substances. In the tilling of the soil, proper persons should be appointed to oversee a certain number of students and should work with them. Thus the teachers themselves will be helped to become men who can carry responsibilities as burden-bearers. The Lord Himself gives His presence to this line of education. . . .

Students should not merely be told to do this or do that without being given a lesson that will teach them the principles underlying the things they are required to do. As they put seeds into the ground, teach them the lesson of the germinating principle of seeds, found in the great lesson Book. Teach them the time to sow, the time to plant trees in their season, and when to prune them. Draw lessons from the day and night, the sunshine and clouds, the former and the latter rains, the harvest. . . .

It is essential that the students in our school obtain an education that they can take with them wherever they go, a knowledge that they can use to the glory of God. True higher education gives power, and the students who receive this education are to consecrate all to God, using their knowledge to search the Scriptures, for this is wisdom that will give an influ-

ence in His work that nothing else can give.   Ignorance is a crime when
light and knowledge can be obtained.   Sanctified knowledge will give much
joy to believers and much light to those who are in the darkness of error.
The education of every student should be turned to the best account in doing
the work of the Lord intelligently.   To every man the Lord has given his
work, according to his several ability. . . .

The Lord has been greatly dishonored in our institutions of learning
when His Word has been made only a book among books.   The very Book that
contains infallible wisdom has scarcely been opened as a study book. . . .

Students and teachers are to regard themselves as being in partnership.
It will be of no benefit or blessing to the school for any of those who act
as teachers to draw themselves apart. Work in Christ's lines. Talk to each
other and pray with each other as Christians.   Stand under the yoke of
Christ. "Learn of Me," said the great Teacher, "for I am meek and lowly in
heart: and ye shall find rest unto your souls. For My yoke is easy, and My
burden is light" (Matthew 11:29,30). I am instructed to speak to our teachers, urging them to become elevated, sanctified, ennobled, by heeding the
invitation, "Come unto me. Take upon you My yoke of restraint and obedience.". . . A study of God's Word will make all students wise unto salvation.--Ms. 55, 1898, pp. 2-4, 7, 9, 10. ("Union With Christ and With Each
Other," May 4, 1898.)

Unselfish Christian Service the Aim of the Highest Education--What are
you here for? Is it to obtain an education that will help you to stand by
the side of Christ in unselfish service? This is the highest education that

you can possibly obtain. The Word of God declares, "Ye are labourers together with God." (See 1 Corinthians 3:9.) "Work out your own salvation
with fear and trembling. For it is God which worketh in you both to will
and to do of His good pleasure" (Philippians 2:12,13). . . .

Christ gives a new character to all who believe. This character,
through His infinite sacrifice, is to be the reproduction of His own. . . .

A great work is to be accomplished by personal labor. Much is comprehended in the command, "Go out into the highways and hedges, and compel them
to come in, that My house may be filled" (Luke 14:23). There is a work to
be done in this line that has not yet been done. . . .

Many more workers ought to be in the field. There should be 100 where
now there is only one. Many who have not been ordained or licensed may work
in their own neighborhoods and in the regions about them. . . .

The Bible is to be the great textbook of education, for it carries in
every page the evidence of its truth. The study of God's Word is to take
the place of the study of books that have led minds away from the truth.--
Ms. 139, 1898, pp. 6, 16, 19, 23. ("An Appeal for Missions," October 21,
1898.)

The Place of the Bible in Education--If the Bible had been made the
book of study in the schools, what a different showing there would be in
society today. The Word of God must be our lesson book if we would travel
heavenward, and in the words spoken by inspiration we are to read our lessons day by day. . . .

Let the students in our school study this Book which has been so universally neglected and set aside for books that are not inspired. Let every

student be taught to read the Word of God with prayerful, earnest interest, lest he shall fail to be a doer of the Word, and his education in science be a useless knowledge; lest he build his house, not upon the eternal Rock, but upon the sand. . . .

All knowledge gained in this life of probation, which will help us to form characters that will fit us to be companions of the saints in light, is true education. It will bring blessings to ourselves and others in this life and will secure to us the future, immortal life with its imperishable riches.

Christ came to our world to restore the moral image of God in man, to elevate and ennoble our mental character, that our pursuits and aims in this life might not be misapplied and lost, and it is of the greatest consequence that every student in our schools obtain that knowledge that will enable him to cooperate with God in the grand work of forming characters after the divine pattern. We may carry with us all the treasure of knowledge that gives us a fitness for the life that measures with the life of God. The fear of the Lord is the beginning of wisdom. Christ came to our world to mold character and give mental power. His teachings were of an entirely practical nature.--Ms. 67, 1898, pp. 1, 2, 9. ("Search the Scriptures," June 9, 1898.)

The Purpose for the Establishment of Avondale College--The school [Avondale College] was established at a great expense, both of time and labor, to enable students to obtain an all-round education, that they might gain a knowledge of agriculture, a knowledge of the common branches of education, and above all, a knowledge of the Word of God. . . .

-173-

Relationships Between Body, Mind, and Spirit--The proportionate taxation of the powers of mind and body will prevent the tendency to impure thoughts and actions. Teachers should understand this. They should teach students that pure thoughts and actions are dependent on the way in which they conduct their studies. Conscientious actions are dependent on conscientious thinking. Exercise in agricultural pursuits and in the various branches of labor is a wonderful safeguard against undue brain taxation. No man, woman, or child who fails to use all the powers God has given him can retain his health. He cannot conscientiously keep the commandments of God. He cannot love God supremely and his neighbor as himself. . . .

Health and a clear conscience will attend those who work faithfully, keeping the glory of God in view. There are many who are mere fragments of men. In Christ is seen the perfection of Christian character. He is our pattern. His life was not a life of indolence or ease. He lived not to please Himself. He was the Son of the infinite God, yet He worked at the carpenter's trade, with His father. As a member of the home firm, He faithfully acted His part in helping to support the family. . . .

Men, women, and children should be educated to labor with their hands. Then the brain will not be overtaxed to the detriment of the whole organism. . . .

Completeness of Christian character is possible. How? "Ye are complete in Him" (Colossians 2:10).--Letter 145, 1897, pp. 3, 6, 9, 10. (To W. C. White, August 15, 1897.)

Dangers of Worldly Higher Education--I am intensely in earnest that our people shall realize that the only true education lies in walking humbly with God. The teachings of the Word of God are opposed to the ideas of those who think that our students must receive the mold of an education that is according to human ideas. Some are departing from the faith as a result of receiving from the world what they regard as a "higher education." The Word of God just as it reads contains the very essence of truth. The highest education is the keeping of the law of God.--Letter 132, 1909, p. 4. (To J. A. Burden, October 11, 1909.)

Suitable Sites for Schools in Rural Areas--We are looking for places on which to establish industrial schools. In charge of these schools we shall place carefully chosen teachers who will teach the children and youth to use their capabilities in a way that will make them of use in the Lord's work. I am urging our people to establish our schools away from the congested cities, and to place in these schools faithful, consecrated teachers who will make the Word of God the beginning and end of all the education given. --Letter 143, 1902, p. 3. (To Mrs. Mary Foss, Sept. 12, 1902.)

Searching for a Site for Pacific Union College--With some of the brethren, I have looked at several locations. At one place there was a large berry-patch that yielded abundantly, but there was little land that could be cultivated. This was not a place suitable for our school. Our school should be located where the students can receive an education broader than that which the mere study of books will give. They must have such a training as will fit them for acceptable service if they are called to do pioneer work in mission fields, either in America or in foreign countries. There must be land enough to give an experience in the cultivation of the soil and to help largely in making the insitution self-supporting. . . .

Consideration of what I saw, and the description given of other parts
of the property,* made it plain that here were many most precious advantages. It was away from the strong temptations of city life. There was
abundance of land for cultivation, and the water advantages were very valuable. All through the mountains there were little valleys where families
might locate and have a few acres of land for a garden or orchard. The many
pipes laid over the grounds made it possible to use water freely both for
the buildings and for the land.

The buildings were to me a very convincing argument in favor of this
property. With the buildings already erected we can begin school work without delay, and the students can receive a most valuable education in putting
up the other buildings that may be necessary. Besides the main building and
the barns, there are two large stone wineries. These can all be used to
good advantage. . . .

Here will be a place for our school, where the youth can obtain just
the education that is essential. In this school which shall be established
we want to demonstrate what the higher education is. We must have the physical and the mental training combined. Our bodies must have exercise.
There have been many deaths because of a lack of suffcent exercise to maintain the health. . . .

We desire our school to be in a retired place. But there is a work to
be done for the community in which we may be located. There are cities and
towns all around that can be worked by the teachers and students. And we
hope this summer to hold a good camp meeting right on this property, and to
arouse an interest among the people of Sonoma to hear more of the truth for
this time.--Ms. 9, 1909, pp. 1-4. ("The Buena Vista Property," Feb. 6,
1909.)

---

*Buena Vista, New Sonoma, Calif., a property offering many advantages, but
without a clear title.

   All-round Education to Be Provided--We are trying to provide means by
which the students in our school may obtain an all-round education by learning to use brain, bone, and muscle equally. This is God's design. As students seek to obtain this education, they become familiar with different
lines of physical work, as well as different lines of study. . . .

   We cannot be in Christ's service, we cannot wear His yoke and bear His
burdens, unless we learn in His school how to love one another as He has
loved us. When this precious attribute is cherished, self dies, and Christ
lives in the soul.--Ms. 84, 1898, pp. 2, 4. ("Notes During Week of Prayer,
No. 4," July 3, 1898.)

   Nature to Be a Lesson Book--The educational advantages of our school
[Avondale College] are to be of a distinct order. This school farm is God's
lesson book. Those who till the soil and plant and cultivate the orchard
are to make the application of nature's lessons, and bring these lessons
learned into their actual spiritual experience. Let every individual bear
in mind that "whatsoever a man soweth, that shall he also reap." The man
who day by day sows objectionable seeds, in words, in deportment, in spirit,
is conforming himself to the same character, and this is determining the
future harvest he will reap.--Ms. 116, 1898, pp. 2, 3. ("Two Great Principles of the Law," Sept. 16, 1898.)

   Lessons to Be Learned From Agricultural Process--As they cultivate the
soil, the students are to learn spiritual lessons. The plow must break up
the fallow ground. It must lie under the rays of the sun and the purifying
air. Then the seed, to all appearance dead, is to be dropped into the pre-

pared soil. Trees are to be planted, seeds for vegetables sown. And after man has acted his part, God's miracle-working power gives life and vitality to the things placed in the soil. In this agricultural process, there are lessons to be learned. Man is not to do slothful work. He is to act the part appointed him by God. His industry is essential if he would have a harvest.--Ms. 71, 1898, p. 2. ("Come Up to the Help of the Lord," June 14, 1898.)

Giving God's Word a Subordinate Position--We have a deep and earnest desire to see all the members of the churches transformed, physically, mentally, and morally. They see men, society, and the world, all in disorder, thinking only of remodeling the fabric. Greater skill, later methods, better facilities, they think will set all things in proper order. Apparently they receive and believe the living Oracles, but they only give the Word of God an inferior position in the great framework of so-called philosophy. It is a secondary consideration with them. That which could stand first is made subordinate to human inventions.--Ms. 58, 1898, p. 9. ("The Mistake of a Low Fee for Tuition," April 17, 1898.)

Unity in Diversity--The Lord endows His workers with power. By the influence of this power they are fitted to be wise directors and teachers, each doing his appointed work. Then the truth goes forth as a lamp that burneth. But God does not design that the teachers of truth shall each be strong on one point. There is to be unity in diversity. Every one is to be earnest in endeavoring to keep the unity of the Spirit in the bonds of peace. One man's thought is not to control, but minds are to be united

under the great Head, as the branches are united to the vine. Believers in
the Saviour who gave His life for them, they are to work together in harmony. There will be no friction, for they will realize that they are called
to the belief and knowledge of the truth as it is in Jesus. Those who are
partakers of the divine nature will be one in spirit with Christ. "For he
that is joined unto the Lord is one spirit" (1 Corinthians 6:17). . . .

Yielding to a desire for diversity has placed the church where God cannot glorify His name through His people. The question is asked, "Why are
not the sick among us healed?" It is because of the lack of unity and love
that exists in the church.*   Perfection of character means perfection in
unity. "That they all may be one," Christ said, "as Thou, Father, art in
Me, and I in Thee" (John 17:21). What possibilities are before us. Shall
not our faith grasp them?--Ms. 158, 1898, pp. 6, 7, 9. ("The Gift of the
Holy Spirit," Dec. 7, 1898.)

*Ellen White elsewhere writes at length concerning prayer for the heal-
ing of the sick and sets forth several reasons why we should not look to
this as the only method to pursue. See MM pp. 13-16; EGW Biography, Vol. 5,
pp. 385-388.

The Quality of Students to Be Trained for the Ministry--In our schools
we want to educate workers, for God wants workers. There are many who think
that if there is a man who cannot make a success at anything else he would
make a minister, but we do not want such men. We want men who can think,
plan, and devise. Do you think a minister who is employed in visiting needs
no ability and tact? If there was ever a place where there should be thinking and acting done, it is in the upbuilding of the kingdom of our Lord
Jesus Christ. Therefore, we want useful persons, and those who have made a
success in other things.

Physical Labor-When you send your children to school, don't tell them
you don't want them to do any manual labor. The physical labor is just what

they need. [Tell them] that they will not only develop the mind, but that they will have physical power as well as mental, that they will not have a one-sided education. . . .

Culinary Arts--There should be in our colleges domestic duties. Good cooking is in demand everywhere, but people have come to regard the act of cooking as something to be looked down upon. And can we marvel at it when we see how the servant girl is treated? When my children would not talk to my cook and associate with her, I would take them and say, Now children I want to talk with you a little. I appreciate my seamstress and I appreciate my copyist, but I appreciate my cook above everyone else of the helpers in my family, because the cook, if educated to her business, knows how to pre-pare good cooked food for the stomach; therefore, my cook stands higher than my seamstress or copyist. And if there is any preference to be given it is to my cook. . . .

I am glad that in South Lancaster School there has been manual labor brought in, and we ought to prize this as the very highest method.--Ms. 19, 1887, pp. 5-7. ("Practical Education," August 18, 1887.)

Physical and Mental Training to Be Combined--The education to be gained in the felling of trees, the tilling of the soil, and the erection of build-ings, as well as the studies of the classroom, is what our youth should seek to obtain. Tentmaking also should be taught. Buildings should be erected, and masonry should be learned. Farther on, a printing press should be con-nected with the school, that an education may be given to students in this line of work.

There are many things which lady students may also engage in, such as cooking, dressmaking, and gardening. Plants and flowers should be cultivated, strawberries should be planted. Thus the lady students may be called out-of-doors to gain healthful exercise, and to be educated in useful labor. Bookbinding also, and a variety of trades, should be taken up. These will not only give exercise to brain, bone, and muscle, but they will also give knowledge of great value. The greatest curse of our world today is idleness. The students coming to our schools have had an abundance of amusement, which serves merely to please and gratify self. They are now to be given a different kind of education, that they may go forth from the school prepared for any service. . . .

Medical-Missionary Work and Business Training--It is also very essential that students understand the principles of medical-missionary work, for wherever students may be called, they need a knowledge of the science of how to treat the sick. This will give them a welcome anywhere, because there is suffering of every kind in every part of the world.

It is an important matter that students be given an education that will fit them for successful business life. In many schools the education given is one-sided. In our schools the common branches should be fully and thoroughly taught.--Ms. 172, 1898, pp. 3-5. ("Character and Work of Avondale School.")

Madison School an Example of Combining Physical Labor With Book Study--The Lord has given to the Southern field object lessons of different kinds. The education being given to the students at Madison, which trains the youth to build, to cultivate the land, and to care for cattle and poultry, will be of great advantage to them in the future. There is no better way of keeping the body in health than to follow the plan of training that the Madison school is carrying out. This is the same kind of work as we were instructed to do when we purchased the land for our school in Australia. The students had their hours for study and their hours for work on the land. They were taught to fell trees, to plant orchards, to cultivate the soil, and to erect buildings, and this training was a blessing to all who engaged in it.

The Lord in His providence has brought about the establishment of the Madison school through the efforts of Brethren [E. A.] Sutherland and [P.T.] Magan, and a few faithful associates. Their labors have been performed under no ordinary circumstances. These men had an experience at Berrien Springs which was a severe one, but the Lord brought them safely through it and made it a means of blessing to them. They felt that they must go to the South and labor for this needy field. They went out not knowing whither they were going, and the Lord guided them to Madison, a beautiful place of 400 acres. For a time the way for the establishment of the work seemed hedged up. The Lord led His servants through a trying experience, but He saw the end from the beginning. When some of their brethren expostulated and labored to discourage them, the Lord encouraged. And the results of the efforts put forth at that place we can see; The Lord's blessing has rested upon their efforts.

The work that the laborers have accomplished at Madison has done more to give a correct knowledge of what an all-round education means than any other school that has been established by Seventh-day Adventists in America. The Lord has given these teachers in the South an education that is of highest value, and it is a training that God would be pleased to have all our youth receive.

The close confinement of students to mental work has cost the life of many precious youth. The Madison school, in its system of education, is showing that mental and physical powers, brain and muscle, must be equally taxed. The example that it has given in this respect is one that it would be well for all who engage in school work to emulate. If the physical and mental powers were equally taxed, there would be in our world far less of corruption of mind and far less feebleness of health.--Letter 168, 1908, pp. 3, 4. (To J. E. White and wife, May 26, 1908.)

The Establishment of Avondale College--Well, the school [Avondale College] has made an excellent beginning. The students are learning how to plant trees, strawberries, etc.; how they must keep every sprangle and fiber of the roots uncramped to give them a chance to grow. Is not this a most precious lesson as to how to treat the human mind, and the body as well, not to cramp any of the organs of the body, but give them ample room to do their work? The mind must be called out, its energies taxed.

We want men and women who can be energized by the Spirit of God to do a complete work under the Spirit's guidance. But these minds must be cultivated, employed to do thorough work, not lazy and dwarfed by inaction. Just so men and women and children are wanted who will work the land, and use their tact and skill, not with a feeling that they are menials, but that they are doing just such noble work as God gave to Adam and Eve in Eden, who love to see the miracles wrought by the Divine Husbandman. The human agent plants the seed and God waters it, and causes His sun to shine upon it, and up springs the tiny blade. Here is the lesson God gives to us concerning the resurrection of the body and the renewing of the heart. We are to learn of spiritual things from the development of the earthly. . . .

The spiritual lessons to be learned are of no mean order. The seeds of truth sown in the soil of the heart will not all be lost, but will spring up, first the blade, then the ear, then the full corn in the ear. God said in the beginning, "Let the earth bring forth grass, the herb yielding seed, and the fruit tree yielding fruit." God created the seed as He did the earth, by the divine word. We are to exercise our reasoning power in the cultivation of the earth, and to have faith in the word of God that has created the fruit of the earth for the service of man.

The cultivation of our land requires the exercise of all the brain power and tact we possess. The unworked lands around us testify to the indolence of men. We hope to arouse to action the dormant senses. We hope to see intelligent farmers, who will be rewarded for their earnest labor. The hand and head must cooperate, bringing new and sensible plans into operation in the cultivation of the soil. We have here seen the giant trees felled and uprooted, we have seen the ploughshare pressed into the earth, turning deep furrows for the planting of trees and the sowing of the seed. The students are learning what ploughing means, and that the hoe and the shovel and the rake and the harrow are all implements of honorable and profitable industry. Mistakes will often be made, but every error lies close beside truth. Wisdom will be learned by failures, and the energy that will make a beginning gives hope of success in the end. . . .

For both children and men, labor combined with mental taxation will give the right kind of all-round education. The cultivation of the mind will bring tact and fresh incentive to the cultivation of the soil.

The more intelligent a man becomes, the more religious influence should be radiating from him. And the Lord would have us treat the earth as a precious treasure, lent us in trust.--Letter 47a, 1895, pp. 5-8. (To J. H. Kellogg, August 27, 1895.)

Purchase of Sunnyside--The plat of land I am to purchase [Sunnyside, Cooranbong, Australia] costs me $1,350. I have forty acres and it was sup- posed I would have twenty; but I want to embrace as much as forty acres, for some must be left as woodland and a portion for grazing and cultivation. Sometimes I think forty is scarcely sufficient. The purchase of this land is really a necessity for the school, and everything seems to be struggling to advance. Why we are here is that we shall have a suitable place to have the children who attend school receive all the benefits of a healthful, beautiful location, and our influence will be a help to many souls if we continue in the love of God. . . .

You will be interested to learn that the industrial department is work- ing successfully. Study and labor combined is working wonderful changes in the physical, mental, and moral [nature of the students]. Students are im- proving in every way.-- Letter 88a, 1895, pp. 3, 9. (To J. E. White, April 4, 1895.)

The Land Is to Be Our Lesson Book--Plans were laid to build cottages on the school campus [Avondale College]. I was glad I was here at the time that this subject was brought up, for I had something to say. I told them that the grounds were not to be occupied by buildings. The land is to be our lesson book. After being cleared, it is to be cultivated. Orange, lemon, peach, apricot, nectarine, plum, and apple trees are to occupy the land, with vegetable gardens, flower gardens, and ornamental trees. Thus this place is to be brought as near as possible to the presentation that

passed before me several times, as the symbol of what our school and premises should be. Dwelling houses, fenced allotments for families were not to
be near our school buildings. This place must by the appointment of God be
a representation of what school premises should be--a delight to the eyes.

The open book of nature is to be the student's study. Schools should
be established away from the cities. I have more invested in this land than
any other person. I am carrying students through school, paying their expenses that they may get a start. This gives me an influence with teachers and
learners. The land was laid out in lots. Houses were to be built, as in a
village. But I tell them that buildings are not to be crowded upon the land
around the school buildings. This is God's farm, and it is sacred ground.
Here the students are to learn the lesson, "Ye are God's husbandry; ye are
God's building." The work that is done in the land is to be done in a particular, thorough, wise manner. From the cultivation of the soil and the
planting of seed, lessons in spiritual lines may be learned.

All kinds of industrial employment are to be found for the student.
The students are constantly to learn how to use brain, bone, and muscle,
taxing all harmoniously and equally.--Letter 84, 1898, pp. 8, 9. (To J. H.
Kellogg, October 5, 1898.)

Schools in the Last Days--"I [the Lord] will instruct the ignorant, and
anoint with heavenly eyesalve the eyes of many who are now in spiritual
blindness. I will raise up agents who will carry out My will to prepare a
people to stand before Me in the time of the end. In many places that ought
to have been provided before with sanitariums and schools, I will establish
My institutions, and these institutions will become educational centers for
the training of workers." . . .

When opportunity offers, our people should purchase properties away from the cities, on which are buildings already erected and fruit orchards already in bearing. Land is a valuable possession. Connected with our sanitariums there should be lands, small portions of which can be used for the homes of the helpers and others who are receiving a training in medical-missionary lines.--Ms. 109, 1902, pp. 7, 8. ("The Favor of God of More Value Than Worldly Honor," August 11, 1902.)

Blueprint for SDA Health-Care Institutions--Our sanitariums are established as institutions where patients and helpers may serve God. We desire to encourage as many as possible to act their part individually in living healthfully. We desire to encourage the sick to discard the use of drugs, and to substitute the simple remedies provided by God, as they are found in water, in pure air, in exercise, and in general hygiene. . . .

Our sanitariums are to be centers of education. Those who come to them are to be given an opportunity to learn how to overcome disease, and how to preserve the health. They may learn how to use the simple agencies that God has provided for their recovery, and become more intelligent in regard to the laws of life. . . .

Jesus Christ is the Great Healer, but He desires that by living in conformity with His laws, we may cooperate with Him in the recovery and the maintenance of health. Combined with the work of healing, there must be an imparting of knowledge of how to resist temptations. Those who come to our sanitariums should be aroused to a sense of their own responsibility to work in harmony with the God of truth. . . .

God would have us turn away from the fashions and the foolishness of this world. He would have us be a blessing to the community in which we live. Every Christian should be a means of disseminating the light of God's Word. God has given us minds, that we may understand, and it is our duty and our privilege to live in harmony with Him and with the laws that He has established.--Ms. 115, 1907, pp. 1-3. ("Why We Have Sanitariums," October 20, 1907.)

Why Sanitariums Are Established--We may preserve our health if we will use good common sense. That is why we have established sanitariums in so many places, that a proper education might be given.--Ms. 43, 1908, p. 11. ("Lessons From the Fifty-eighth of Isaiah," March 14, 1908.)

The Purpose and Objectives for the Establishment of Loma Linda--Loma Linda is to be not only a sanitarium, but an educational center. A school is to be established here for the training of gospel medical—missionary evangelists. Much is involved in this work, and it is very essential that a right beginning be made. The Lord has a special work to be done in this field. He instructed me to call on Elder and Mrs. [S. N.] Haskell to help us in getting properly started a work similar to that which they had carried on at Avondale [College]. Laborers of experience have consented to unite with the forces at Loma Linda to develop the school that must be carried on there. As they go forward in faith, the Lord will go before them, preparing the way.

In regard to the school, I would say, Make it especially strong in the education of nurses and physicians. In medical-missionary schools, many workers are to be qualified with the ability of physicians to labor as medical—missionary evangelists. This training, the Lord has specified, is in harmony with the principles underlying true higher education. We hear a great deal about the higher education. The highest education is to follow in the footsteps of Christ, patterning after the example He gave when He was in the world. We cannot gain an education higher than this; for this class of training will make men laborers together with God. . . .

In the work of the school, maintain simplicity. No argument is so powerful as is success founded on simplicity. You may attain success in the education of students as medical missionaries without a medical school that can qualify physicians to compete with the physicians of the world. Let the students be given a practical education. The less dependent you are upon worldly methods of education, the better it will be for the students. Special instruction should be given in the art of treating the sick without the use of poisonous drugs and in harmony with the light that God has given. In the treatment of the sick, poisonous drugs need not be used. Students should come forth from the school without having sacrificed the principles of health reform or their love for God and righteousness. . . .

It is well that our training schools for Christian workers should be established near our health institutions, that the students may be educated in the principles of healthful living. Institutions that send forth workers who are able to give a reason for their faith, and who have a faith that works by love and purifies the soul, are of great value. I have clear instruction that, wherever it is possible, schools should be established near our sanitariums, that each institution may be a help and strength to the other. He who created man has an interest in those who suffer. He has

directed in the establishment of our sanitariums and in the building up of
our schools close to our sanitariums that they may become efficient mediums
in training men and women for the work of ministering to suffering humanity.
. . .

If we had faithfully followed from the first the instruction regarding
city work, means would have come in for us to establish in these places
schools and small sanitariums where we could treat the sick and preach the
gospel and educate the people in Bible truth. We would have had means to
sustain all the enterprises for missionary work that we could carry forward.
--Ms. 39, 1909, pp. 2, 3, 6, 7. ("The Loma Linda College of Medical Evangelists," June 1, 1909.)

We are not in this school work to make money; we are here to give the
youth a well-balanced education. To this end they must educate their muscles as well as their minds for service. The physical powers should be
brought into exercise that the brain powers may not be overtaxed. We want
this school to stand forth as an example in every way; these buildings
should be perfect in their equipment.--Ms. 31,1909, pp. 4, 5. ("Industrial
Cooperation," April 17, 1909.)

The Work of the Madison School--Much acceptable work has been done in
Madison. The Lord says to you, "Go forward." Your school is to be an
example of how Bible study, general education, physical education, and sanitarium work may be combined in many smaller schools that shall be established in simplicity in many places in the Southern States.

My brethren in responsible places, mourn not over the work that is being done at Madison to train workers to go forth into the highways and the

hedges. It is the will of God that this work should be done. Let us cease to criticize the servants of God engaged in this work, and humble our own hearts before the Lord. Let us strengthen this company of educators to continue the good work in which they are engaged, and labor to encourage others to do a similar work. Then the light of truth will be carried in a simple and effective way, and a great work will be accomplished for the Master in a short time. . . .

Educate the children to do missionary work, and to bring their offerings to God. Let us awake to a sense of the spiritual character of the work in which we profess to be engaged. . . .

It is a sin for one who knows the truth of God to fold his hands and leave his work for another to do. It is a sin for any to criticize and find fault with those who in their manner of working do not exactly meet their mind. Let none blame or censure the men who have labored at Madison. In the place of complaining at your brother's work, take up your own neglected work. Instead of picking flaws in your brother's character, search your own heart, confess your sins, and act honestly with God. Let there be condemnation of self for the work that lies undone all about you. Instead of placing impediments in the way of those who are trying to accomplish something in the South, let your eyes be opened to see that time is passing, and that there is much for you to do. . . .

Brethren [E. A.] Sutherland and [P. T.] Magan should be encouraged to solicit means for the support of their work. It is the privilege of these brethren to receive gifts from any of our people whom the Lord impresses to help. They should have means--God's means--with which to work. The Madison enterprise has been crippled in the past, but now it must go forward. If

this work had been regarded in the right light, and had been given the help
it needed, we should long ere this have had a prosperous work at Madison.
Our people are to be encouraged to give of their means to this work which is
preparing students in a sensible and creditable way to go forth into neglected fields to proclaim the soon coming of Christ.

The Lord directed Brethren Sutherland and Magan, as men of sound principles, to establish a work in the South. They have devised and planned and
sacrificed in order to carry forward the work there on right lines, but the
work has been greatly delayed. The Lord guided in the selection of the farm
at Madison, and He desires that it be managed on right lines, that others,
learning from the workers there, might take up a similar work, and conduct
it in like manner. Brethren Sutherland and Magan are chosen of God and
faithful, and the Lord of heaven says of them, I have a special work for
these men to do at Madison, a work of educating and training young men and
women for mission fields. The Spirit of the Lord will be with His workers
if they will walk humbly with Him. He has not bound about and restricted
the labors of these self-denying, self-sacrificing men. . . .

The school at Madison not only educates in a knowledge of the Scriptures, but it gives a practical training that fits the student to go forth
as a self-supporting missionary to the field to which he is called. In his
student days he is taught how to build simply and substantially, how to cultivate the land, and to care for the stock. To this is added the knowledge
of how to treat the sick and care for the injured. This training for medical-missionary work is one of the grandest objects for which any school can
be established. There are many suffering from disease and injury, who, when
relieved of pain, will be prepared to listen to the truth. Our Saviour was

a mighty Healer. In His name there may be many miracles wrought in the
South and in other fields through the instrumentality of the trained medical
missionary. Therefore it is essential that there shall be a sanitarium connected with the Madison school. The educational work at the school and the
sanitarium can go forward hand in hand. The instruction given at the school
will benefit the patients, and the instruction given to the sanitarium
patients will be a blessing to the school.

The class of education given at the Madison School is such as will be
accounted a treasure of great value by those who take up missionary work in
foreign fields. My brethren, let no hindrance be placed in the way of men
and women who are seeking to gain such an education as those at the Madison
School are receiving. If many more in other schools were receiving a similar training, we as a people would become a spectacle to the world, to
angels, and to men. The message would quickly be carried to every country,
and souls now in darkness would be brought to the light. . . .

Those who have received an all-round education will have a great advantage wherever they are. The Lord reveals divine wisdom in thus leading His
people to the training of all their faculties and capabilities for the work
of disseminating truth.--Letter 32, 1908, pp. 4-10. (To Brethren in Positions of Responsibility, January 6, 1908.)

The Meaning of an All-sided Education--The grace of God takes men as
they are and works as an educator, using every principle on which an all-
sided education depends. The steady influence of the grace of God trains
the soul after Christ's methods, and every fierce passion, every defective
trait of character is worked upon by the molding influence of the Spirit of

Christ, until new motive power becomes filled with the Holy Spirit of God, after the likeness of the divine similitude.

Never forget that thoughts work out actions. Repeated actions form habits, and habits form character. . . . The Bible is to be the rule of life. It is marvelous in the eyes of the universe of heaven that men who teach the Word do not always practice the truth. Few realize what it means to be complete in Christ Jesus, the revealed will of God. His Word is not dishonored by being brought into practical life to form habits which will develop character.--Letter 85, 1896, p. 4. (To O. A. Olsen, March 16, 1896.)

Physical Exercise Needed-It is essential that every minister of the gospel should take physical exercise, and that every teacher and every student in our schools should cultivate their physical strength and live in such a way that disease shall not fasten upon them, so that the impression will go out that education is incompatible with good health.--Ms. 60, 1894, p. 6. ("Beneficent Action a Proof of Sincere Love," cir. 1894.)

Cooperation Between Schools and Sanitariums--The question has been asked if it would be well to establish our college [Pacific Union College] so near to the St. Helena Sanitarium. Recently I have written much regarding the advantages of our schools being established close to our health institutions, that the older students may have the benefits of the united instruction in the work of ministry and the care of the sick. Our schools should be near our sanitariums, but not so close as to interfere with their work. If the instruction that has been given regarding this matter is followed, the students will reap great advantages. . . .

Then, too, for their own welfare the students should have wise instruction regarding the principles of healthful living. This should be considered an important part of their education, even though they never expect to go
out as missionaries. In the primary school the children should be taught to
form habits that will keep them in health. All should have an intelligent
knowledge of how to preserve health, for thus much suffering may be avoided.
These are some of the reasons why our schools should be located in easy access of our sanitariums. Students are to be taught how to keep in health,
and free from the ills that are prevalent, but which, by the exercise of
care and wisdom, may be avoided.

Some of the meetings held in the sanitariums for the instruction of the
patients, may be made occasions of valuable instruction to the students.
Many benefits will accrue by our sanitariums and schools being closely related. Both should blend, each helping the other as far as it is possible.

I have written in regard to the Madison School, that this should be the
plan of the work there, the educational work to blend with the medical. The
interest of each institution in the other will prove a great blessing to
each, a blessing which it is not possible to define clearly. . . .

Let parents understand that the training of their children is an important work in the saving of souls. In country places abundant useful exercise will be found in doing those things that need to be done, and which
will give physical health by developing nerve and muscle. Out of the cities
is my message for the education of our children.--Ms. 85, 1908, pp. 1-3.
("Cooperation Between Schools and Sanitariums," June 30, 1908.)

   Establishment of Avondale College--We have located our school in Cooranbong that we may educate and discipline and train the youth to seek the Lord. There must be a work done to discipline the youth for a higher sphere of service. . . .

   Benefits of Exercise--Thousands are sick and dying around us who might get well and live if they would, but their imagination holds them. They fear that they will be made worse if they labor, when this is just the change they need to make them well. Without this, they can never improve. They should exercise the power of the will, rise above their aches and debility, engage in useful employment, and forget that they have aching backs, sides, lungs, and heads. Neglecting to exercise the entire body, or a portion of it, will bring on morbid conditions. Inaction of any of the organs of the body will be followed by a decrease in the size and strength of the muscles, and will cause the blood to flow sluggishly through the blood vessels. Many think they are unable to perform their own domestic duties and so depend upon others. Sometimes it is exceedingly inconvenient for them to obtain the help they need. They frequently expend double the strength required to perform the task in planning and searching for someone to do the work for them. If they would only bring their mind to do these little acts and family duties themselves, they would be blessed and strengthened in it. . . .

   One of the first laws the Creator has established in our being is that of action. Every organ has its appointed work, upon the performance of which its development and strength depend. The normal action of all the organs gives strength and vigor, while the tendency of disuse is toward decay and death. . . .

By the cheerful performance of domestic and other duties, idle daughters of wealth might become useful and happy members of society. For many, such labor is a more effective and profitable "movement cure" than the best invention of the physicians.

Parents should early awaken in their children an interest in the study of physiology, and should teach them what are and what are not correct physical habits. This knowledge is invaluable to the young. They need to understand their own bodies. An education in the things that concern life and health is more important to them than a knowledge of the sciences usually taught in the schools, and should be as early obtained. But there are few of them who have any definite knowledge of the human organism or of the mysteries of life.

Very often parents themselves are ignorant of the living machinery, with the relation and dependence of all its complicated parts. They do not understand the influence of the body upon the mind, or the mind upon the body, and they do not see the need of teaching these things to their children. They venture to assume the sacred family relationship, and to undertake to form the character and habits of their children, when they are ignorant in regard to both the physical and the moral education their offspring should receive, and many seem to be scarcely less indifferent in the matter than are the dumb animals. . . .

There is so close a relation between the mind and the body that it is not possible to secure the health of the one without giving special care to the other.--Ms. 44, 1900, pp. 2, 10-13, 20. ("Jots and Tittles," copied July 24, 1900.)

Sound Constitutions Needed--No one can submerge his identity in another. He must know himself, and give himself a favorable chance to come forth with an unbroken constitution, with a clear mind, with well-balanced nerves, and a good digestion. With these, he will be fitted to do the work he has qualified himself to do. If he disqualifies himself by imprudence, by eating hurriedly, because he has little time to spend, he is unfitting himself for ever doing sound, wholesome work.

This matter is worthy of consideration. We should keep the words of Christ ever before us. "Ye are not your own; ye are bought with a price; therefore glorify God in your body and in your spirit, which are God's" (See 1 Corinthians 6:20). The first and highest and most acceptable missionary work that the student can do is to obey God in all he undertakes, in every action of the wonderful machinery God devised in the formation of man. He is not to treat himself indifferently. He is to know himself and work with an intelligent knowledge of what he can do, and do safely, and what he should avoid in eating and in working. A disordered stomach means a disordered mind. . . .

Give yourself proper time to sleep. They who sleep give nature time to build up and repair the weary waste of the organs. [1 Corinthians 3:9-11, 16, 17 quoted.]--Letter 116, 1898, pp. 1, 2. ("Students to Understand Themselves,"no date.)

Knowledge of God Essential--Worldly education cannot make a symmetrical, perfect man. It must be combined with the wisdom that cometh from above. An intelligent knowledge of God and of Jesus Christ, whom He hath sent, is the essential knowledge, for "this is life eternal, that they might know Thee the only true God, and Jesus Christ, whom Thou hast sent" (John 17:3).--Letter 19, 1895, p. 4. (To S. N. Haskell, Nov. 6, 1895.)

Manuscript Release #884

Prophets Subject to Human Error

There is a letter I will let you have, which I supposed was the one you now have, but please keep these letters to yourself. When I see them and understand what I have done in mistake then I will send you letters that would not do any harm to be circulated. Now will you please strictly heed my request?

I can write no more now. It is near the Sabbath, and I must close up this matter. Brother Harper, that discourse given in the Congregational church was free for you to read and let others read, but the personal letter to Elder _____ was not designed to be made public. Return it to me if you please and keep no copy of the same. I will expect this to be done.--Letter 353, 1906, p. 1. (To Walter Harper, Nov. 9, 1906.)

White Estate
Washington, D. C.
August 22, 1981

THE KELLOGG PANTHEISM CRISIS

I awoke about half past one o'clock. I am being deeply impressed that we have come to an important crisis. I cannot keep silent at such a time as this.--Ms. 175, 1903, p. 2. (Diary, August 3, 1903.)

I am now instructed to prepare for publication the messages of warning that have been given over and over again for years to keep Dr. [J. H.] Kellogg from following another leader.--Letter 172, 1903, p. 3. (To W. C. White, August 4, 1902.)

After taking your position firmly, wisely, cautiously, make not one concession on any point concerning which God has plainly spoken. Be as calm as a summer evening, but as fixed as the everlasting hills. By conceding you would be selling our whole cause into the hands of the enemy. The cause of God is not to be traded away. We must now take hold of these matters decidedly.--Letter 216, 1903, p. 6. (To the Leaders in Our Medical Work, August 4, 1903.)

White Estate
Washington, D. C.
August 20, 1981

PROFESSOR G. H. BELL

The Bell School--In regard to Brother Bell's school, I know not. Write us more definitely terms and studies.--Letter 8, 1868, p. 2. (To J. E. White, March 9, 1868.)

We feel so great an interest for Lena. We propose to have her and her sister who is at Brother Olmstead's come to Battle Creek, and we will have a care for them and labor especially for their salvation. We will have them attend Brother Bell's school. He may do them good. Perhaps we may, in the strength of God, remove this prejudice that has closed about this poor child.--Letter 1, 1870, pp. 4, 5. (To Brother King, Feb. 19, 1870.)

Criticisms of Professor Bell--In reference to Brother Bell: He may move unwisely, but it would not do to separate him from that college. Small matters may arise that need correcting in Brother Bell, but I should not make any move without [unless] most positive inconsistencies arise. Excuse me from expressing myself thus freely. You are on the ground and if you converse with Brother Bell yourself, you may learn that there are two sides to the story. There are so many ever ready at Battle Creek to load our guns. We should take nothing as sure until we are most thoroughly convinced ourselves. We believe that God will guide you in judgment.

We feel anxious to learn how matters stand in Battle Creek. Do not put too much confidence in Brother N. He lacks experience. He will work

against his own influence. In his management in school he has some peculiar
ways that injure his influence as a teacher very much. I have not conversed
with Mary and Willie as to what I have written, but speak of things that I
know myself from high authority.--Letter 3, 1876, pp. 2, 3. (To James
White, April 4, 1876.)

Praise and Criticism of Professor Bell--You all know my position in regard to the matters that have occurred at Battle Creek in reference to the
school, if you have heard or read the letter I sent. If you have not,
please carefully read the contents of this long letter.

You know that I have spoken very plainly to Brother Bell in regard to
his defects. I have not in all the trouble at Battle Creek, received one
word from Brother Bell. If any of the parties who were in trouble had
wanted to know if I had any light from God in reference to the matters that
were questionable, they could have written to me.

While I do not consider Brother Bell has taken altogether a right course
in the school and has shown a weakness of character, I know that most of
those who have been so zealous in this matter, ready to condemn him, ought
to have been confessing their sins before God and purifying their characters
and making diligent work lest they fail of the grace of God, and find at
last they were guilty of worse faults than those they condemn in Professor
Bell. I have not the least countenance to give to Satan's rebuking or re-
proving sin, but he has done it and others follow his example.

God gave you light long ago to prevent this state of things, but the
church at Battle Creek paid no heed. They have developed the feelings existing in hearts unsanctified by the grace of God. I rebuke the satanic

spirit in the name of the Lord. There has been a wrong course pursued on both sides. There has been much talk and much feeling and great lack of wisdom with both parties. But those who have pursued the course they have toward Professor Bell have done a work they will one day wish they had not done, for it savors of the spirit of the prince of the power of darkness.

I think Brother S has made a mistake in having so much to say in exaltation of Professor Bell and Edith Sprague. I cannot harmonize with this. Will Brethren G and S please remember how they have felt and what they have said in reference to my husband calling names, and elevating this one and that one in the public print. Are they doing any wiser? I learn it is much easier to question and condemn than to do better yourselves. All this extolling Brother Bell and Edith Sprague I know is not right. Those who can read human nature and reason upon this matter must see the influence of such pieces in print upon those who have pushed and crowded Brother Bell. It is to make them crowd the harder, to make out a case. The least said on both sides in revealing differences of opinion, the better will it be for themselves, the better for the cause of truth, and in every way better for the ones you would extol.

I am thoroughly disgusted with speaking in praise of any man or woman. They have not humility and grace to bear it. Unless Professor Bell walks humbly before his Saviour, he will stumble and fall. I see more to cause grief in his course than to elicit praise.--Letter 11, 1882, pp. 1, 2. (To G. I. Butler, C. W. Stone, A. B. Oyen, and J. H. Kellogg, May 5, 1882.)

White Estate
Washington, D. C.
October 6, 1981

REGULARITY PART OF TRUE RELIGION

The work of God must not be done by fits and starts. It will not be placed on vantage ground by following a sudden impulse. On the contrary, it is positivey necessary to follow the good work patiently, day by day, progressing in our ways and methods. One should get up at a regular hour. If during the day the work is neglected, and the following night is spent in making up for lost time, the morrow and following day will show, as a result, a wearied brain and a general fatigue which constitute positive violations of the law of life and health. There should be regular hours for rising, for family worship, for meals and for work. And it is a religious duty, in every one of our institutions, to maintain this by precept as well as by a firm example. Many squander the most precious hours of the morning hoping that they can terminate the work thus neglected during the hours which should be devoted to sleep. Godliness, health, success, everything suffers from this lack of true religious system.--Ms. 24, 1887, p. 5. ("Testimony for the Workers of the Publishing House at Basle," Feb. 14, 1887.)

White Estate
Washington, D. C.
October 6, 1981

Manuscript Release #888

FALSE TEACHERS WILL ARISE IN OUR MIDST

False theories will be mingled with every phase of experience and advocated with satanic earnestness in order to captivate the mind of every soul who is not rooted and grounded in a full knowledge of the sacred principles of the Word. In the very midst of us will arise false teachers, giving heed to seducing spirits whose doctrines are of satanic origin. These teachers will draw away disciples after themselves. Creeping in unawares, they will use flattering words and make skillful misrepresentations with seductive tact. . . .

The Lord is guarding His people against a repetition of the errors and mistakes of the past. There have always abounded false teachers who, advocating erroneous doctrines and unholy practices, and working upon false principles in a most specious, covered, deceptive manner, have endeavored to deceive, if possible, the very elect. They bind themselves up in their own fallacies. If they do not succeed, because their way becomes hedged by warnings from God, they will change somewhat the features of their work, and the representations they have made, and bring out their plans again under a false showing. They refuse to confess, repent, and believe. Confessions may be made, but no real reformation takes place, and erroneous theories bring ruin upon unsuspecting souls, because these souls believe and rely upon the men advocating these theories.--Ms. 94, 1903, pp. 10, 12. ("Lessons From the Past," Aug. 27, 1903.)

White Estate
Washington, D. C.
October 6, 1981

THE SANCTUARY DOCTRINE AND THE SHAKING

The McCullagh Apostasy, the Sanctuary Doctrine, and the Shaking--Brother Haskell spoke, taking for his subject the sanctuary question, which is present truth. McCullagh makes derision of this subject, thus showing that the counsel given him to seek to know more of present truth, and stating that he had only a superficial knowledge of it, was correct. He knows very little of the precious truth for this time, because he has not sunk the shaft deep into the mine of truth to discover the precious ore.

God's Spirit has illuminated every page of Holy Writ, but there are those upon whom it makes but little impression, because it is imperfectly understood. When the shaking comes, by the introduction of false theories, these surface readers, anchored nowhere, are like shifting sand. They slide into any position to suit the tenor of their feelings of bitterness. This is the way McCullagh has done. He has indulged his feelings against me, without intimating to me one word in regard to his difficulties.

I am so grateful to God that the Word of God is plain and clear when our hearts are in harmony with it. Without the Word, what a starving people we would be in this world which is as desolate as a wilderness to the soul. But now springs of water break out in the desert. We may drink of the living streams which proceed from the throne of God.

Daniel and Revelation must be studied, as well as the other prophecies of the Old and New Testaments. Let there be light, yes, light in your dwellings. For this we need to pray. The Holy Spirit, shining upon the sacred page, will open our understanding that we may know what is truth.

We can appropriately say, as said the disciples when Jesus walked with them on their way to Emmaus after He had risen from the dead, Then opened He their understanding, that they might understand the Scriptures. "And they said one to another, Did not our hearts burn within us, while He talked with us by the way, and while He opened to us the scriptures?" (Luke 24:32).

Less talk about things of no profit, with much more talk of Jesus, and of the Word of Life, would give spiritual enlightenment and great joy in the soul. Then we would be steadfast, unmovable, always abounding in the Word of the Lord.--Letter 141, 1897, pp. 14-15. (To W. C. White, May 5, 1897.)

White Estate
Washington, D. C.
October 6, 1981

COUNSELS TO A. T. JONES

Dear Brother: I did not feel free to bring into the testimony I read while I was in Oakland all that had been shown me concerning your work. But I must tell you plainly that your views in regard to church discipline are not in harmony with the Word of God. You are wide of the mark. God calls upon you, my brother, to weigh your words carefully before you speak them to the congregation.

You have been given great light upon the Bible. God has helped you to make truth appear in its true bearing before the people, but this is no excuse for you to speak words that have no foundation in the Word of God; words that, if carried out, would bring our churches to the place where they would need the reproof, "My house shall be called a house of prayer; but ye have made it a den of thieves" (Matthew 21:13).

The names of those who sin and refuse to repent should not be retained on the church books, lest the saints be held accountable for their evil deeds. Those who pursue a course of transgression should be visited and labored with, and if they then refuse to repent, they should be separated from church fellowship, in accordance with the rules laid down in the Word of God.

[Matthew 5:23,24; 18:15-17; 1 Cor 5:9,10; Romans 1:16-18; 2 John 9-11 quoted.]

Brother Jones, instruction has been given to me to the effect that you are careless in your speech, and that your words must be more carefully chosen. You must remember that you are certainly dishonoring God when you use His entrusted talent of speech, which should be consecrated and holy, in such a way that it is a stumbling block to our people. Those who refuse to hear the admonitions and warnings given by God's faithful messengers are not to be retained in the church. They are to be disfellowshipped, for they will be as Achan in the camp of Israel--deceived and deceiving.

Who, after reading the record of Achan's sin and punishment, can think it according to the will of God that those who do wickedly, refusing to re- pent, are to be retained in the church? To retain them would be an insult to the God of heaven.

Elder Jones, I am much pained by your incautious statements. You speak rashly. You are not sanctified by the truth you handle. Your spirit needs to be refined. Then Christlike words will flow from a heart imbued with the Holy Spirit. You are too self-confident, too sure that everything you say possesses a power which will obtain assent to it from those who hear.

Unless you are converted, your unguarded statements will destroy the force of the most powerful sermons you can preach, for they reveal that you are not speaking under the influence of the Holy Spirit, but that "another spirit" has taken possession of you. All in your words and actions that is coarse and rough, all that savors of a reckless self-confidence, greatly injures the force of the truth that you proclaim. Unless you change, your careless speech will make fruitless the most precious truths.

Speak guardedly. When your words are weighted with the Holy Spirit, when you stand where you should as a man who is proclaiming the sacred truths of the Word of God, your unsuspected weaknesses of character will not be developed as something worthy of imitation. If you keep humble before God, self will not appear. It will be unmistakably seen that Christ is abiding in the heart, sanctifying the life. Show by your careful, holy profession that you are receiving into your soul the water of life, to send it forth to others in sweet, living currents. The religion of Calvary and the gospel is a triumphant argument to the transforming power of the grace of Christ. Unless your spirit is decidedly changed, your course will greatly detract from your influence. God does not want the ways and words of A. T. Jones to be woven into your discourses. You must come to the feet of Jesus. "Learn of Me," says the divine Teacher, "for I am meek and lowly in heart, and ye shall find rest unto your souls. For My yoke is easy, and My burden is light."

Cover yourself with the righteousness of Christ. Let not unadvised words and actions injure your influence. Do not think that your course of action is perfect, and that no one should question it. Our people will certainly question your course unless they see that you are moving under the influence of the Holy Spirit in all meekness and lowliness of heart. The sharp way in which you sometimes bear down on others will tell upon you. You need to be melted over by the Spirit of God. You need to cherish the gentleness of Christ.--Letter 215, 1902, pp. 1-4. (To A. T. Jones, May 7, 1902.)

Manuscript Release #891

ALPHA AND OMEGA

The Alpha of the Omega--There are times when important movements must be made in a crisis that the Lord permits--the development of an evil work which has long been in minds and hearts. The work of advancement in the proclamation of truth has at such times been greatly hindered [by] specious workings, which are the Alpha of the Omega, which means very much to the people who are in any way connected with parties who have received the warnings of the Lord, but refused to heed them. . . .

Omega to One of the Most Subtle Delusions--We are now to be on guard, and not drawn away from the all-important message given of God for this time. Satan is not ignorant of the result of trying to define God and Jesus Christ in a spiritualistic* way that sets God and Christ as a nonentity. The moments occupied in this kind of science are, in the place of preparing the way of the Lord, making a way for Satan to come in and confuse the minds with mysticisms of his own devising. Although they are dressed up in angel robes they have made our God and our Christ a nonentity. Why?--because Satan sees the minds are all fitted for his working. Men have lost track of Christ and the Lord God, and have been obtaining an experience that is Omega to one of the most subtle delusions that will ever captivate the minds of men. We are forbidden to . . . set the imagination in a train of conjecture.--Diary, #48, pp. 153, 163, Aug. 25 and Aug. 28, 1904.

*Used here in reference to a system of interpretation, not spiritism popularly called spiritualism.

Ellen White Impressed to Delay Sending to J. H. Kellogg Messages
Received in Europe--At times I have felt that I must print all the warnings
given me for Dr. [J. H.] Kellogg, especially some that were given me while
in Europe. But I have not yet done this,because I have been impressed to
wait. If I should make a strong move in this direction, the battle would be
on. Those who are opposing the light God has given would feel that they had
been attacked, and would claim that they were compelled to make moves that
otherwise they would not have made. And it would take much of our time to
meet the issue.

Let us hold on patiently for a little while, and let the elements break
forth that are strugggling into life. Let not too many articles be published in the Review and Herald that are of a character to stir up strife.
. . .

Satan's Deceptive Science Will Overcome Us Unless We Are Conformed to
Christ's Will--Unless the heart, mind, soul, and strength are completely
conformed to the will of Christ, the science studied will not give entrance
into the narrow way and the strait gate that lead to eternal life. Strait
is the gate and narrow is the way that leadeth unto life, and few there be
that find it. Because broad is the way, and wide is the gate that leadeth
to destruction, and many there be that go in thereat. Those who regard it
as a valuable science to be sharp, to take advantage of and cheat their
neighbors, are cheating their own soul, and unless they change, they can
never enter the holy city. No crooked dealing, no deceptive science, will
find a place in the heavenly courts. . . .

As I am shown these special things of Satan's science, and how he deceived the holy angels, I am afraid of the men who have entered into the
study of the science that Satan carried into the warfare in heaven. Oh, how

I have longed to be where I should not be compelled to see the same science practiced on this earth by medical practitioners. How my heart has been agonized as I have seen souls accepting the inducements held out to them to unite with those who were warring against God. When they once accept the bait it seems impossible to break the spell that Satan casts over them, because the enemy works out the science of deception as he worked it out in the heavenly courts. He uses human agencies to carry on his work with other human beings. He has worked so diligently with men in our day that he has won the game again and again.

Never Leave a Soul Unwarned--What, I ask, can be the end? Again and again have I asked this, and I have always received the same instruction-- Never leave a soul unwarned. Those who are bound in Satan's toils are the most confident and the most boastful. They will protest at the thought that they are ensnared, and yet it is the truth.--Letter 311, 1905, pp. 10, 11. (To A. G. Daniells, W. W. Prescott, and their associates, Oct. 30, 1905.)

Christ Refuted Satan's Boast That No One Could Live a Spotless Life-- Christ came to suffer in man's behalf, for Satan had made the boast that no one could withstand his devising and in this world live a spotless life. Clothed with human nature, the Redeemer subjected Himself to all the temptations with which human beings are beset, and He overcame on every point. The record of His life is given to the world, that no one need be in doubt as to the power of the grace of God. To every soul who strives for perfection of Christian character, this world becomes a battlefield on which is fought the controversy between good and evil. And everyone who trusts in Christ will gain the victory.

Do Not Let J. H. Kellogg and A. T. Jones Gain Control of Battle Creek
Tabernacle--Brother [Russell] Hart, I want you to stand rooted and grounded
in the truth. My interest in your father and mother was not a small one.
In the past we have often been united in our labors and I have a deep interest in you. I want to see you bearing an unwavering testimony for the
truth. My position is unchanged.

According to the light given me, unless a decided stand is taken to
safeguard the Tabernacle in Battle Creek, theories will be presented in it
that will dishonor God and His cause. I have been shown that if you understood the matter you would be as decided as I am in the testimony you bear.

I must act in accordance with the light the Lord has given me; and I say
to you that Elder A. T. Jones and Dr. Kellogg will make every effort possible to get possession of the Tabernacle, in order that in it they may present their doctrines. We must not allow that house to be used for the pro-
mulgation of error until our work is done in Battle Creek. The Tabernacle
was built by the Seventh-day Adventist people. It is their property, and
their loyal representatives should control it. On this question I will
stand firm, and if you and others will take a decided stand with us, you
will be doing that which God requires of you at this time.

We must make sure the control of the Tabernacle, for powerful testimonies are to be borne in it in favor of the truth. This is the word of the
Lord to you and to others. Elder A. T. Jones will work in every possible
way to get possession of this house, and if he can do so he will present in
it theories that should never be heard. I know whereof I speak in this
matter, and if you could have seen the end from the beginning, if you had
believed the warnings that have been given, you would have moved understandingly.

I am glad that you wrote, so that I can express myself to you. I want you to understand that as long as the Lord gives me testimonies to bear, I will bear them, whether men will hear, or whether they will forbear. I have been clearly shown that we must safeguard the Tabernacle.

The Lord has a message for the people in Battle Creek, and I may act a part in giving them this message. I am in my eightieth year, but my mind is clear. My faith is strong. May the Lord give you clear light, that you may not be numbered among those who have been seduced from the truth, is my prayer.--Letter 38, 1907, pp. 5-7. (To Russell Hart, Feb. 4, 1907.)

White Estate
Washington, D. C.
November 12, 1981

PROBLEMS IN BATTLE CREEK IN 1898

Problems at the SDA Offices of Publication Not to Be Taken to Worldly
Men--Pure, uncorrupted motives and principles must become a controlling
power in our offices of publication. At your board meetings angels of God
have covered their faces, that they might not behold the wrongs devised.
Yet I have still an appeal to make: Stop where you are. You have no more
right to the large wages you demand than have I or your brethren. If you
obtain them by fraud, by carrying your case to worldly men, please read your
Bible, and see what it says on this subject.--Letter 41, 1898, p. 15. (To
A. R. Henry, May 16, 1898.)

Church Members Who Appeal to Worldly Courts Show They Have Chosen the
World for Their Judge--The world and unconverted church members are in sympathy with each other. Some, when God reproves them for wanting their own
way, make the world their confidence, and bring church matters before the
world for decision. Then there is collision and strife, and Christ is crucified afresh and put to open shame. These church members who appeal to the
courts of the world show that they have chosen the world as their judge, and
their names are registered in heaven as one with unbelievers. How eagerly
the world seizes the statements of those who betray sacred trusts!

This action of appealing to human courts, never before entered into by
Seventh-day Adventists, has now been done. . . .

Hope for Those Who Repent--There is hope for all who will hear the truth
and repent of their evil works. When from unfeigned lips the earnest prayer

goes up, "Create in me a clean heart, O God," the answer comes in the promise, "Then will I sprinkle clean water upon you, and ye shall be clean:
from all your filthiness, and from all your idols, will I cleanse you. A
new heart also will I give you, and a new spirit will I put within you: and
I will take away the stony heart out of your flesh, and I will give you an
heart of flesh. And I will put My spirit within you, and cause you to walk
in My statutes, and ye shall keep My judgments, and do them" (Ezekiel
36:25-27).

These are the words of the Lord, and if the blindness of those who have
betrayed the cause of God into the hands of our enemies is ever removed they
will understand this scripture. . . .

The Lord and Heaven Rejoice in Medical-Missionary Work Being Done--The
Lord and all heaven rejoice to see this work being done in medical missionary lines. The churches are to blend with this work, that they may be kept
in a healthy condition, guarding the Lord's purchased possession as faithful
sentinels.--Ms.64, 1898, pp.11-14.("The Danger of Rejecting Light," May 19,
1898.)

J. H. Kellogg's Medical-Missionary Work Commended--Doctor Kellogg is doing the very work which God has given to the church in Battle Creek--the
last call to the supper He has prepared.

In order to be carried forward aright the medical-missionary work needs
talent and wise discrimination. But can this work be done while those in
responsible places--presidents of conferences, and ministers--bar the way?
I say to the president of the Michigan Conference, to Elder _____ and to
others, Remove the stumbling block that you are surely placing before the
people.

The people in Battle Creek have not exercised their talents in devising and planning how they may plant the standard of truth in regions where decided efforts should be made, and the Lord has moved upon Doctor Kellogg to do the work offered to those in Battle Creek, which they did not choose to accept. . . .

Those who are doing medical-missionary work in Battle Creek should have the full sanction and cooperation of the church. . . .

Time is short, and there is a great work to be done. If you feel no interest in the work that is going forward, if you will not encourage medical missionaries to work in the churches, they will do it without your consent, for this work must and will be done. Brother _____, Brother _____, Brother _____, Brother _____, in the name of the Lord, I call upon you to take your position on the Lord's side. Do not be found fighting against God.--Letter 51, 1898, pp. 1, 2, 6. (To Brethren in Battle Creek, June 6, 1898.)

God Will Not Be the Counselor of Those Who Take SDA Problems to Worldly Lawyers--You who are engaged in opening the things connected with our work to lawyers, will realize that those who trust the things connected with our work to those who know not God, will be left to trust to the law, and will have all the law they want until their souls are satisfied. God will not be their Counselor.--Letter 51a, 1898, pp. 1, 2. (To Uriah Smith and G. A. Irwin, June 6, 1898.)

White Estate
Washington, D. C.
Nov. 12, 1981

CHRIST OUR EXAMPLE IN SOUL-WINNING

No teacher ever placed such signal honor upon man as did our Lord Jesus Christ. He was known as "the friend of publicans and sinners." He mingled with all classes and sowed the world with truth. In the market place and in the synagogue He proclaimed His message. He relieved every species of suffering, both physical and spiritual. Beside all waters He sowed the seeds of truth. His one desire was that all might have spiritual and physical soundness. He was the friend of every human being. Was He not pledged to bring life and light to all who would receive Him? Was He not pledged to give them power to become the Sons of God? He gave Himself wholly and entirely to the work of soul saving.

Selfishness He sternly rebuked, sparing not even His disciples. "All ye are brethren," He would say to anyone seeking the highest place. Those who were unjust and unfair in their dealings writhed under His parables. He shielded no one, however high his position, who had been guilty of hypocrisy or fraud.

To save a fallen race, Christ gave Himself to a death of shame and humiliation. Since human beings are of such value, let us take heed how we speak of one another. Those who would enjoy the approbation of the great Head of the church must treat their fellow beings as Christ would treat them were He in their place. In their dealings with one another they must reveal the love that Christ revealed for them when they were at enmity with God. The command is upon every soul who receives Christ to show to the world that Christ has given them power to become the sons of God, power to love one another as He has loved them. . . .*

It is faith and prayer that cast out evil spirits. We may ask Christ with full assurance of faith for enlarged capacity for service, for increased power to help souls. But let us remember constantly that it is through the Holy Spirit that we receive power and efficiency.

He who makes advancement in the school of Christ in this lower life will at last pass through the pearly gates of the city of God, to enter the higher school, there to receive instruction from the divine Teacher.--Ms. 82, 1903. (Diary, "The Promise of the Spirit," September 25, 1902.)

*The material included in Manuscript Release #290 appears at this point.

White Estate
Washington, D. C.
Nov. 12, 1981

THE SYDNEY SANITARIUM

Wahroonga an Ideal Location for the Sanitarium--Our brethren have selected a site for our new sanitarium. It is about thirteen miles from
Sydney, and is in an excellent, healthful location. The altitude is about
six hundred feet, and the place receives the cool, life-giving breeze from
the sea. Thus, while in the low-lying towns the atmosphere is impure, hot,
and oppressive, here it is pure, cool, and refreshing. Excellent roads, and
beautiful, picturesque scenery afford opportunity for pleasant drives.
Freedom from the dust and the smoke, the din and the confusion, of the city
will be most grateful to the brain-weary and the sick.

It was not God's purpose that people should be crowded into cities, huddled together in terraces and tenements. In the beginning He placed our
first parents in a garden, amidst the beautiful sights and sounds of nature,
and these sights and sounds He desires men to rejoice in today. The more
nearly we can come into harmony with God's original plan, the more favorable
will be our position for the recovery and preservation of health.

Our retired location will offer comparative freedom from many of the
temptations of city life. Here are no liquor-selling hotels or dram-shops
on every corner to tempt the unfortunate victim of intemperance. And the
pure sights and sounds, the clear, invigorating air, and the sense of God's
presence pervading all nature, tend to uplift the mind, to soften the heart,
and to strengthen the will to resist temptation.

While affording the benefits of country life, our sanitarium will be sufficiently near Sydney to secure the advantages of connection with the city. There are two railway lines leading into Sydney. The stations are about twenty minutes' drive from the sanitarium farm, and trains run almost hourly into the city. Five or six little villages within a few miles of our site are fast filling up with the residences of businessmen from the city. This district seems destined to be the most desirable of all the suburbs of Sydney. Not a person who has seen our location of land has one word of criticism to offer. All are surprised that we have purchased it so cheaply. We are sure that it possesses advantages above any other place we have seen.

Appeal for Means ith Which to Build--Our new building should be erected at once. But we have not on hand sufficient means either to pay for the land or to erect the building. We thank the Lord that our brethren and sisters in America have had their hearts stirred to help the cause in Australia. But we are reluctant to draw upon them largely now, because they have so many missions in foreign countries to help. Dr. J. H. Kellogg and a few others have done what they could personally in donations for the sanitarium. For this we thank them on behalf of our people in this country. Now shall we not in Australia make an earnest effort to help ourselves?

We had hoped ere this to have a sanitarium established and in running order; the hindrance has been the dearth of means. We are now paying more than two hundred pounds a year for a rented house. We hope that soon this amount may be devoted to paying for a building of our own in a healthful location, away from the confusion of the city. . . .

Again I ask my brethren in Australia and wherever this appeal may go, Will you help us with your gifts in our emergency? Will you help in erecting a memorial for the Lord in Sydney? Such an institution will give character to our work. It will bring the truth before many persons of the higher classes, who might never see the light of truth but for the Lord's agencies in medical-missionary lines. Through this instrumentality Jesus, the Prince of life, will be uplifted before those who are suffering and are subdued by affliction. As their hearts are softened by the grace of God, some will listen to the gospel, and will see its claims upon them. They will give ear to the last message of mercy to the world, "Come, for all things are now ready."

My brethren, what will you do to forward this work? How much will you lay up as treasure in heaven by contributing toward the erection of a sanitarium? When the building is completed, it will give us facilities to educate and train workers who can carry forward the same work in other places, and thus the blessing will be extended .

In this enterprise all may bear a part. As the sanitarium shall do its work of beneficence, will you not rejoice to be able to say, "With the means the Lord entrusted to me, I helped to establish that institution, which is now doing such a wonderful work in restoring the sick"?

We ask that everyone now will do his best. You may have the same privilege as had the Macedonians. You may surprise the Lord's servants by the liberality of your gifts.--Ms. 12, 1900, pp. 5-11. ("Who Will Help?" Jan. 31, 1900.)

Both Donations and Loans Sought From Church Members--The time has come for us to arise and build the sanitarium without waiting for anyone. This work is the work of the Lord, and it should have been done before this. The building of the sanitarium has long been contemplated, but the work has been delayed from positive necessity. The school buildings had to be erected, and this called for the means. We need now to walk by faith. The Lord will help us if we will arise and build.

The light which the Lord has been pleased to give me is that in the work of establishing the sanitarium, we should ask our people for donations and loans. All the donations possible are to be obtained, and then our brethren are to be asked to loan their money, without interest or at a low rate of interest. But we are not to borrow money from the banks, even though we are obliged to put up the building piece by piece. In this matter let us work with an eye single to the glory of God.--Ms. 42, 1900, p. 1. ("Words of Instruction Regarding the Sanitarium at Wahroonga," July 23, 1900.)

Better Facilities Needed--The sanitarium in Sydney is now full. But the higher class of patients, those who can afford to pay well, will remain only long enough to take their treatment. They do not like the building or the rooms, and they will not stay any longer than they can help.--Letter 50, 1900, p. 1. (To Brother Murphet, March 20, 1900.)

The Sydney Sanitarium Will Advance God's Work in Australia--We are now in California, and yet our interest in the work in Australia is not diminished. I am just as desirous now that the work in Australia shall go forward as I was when I was there. The work of the Lord in that place is in no way to decrease because we are not there. We feel an earnest desire that the work on the sanitarium shall advance as fast and as solidly as possible. I hope that you will help all you possibly can by gifts and by loans. Do this for the sake of our Lord Jesus Christ, and a rich blessing will be granted you.

I have a request to make of you. Will you and your son visit Cooranbong and the place where the new sanitarium is being erected? May the Lord help you to help the men who are trying to do their best for the advancement of His cause. I am glad that you have invested some of the Lord's money in the sanitarium; but it will be a hard pull if our brethren and sisters in Australia do not do more than they have done. All should do their best. There should be no failure in the work of erecting the sanitarium on the land purchased for it.

A great work is to be done in Australia, and one important way of advancing this work is the establishment of a sanitarium where the sick can be cared for. All classes of people will come to the sanitarium, those in high positions of trust as well as the more lowly, and the Lord will impress their minds. If there ever was an object where the means locked up in banks would be well invested, it is in such an institution, where the sufferings of humanity will be relieved, and the work conducted on the strictest temperance principles.

The Lord calls upon those to whom, as His stewards, He has entrusted means to do their best. My heart is in the work. I am very anxious to see the sanitarium in running order. Therefore, my brother, we thank you for what you have done, and ask you to help still further if you possibly can. You will be putting your money into a safe bank, which will yield a rich return, if not in this life, in the life eternal.

The building of the sanitarium is the will of God. The work is His work, and we greatly desire that sufficient means shall come in to complete the building. It is to be erected economically, without extravagance or display, but according to the mind of God, so that it will be a memorial for Him among other institutions of the kind. It is to be controlled and conducted on strictly religious principles, and many souls will be saved. Many will believe the truth and keep the Sabbath of the fourth commandment. Thus all classes can be reached, high and low, rich and poor.

Every dollar invested for Christ's sake will bring blessing to the giver and to suffering humanity. I am thankful for what you have done. Cannot you help still more?--Letter 130, 1900. (To Brother Murphet, October 16, 1900.)

White Estate
Washington, D. C.
November 12, 1981

MINNEAPOLIS GENERAL CONFERENCE AND ITS AFTERMATH

The Sinfulness of an Unloving Spirit--I never can express with pen or voice the work that I discerned was laid out before me on that occasion when I was beside my dying husband. I have not lost the deep views of my work, as I sat by the bed of my husband with his dying hand in mine. . . .

I have pledged myself by a solemn vow to God that wherever this spirit of contempt and unkindness and want of love should exist, I would lay it out in clear lines before my brethren, show them the sinfulness of their course, and with decided testimony turn the current if possible.--Ms. 21, 1888, pp. 3, 6. ("Distressing Experiences of 1888," probably written at Minneapolis.)

The Spiritual Blindness of Many at Minneapolis--There was, I knew, a remarkable blindness upon the minds of many [at Minneapolis], so that they did not discern where the Spirit of God was and what constituted true Christian experience. And to consider that these were the ones who had the guardianship of the flock of God was painful--the destitution of true faith, the hands hung down because not lifted up in sincere prayer! Some felt no need of prayer. Their own judgment, they felt, was sufficient, and they had no sense that the enemy of all good was guiding their judgment. . . .

The Lord was testing and proving His people who had had great light whether they would walk in it or turn from it under temptation, for but few know what manner of spirit they are of until circumstances shall be of a character to test the spirit which prompts to action. In many the natural heart is a controlling power, and yet they do not suppose that pride and prejudice are entertained as cherished guests, and work in words and actions against light and truth.

Our brethren who have occupied leading positions in the work and the cause of God should have been so closely connected with the Source of all light that they would not call light darkness and darkness light. They had the example of those before them who had claimed to believe the truth, but who, when mercifully reproved for sin and errors, gave loose rein to their own natural temperament and opposed the work of the Spirit of the Lord. They had seen these go farther and farther in darkness until they became apostates to the truth. And they do not discern that they are in the greatest peril, if, notwithstanding the course and marked example of others, they blindly stumble into the same path of doubt, unbelief, and rejection of light sent of God, because it does not coincide with their ideas.--Ms. 24, 1888. ("Looking Back at Minneapolis," cir. Nov. or Dec., 1888.)

A Reformation Needed After the 1888 General Conference-- The Lord was working [at Minneapolis] and I must be faithful to speak the words given me of God, although I was passing through the most grievous trial of my life, for, from this hour, that confidence which I had hitherto had that God was leading and controlling the minds and hearts of my brethren was not as heretofore. I had felt that when a call came to me, "We want you at our meeting, Sister White; your influence is needed," I should not consult my choice

or my feelings, but should arise by faith and try to act my part and leave
the Lord to do the work that was essential to be done. Now a greater burden
falls upon me. From this time I must look alone to God, for I dare not rely
upon the wisdom of my brethren. I see they do not always take God for their
Counselor, but look in a large degree to the men they have set before them
in the place of God. . . .

I then felt my spirit stirred within me, and I bore a very plain testimony to these brethren. I told them a little of how matters had been carried at Minneapolis and stated the position I had taken, that pharisaism had
been at work leavening the camp here at Battle Creek, and the Seventh-day
Adventist churches were affected, but the Lord had given me a message and
with pen and voice I would work until this leaven was expelled and a new
leaven was introduced, which was the grace of Christ.

I was confirmed in all I had stated in Minneapolis, that a reformation
must go through the churches. Reforms must be made, for spiritual weakness
and blindness were upon the people who had been blessed with great light and
precious opportunities and privileges. As reformers they had come out of
the denominational churches, but they now act a part similar to that which
the churches acted. We hoped that there would not be the necessity for
another coming out. While we will endeavor to keep the unity of the Spirit
in the bonds of peace, we will not with pen or voice cease to protest
against bigotry. . . .

I stated that the course that had been pursued at Minneapolis was cruel-
ty to the Spirit of God; and those who went all through that meeting and
left with the same spirit with which they came to the meeting, and were
carrying on the same line of work they did at that meeting and since they

had come from it, would--unless they were changed in spirit and confessed their mistakes--go into greater deceptions. They would stumble and know not at what they were stumbling. I begged them to stop just where they were. But the position of Elder A and Elder B influenced them to make no change, but stand where they did. No confession was made. The blessed meeting closed. Many were strengthened, but doubt and darkness enveloped some closer than before. . . .

If my brethren had sensed their own weakness, their own inability, and had never lost sight of this, they would have humbled their hearts before God, confessed their errors, and come into light and freedom. . . .

Many are ignorant of the deception which palms off falsehood for truth. They entertain ideas that men may be saved by their own merit. A false religion has come in among us, a legal religion. We will not keep silent. The church must be roused. We will secure halls in the cities and put out handbills and the people shall be enlightened. . . .

We are years behind, and yet men in responsible positions will in their blindness keep the key of knowledge, refusing to enter themselves and hindering those who would enter. . . .

A difference in the application of some few scriptural passages makes men forget their religious principles. Elements become banded together, exciting one another through the human passions to withstand in a harsh, denunciatory manner everything that does not meet their ideas. This is not Christian, but is of another spirit. And Satan is doing his utmost to have those who believe present truth deceived on this point, for he has laid his snare to overcome them, that those who have accepted unpopular truth, who have had great light and great privileges, shall have the spirit that will

pervade the world. Even if it is in a less degree, yet it is the same principle, which, when it has a controlling power over minds, leads to certain
results. There is pride of opinion, a stubbornness that shuts the soul away
from good and from God.--Ms. 30, 1889, ("Experience Following the Minneapolis Conference," late June, 1889.)

Need for Heavenly Wisdom in Combating Error--We see more and greater
need of close communion with God and greater need of unity. Let us devote
much time to seeking for heavenly wisdom. Let us be much with God in prayer. We want Bible evidence for every point we advance. We do not want to
tide over points as Elder Canright has done with assertions.

What we want in every conflict is not words to condemn, but the sword of
the Spirit. We want the truth as it is in Jesus. We want to be filled with
all the fullness of God and have the meekness and lowliness of Christ.

We have a wily foe who will seize your sword and turn it against you,
unless you know how to use it skillfully. But let none feel that we know
all the truth the Bible proclaims.--Letter 13, 1887, p. 4. (To G. I. Butler
and Uriah Smith, April 5, 1887.)

Righteousness by Faith Needed at the 1889 Camp Meetings-- I think that
Elder A. T. Jones should attend our large camp meetings and give to our
people, and to outsiders as well, the precious subject of faith and the
righteousness of Christ. There is a flood of light in this subject, and if
he goes to the canvassers' meetings only, how can the light come before the
largest number? You cannot expect that any of the canvassers can present
this matter in the light in which he presents it. I think that it is

robbing the churches of the light and the message for the present time for him not to attend the camp meetings. Let the outsiders understand that we preach the gospel as well as the law.--Letter 1, 1889, p. 6. (To W. C. White, April 7, 1889.)

Ellen White's Work at the Ottawa, Kansas, Camp Meeting--I have good news to report this morning. There has been a break in the meeting. Praise the Lord. He is at work for His people. We have felt surely that the enemy of Christ and all righteousness was upon the ground. There were some ministers from Iowa who came armed and equipped to leaven the camp with the very same spirit that was so prominent in Minneapolis. . . .

Wednesday I attended the early morning meeting and bore a decided testimony and entreated all present not to act over Minneapolis, and not to be like those Paul describes in Hebrews 4:2. I then entreated them to humble their hearts before God and put away their sins by repentance and confession, and receive the messages God sends them through His delegated servants. . . .

In the night season, one of God's messengers stood by my side and asked:

"Did not I raise you up when you were sick nigh unto death in Healdsburg? Did not I put My Spirit upon you and sustain you to bear your testimony in Oakland? Did not I your Lord strengthen you to come the long journey to this place? Have I not kept your mind in peace amid the strife and confusion of tongues, and now I have a work for you to do in this place. My everlasting arms are beneath you. I have given you a message to bear. I will show you many things."

I was conducted to the house where our brethren made their homes, and there was much conversation and excitement of feelings and some smart, and as they supposed sharp, witty remarks. The servants whom the Lord sent were caricatured, ridiculed, and placed in a ridiculous light. The comment of words passed upon me and the work that God had given me to do was anything but flattering. Willie White's name was handled freely and he was ridiculed and denounced, also the names of Elders Jones and Waggoner.

Voices that I was surprised to hear were joining this rebellion and those with whom I had labored in past years without any evidence, or any sure knowledge of any change in Sister White, were hard, bold and decided in denouncing her. And of all those so free and forward with their cruel words, not one had come to me and inquired if these reports and their suppositions were true. I was represented as telling things untrue, when I made the statement that not a word of conversation had passed between me and Brethren Jones and Waggoner nor my son Willie upon the law in Galatians. If they had been as frank with me as they were in talking with one another against me, I could have made everything plain to them in this matter. I repeated this several times, because I saw they were determined not to take my testimony. They thought we all came to the conference with a perfect understanding and an agreement to make a stand on the law in Galatians.

After hearing what I did my heart sank within me. I had never pictured before my mind what dependence we might place in those who claim to be friends, when the spirit of Satan finds entrance to their hearts. I thought of the future crisis, and feelings that I can never put into words for a little time overcame me. [Mark 13:9,12,13 quoted.]

All this passed through my mind like a flash of lightning and I was sensible how little trust or dependence could be put in the friendship of men,
when human thoughts and human passions bear sway. Just as sure as the enemy
is permitted to bear sway, then we may expect anything. Human friendship,
bonds, and ties of relationship are severed, and why? Because there is a
difference of opinion in interpretation of the Scriptures. It is the same
spirit which condemned the Lord of life and glory. . . .

And what created all this stirring up of human passions which was bitterness of spirit, because some of their brethren had ventured to entertain
some ideas contrary to the ideas that some others of their brethren had
entertained, which were thought from their understanding to be inroads upon
ancient doctrines?

The guide who accompanied me gave me the information of the spiritual
standing before God of these men who were passing judgment upon their brethren. They were not keeping their own souls in the love of God. Had they
been growing in grace and the knowledge of our Lord and Saviour Jesus
Christ, they would have distinguished light from darkness, and truth from
error.

I had declared my intention of leaving the meeting as soon as the Sabbath should close, but when I was assured I had a work to do to stand at my
post, that God had given me a message to bear in His name, and if even I had
foreseen the consequences, I could not be clear before God and have my
peace. My work must not cease here, for my testimony of this character must
continue as God should direct until these wrongs were expelled from the
churches. Unless the faithful testimonies are continued to be repeated in

the ears of the people of God, the mold that has been left upon the work would not be removed.

There have been, I was informed, misunderstandings not only of the testimonies, but of the Bible itself. Men have exalted themselves and esteemed themselves too highly, which leads to the denouncing of others and passing judgment upon their brethren. Envy, jealousy, evil speaking, evil surmising, judging one another, has been considered a special gift given of God in discernment when it savors more of the spirit of the great accuser, who accused the brethren before God day and night. There has been a spirit of pharisaism, a hard, unsympathetic spirit toward the erring, a withdrawing from some and leaving them in discouragement, which is leaving the lost sheep to perish in the wilderness. There has been a placing of men where God alone should be.--Letter 14, 1889, pp. 4-6. (To Dear Children of the Household, May 12, 1889.)

Ellen White's Concerns While at Ottawa, Kansas--If I can possibly get off from the appointment to the Scandinavians I will do it and return home and see what you are all about. I shall be glad to have No. 33* out, for the people need it. I am up writing at three o'clock in the morning. There are many questions to be considered and settled. It is understood that you are going to the Kansas meeting. I cannot lay out the matter clearly in my mind.

I have had some thoughts like this about Iowa: [J. H.] Morrison and [Henry] Nicola have run the conference until there is but little life and soul in it. Now whether Elder [A. T.] Jones and I ought not to attend that conference and bring to the poor sheep and lambs food, is the question.

---

*Now Testimonies for the Church, Vol. V, pp. 477-754.

I never saw the condition of things as since coming here. The people seemed to be in a maze. They could not seem to get hold of the subjects presented until last Thursday; then there was a break, and since that time the meetings have increased steadily in interest and the people have been greatly benefited. Brother [R. M.] Kilgore is a free man. He no longer sees men as trees walking. His trumpet will give a certain sound. He is a converted man.

Brother Tait is another who has been greatly blessed and will give the trumpet a certain sound. Brother [J. F.] Ballenger has been in great distress of mind, but he is now free and has a new conversion. It does my soul good to see these old men and young men drinking in of the Spirit of God and planting their feet on solid Rock.

I have so desired that Frank [Belden] and yourself would share in the benefits of this meeting, for if you both act a part in the work of God, then you both need to be supplied with divine grace, that your works shall be wrought in God. I see the great need of less of self and more--a great deal more--of Jesus, and young and old have been getting hold from above and becoming acquainted with faith and the righteousness of Christ.

Well, I must write no more now.

[Later:] We want the Testimony out as soon as possible. I think I shall not wait here any longer, although they want me to do so. As far as anyone to consult with is concerned, I am alone. I scarcely see Fannie [Bolton]; only in meeting and a few moments in the evening. I do not know what she is doing, except to attend the meetings, which I am confident means to her very much. I shall not have her travel with me. This Kansas meeting is somehow to me inexplainable. I cannot understand it--that four weeks' work should be put in in one place, and then other places where my testimony is much needed be passed by.

I have been really worried over this matter of Iowa--whether I ought not to go there, and Elder Jones go, and leave some other places. I should have to give up Pennsylvania. Had I thought you would not have attended this meeting at all, I should have made calculations accordingly. Now I do not know what to do. I verily believe it was the work of the enemy that you have not been here all through this meeting. You might have waited here for news from Emma if she was worse, and then matters might have shaped themselves so that you would have had the benefits of this meeting, which I knew you needed. I am sorry, so sorry; but I must close.--Letter 14a, 1889, pp. 1, 2. (To J. Edson White, cir. April 7, 1889.)

The Spirit of Picking Flaws--Now, brethren, I want to tell you, when the Spirit of God comes into our midst, it will strike the minds that are ready to receive it. But if their minds are not open to receive it, they are all ready to pass judgment upon the messenger and the words spoken. In the place of coming to God and asking Him to give them a new heart and a new mind, that the transforming influence of the grace of God shall be upon them, they commence to find fault and pick flaws. It does not strike them, and it must harmonize with their ideas and they will stand right there until these things are culled out of the way, and they place themselves right there to judge. This is the way it was at Minneapolis.

It is because I know that the very same spirit is here, and that we should not give place to it for a moment that I say these things. I know that while the Spirit of God will make impressions upon human minds, the enemy will come in and make the most of any little thing that it is possible to make and the leaven will begin to work because the devil wants it so. Now brethren and sisters I want to place you on your guard. I want to ask you if you are satisfied with your coldness, your unbelief, your backslidings. Have you not had enough of it? If not, the devil will give you all you desire. We don't want any more.

We see that we are in no better condition than the Jewish people. God gave them clear light that they might stand as His holy, peculiar people. He had given them the prophets, and then Christ Himself came in order that He might present the truth to them. But when His own nation rejected Him, He turned away. He told them, "Ye have ears, but ye hear not, eyes have ye but ye see not." (cf. Jer. 5:21.) Then they inquired, "Are we blind also?" Christ said, "If ye were blind no sin would be attached, but it is because light has come and ye choose darkness rather than light." (See John 9:41.) Was it a real darkness? No, it was not. The light of truth had shone upon them, but Satan was throwing his blinder before their eyes, and they received it not.

Now, Brethren, there is a blessing here for you. You may think it strange that I speak to you about these things, but it is my duty. We never want this thing acted over again on God's earth; and if God gives me strength I will lift up a standard against the enemy. I have a work to do, and if God gives me strength I will do it. I want you to inquire, How is it with my soul? Will you take the light, or will you stand complaining?

It is time we should know where we are. We should have a chance to pray and talk and seek God. What we want is the Lord, and we don't want anything else. But we have it here in these words of Zechariah. Joshua stood before the Lord, and Satan stood there at his right hand to resist him. "The Lord rebuke thee," He said, "is not this a brand plucked out of the fire?" (Zechariah 3:2).

Now here are the people of God and God wants you to be getting ready for the great day of salvation, that you may be getting others ready. He wants you to have a fitting-up, that you may have a message for the people that will cut its way through the fleshy heart, and that you may go crying through the porch and the altar, "Spare thy people, O Lord, and give not thine heritage to reproach" (Joel 2:17). Now open your ears to the truth you have had and put away your doubts, unbelief, and Christless surmisings.

God wants you to come and drink of the clear waters of the streams of Lebanon, and when you have drunk yourselves you will want to call others to drink. Convert after convert is presented to me who does not know what it is to have faith in Christ. It seems they are ready to die; there is no light in them; they are dying for want of food.

I went to a meeting where I could stay only three days, and in that time I spoke to them seven times. They begged me to stay longer; they seemed starved, and they would get up and talk of how they wanted this truth and this light, but the devil was ready to bring in something to shut out the light, and many are ready to have it so. They don't know what the pure atmosphere is, but may the Lord help us that the clear light of His glory may surround us. May God help us to stand on vantage ground before the enemy that we shall have our minds broken off from things below and get hold from above.

Christ, when talking to the people of His time, told them that they had blinded their eyes and closed their ears lest they should see with their eyes and hear with their ears and be converted and He should save them. (Matthew 13:15.) Light had been given them, but they would not receive it. Darkness was upon them, and they would come and pick the little flaws, and draw the minds of the people away from the solemn truth that was for them. Now, how will it be with us? We don't want to kill ourselves here laboring for you, but will you labor for yourselves? We want to know whether we will have the rich blessing of the Lord resting upon us, and we realize that He sheds His rich light and glory upon us. This is my prayer.--Ms. 2, 1889, pp. 2-4. ("Picking Flaws," May 12, 1889.)

The Need for Humility-- Brethren and sisters, just as surely as we begin to look earnestly to Jesus and uncover our souls to Him, we shall go down deep into the valley of humiliation; and just so surely as we go down, we shall rise up again. The more humbly we live before God, the nearer we will come to Him, and the more distinct will be our view of Jesus Christ and His matchless light.

"But we all, with open face beholding as in a glass the glory of the Lord, are changed into the same image from glory to glory" (1 Cor. 3:18). Now you see how important it is that we are beholding this. The enemy has come in and his dark shadow has been thrown athwart our pathway, so that we dwell on the dark side and talk of gloom until our way seems almost hope-less, and we stumble along without courage, hope or love. But we do not

want this to be so. We want this shadow to be swept away, and it will be if
we look beyond the darkened shadow to the brightness beyond in Christ Jesus.
. . .

Have we received a bright thought? If so, we are not to think that it
is because of any wonderful smartness or intelligence in ourselves. It is
because God is the author of it. If anyone tells you you have preached a
good sermon, tell him the devil told you that before he did, and for him not
to be an agent for the devil. There is pride in our hearts that must be
emptied out, and then Jesus Christ will come in and take possession of our
whole heart. I love my Saviour this morning because He first loved me. If
there is anything in my life, my words, my teachings that is good, it is
because Christ has put it there. It is not because of any goodness in me,
and there is no glory to be directed to myself.

The fruit of the spirit is love, joy, peace, longsuffering, gentleness,
goodness, faith; against these there is no law. We should experience this,
and then we will not be under the bondage of the law of God by any means.
You are free in Christ Jesus. We shall walk in liberty, because our will is
in harmony with the will of God and we love all His commandments. . . . It
is our privilege to go on from strength to strength and from glory to glory.
Do not think that,because we have a glimmer of the light of God,that we have
it all.--Ms. 3, 1889, pp. 1-3. (Morning Talk at Ottawa, Kansas, May 14,
1889.)

Preparation for Christ's Coming--We take the words of Brother [O. A.]
Olsen in regard to the coming of the Lord, and we think how it has been pre-

sented to us in a striking manner that the end of all things is at hand, the Lord is at the door. What influence has it had to solemnize our minds, and arouse in us an earnestness to separate from us everything that is offensive to God? Then to think that after all He is nearer now than when we first believed. The day of the Lord is right at hand, and it is not safe for us to delay His coming. . . .

Let us thank God today that we are not yet before the judgment seat of God, but we have an Intercessor, One who has loved us so that He gave His own precious life for us individually. just as though there were not another soul in the universe. He died for us and we are of infinite value to Jesus Christ. How can we measure the sacrifice He has made for us? . . .

It is not that you come out in words and deny Him, but in your actions you deny Christ so that He is ashamed to call you brethren. We want every one of us to be consecrated to God. Let the plowshare go deep and uproot all this pharisaism and let this self-righteousness be torn all to pieces. The very best way to have this done is to fall on the Rock and be broken. Just as soon as you see that there is nothing in you that is righteous; just as soon as you have a dread of sin, you will fall on the Rock, and then it is that Christ can take you and mold you and fashion you into a vessel of honor. But just as soon as you allow your thoughts and feelings to be turned against one another, this is unlike Christ, and just so sure it is that you are not vessels unto honor, but dishonor. You don't give God a chance. You are trying to fashion yourself after a mold of your own imagination, but you need to take that out of your mind and keep Christ before you every day.

When you rise up, and when you sit down, when you go out, and when you come in, you need to exercise Christian politeness and respect, because you are the purchase of the blood of Christ, and He has died upon Calvary's cross that we might live. Christ Himself has bridged the gulf for us. It is our duty to help those who are downcast. Recollect what their privileges are, and don't talk of the difficulties, but go right to them and try to bind up the brokenhearted. These are right in the church all around us. Never have an idea that you know more than your brethren, but just keep humble. It was this spirit of evil surmising that brought all the weakness into the Jewish nation.-- Ms. 4, 1889, pp. 1, 2. ("Preparation for Christ's Coming," May 14, 1889.)

Evil-surmising Leads to an Unbalanced Intellect--In Minneapolis God gave precious gems of truth to His people in new settings. This light from heaven by some was rejected with all the stubbornness the Jews manifested in rejecting Christ, and there was much talk about standing by the old landmarks. But there was evidence they knew not what the old landmarks were. There was evidence and there was reasoning from the Word that commended itself to the conscience; but the minds of men were fixed, sealed against the entrance of light, because they had decided it was a dangerous error removing the "old landmarks"--when it was not moving a peg of the old landmarks.

The men in responsible positions have disappointed Jesus. They have refused precious blessings, and refused to be channels of light, as He wanted them to be. The knowledge they should receive of God that they might be a light and blessing to others, they refuse to accept, and thus become channels of darkness. The Spirit of God is grieved. Never can the heart be stirred up with envy, with evil-surmising, with evil reports, but the intellect becomes unbalanced, and cannot decide correctly any controverted point. The attributes of Satan which have found entrance to the soul, cannot harmonize with truth.--Ms. 13, 1889, pp. 3, 4. ("Standing by the Landmarks.")

Need for Divine Enlightenment--I tell you now that you must have divine enlightenment. If you do not seek this, Satan will set up his hellish banner right in your homes, and you will be so blinded to the real nature of his deceptions that you will reverence it as the banner of Christ.--Ms. 18, 1888, p. 4. ("Religious Liberty.")

Accepting the Robe of Christ's Righteousness--The Lord blessed the words spoken, and he [Edwin Jones] said he could now better understand that his business was "to look and live," to take the robe woven by Christ Himself in the heavenly loom, and rejoice in the worthiness and righteousness of Christ.--Letter 114, 1890, p. 3. (To O. A. Olsen, June 9, 1890.)

Ellen White's Arduous Labors From 1887 to 1890--I have not spared myself, but I have labored, I may say, day and night without periods of rest. I have been so burdened that I could not sleep. The Lord was setting things before me and He strengthened me to meet the different issues that were arising. . . . I had labored early and late, writing out important matters to meet and correct the prejudice, the misconstruing of things, the misinterpretation of matters. . . .

I have had to vindicate myself and my brethren, press with all my powers against the prejudice, unbelief, false statements and misrepresentations until it almost gives me a nervous chill to think of the blindness and unreasonable pharisaism that has been adjusted as a garment about men in prominent positions. . . .

If my brethren allow me to carry this burden longer in this way I will certainly know that God does not lead them and me. One of us is not moving in God's order. I think it time to call a halt and see what powers are moving us. . . .

Satan will work with masterly power not only among unbelievers, but believers, to close the door that the very special light shall not do its work. What am I to do, Elder Olsen? I have no rest day nor night in spirit.--Letter 115, 1890, pp. 1, 2, 7, 8. (To O. A. Olsen, June 21, 1890.)

Satan's Attempt to Undercut Ellen White's Message--The spirit of resistance that has been exhibited in presenting the righteousness of Christ as our only hope has grieved the Spirit of God, and the result of this opposition has required the delivery of this matter the more earnestly and decidedly. . . .

Satan sees it is his time to make a strike. Fanaticism and errors will prevail, and the men who ought to have stood in the light, their voices heard on the right side of the question, were exercised on the wrong side to oppose that which was of God and resist that message which the Lord sends. Their position is seen to be wrong by very many, and they cry, "Danger, fanaticism," when there is no heresy and fanaticism. When these evils

really appear and they see the peril and try to avoid it. they cannot do it.
. . .

Satan fixed up the matter according to his own devices. Because the message of Sister White in testimonies given did not harmonize with their ideas, the testimonies were made of no account, except when they endorsed their ideas. So persistently have they followed their own ways in this matter, that should reproof be given to the evils that shall arise, the ones reproved will say, "Sister White's testimonies are no longer reliable. Brethren A, B, and other leaders no longer have confidence in them." These men have sown the seed and the harvest will surely follow.--Letter 116, 1890, pp. 1, 2. (To O. A. Olsen, August 27, 1890.)

White Estate
Washington, D. C.
November 12, 1981

PANTHEISM AND THE ALPHA OF HERESIES

The difficulties that have arisen have been very hard to meet, and they are far from being settled yet. One, and another, and still another are presented to me as having been led to accept the pleasing fables that mean the sanctification of sin. Living Temple contains the alpha of a train of heresies. These heresies are similar to those that I met in my first labors in connection with the cause in Maine, New Hampshire, Vermont, then in Boston, Roxbury, New Bedford, and other parts of Massachusetts. Through them the evil one worked upon the minds of men and women.

There was a Mrs. Minor, who had been to Jerusalem. When she returned she advocated some of these sentimental, spiritualistic* sophistries. She invited me to visit her and relate what the Lord had shown me. Brother Nichols took my sister and self to her home in Roxbury, where we found a company of about twenty assembled. Among them were brethren and sisters whom I loved and highly esteemed. They had believed the testimonies that I had borne to the people. But they had been led astray by spiritualistic ideas which were nothing less than a love-sick sentimentalism. The power of

---

*Spiritualism as here used refers to a method of interpretation employed after the Great Disappointment of October 22, 1844, whereby plain truths of the Bible were spiritualized away.

God came upon me as I warned them of their dangers, and some said they had never expected to see so much of the blessing of God this side of the Eden above. I bore them a message similar to the message I have been bearing for the last two months. I was instructed that the ideas they had accepted were but the alpha of a great deception. I had to meet similar delusions in Portsmouth and in Boston.

These doctrines led to free-loveism, and my heart was sorely grieved as I saw the result they brought to those who accepted them. One family who for years had lived happily together was broken up. A man and his wife, well advanced in years, were separated. The husband left his wife and children, and established other family relations. We seemed to be able to do nothing to break the spell upon these persons. The precious truths of the Bible had no influence over them.

This same hypnotic influence is seen working among our people today. Ever since my return to America a heavy burden has rested upon me. Everywhere I see the power of the enemy. Were it not for the armies of the Lord's host, led by Michael, the destruction that Satan would be pleased to witness would come to the people of God. They would be discomfited and brought to shame. But the Lord will work for His people. He will not suffer them to be defeated.

We have a most solemn work to do. I have been instructed that some of our ministering brethren are working with clouded vision. They see men as trees walking.

Unless Brethren Jones, Tenney, Waggoner, and others who have been flattered by the leaders of the medical work are especially worked by the Holy

Spirit, they will never see things as they are.   It is hard for those who have been charmed by seductive, flattering, soul-destroying theories to see where these theories will lead, or to discern wherein their spiritual eyesight has been defective.

Dr. Kellogg has been beguiled by beautiful, philosophical theories that are contrary to the truth.   He is standing as a guide and instructor of youth. But for a long time he has been presented to me as a man walking in strange paths. He has not been working with the Lord. If his blind eyes could be anointed with the heavenly eyesalve, and he would then look at himself in the moral looking glass, he would see his sad condition and understand that unless he breaks his heart before God, and makes an entire reformation, he will surely receive of the judgments of God.   The Lord will not forever bear with his perversity.

I am instructed to say that Dr. Kellogg is not yet soundly converted, and cannot be until by genuine faith he receives Christ as his Saviour. He needs to feel the divine power that will work in him the change of heart represented in the Scriptures as the new birth. Neither his words nor his actions can be depended on. He is surrounded by circumstances that tend to stimulate his pride and increase his vanity. He does not see his peril, nor does he see the dangerous path which he has been following.

If he were openly united with the world, his course would be less dangerous to the people of God.

God reads the heart.   He understands the motives which cannot be discerned by men. The question was asked by one of authority, "How can God accept such a man, though his professions and his assertions be ever so strong?" For a long time he has been deceived by the enemy. After the South Lancaster Conference,* he was for a time in the valley of decision, but since he decided what course he would pursue he has been making many false paths for his feet.

His course in urging the adoption of binding agreements, and in leaning upon the arm of the law instead of upon the arm of God, has led him farther and farther from the truth. Yet the Lord says, "Let him now accept My word. If he will wear My yoke he shall be My chosen physician, My human helper."

At the time of the General Conference in Battle Creek,** the Lord mercifully gave him another opportunity to change his course. He has waited for him to humble his heart. All obstructions were removed, even those that his own course had built up. But he was again deceived by the flatteries and sophistries of the enemy. Last spring he began a work of repentance. But he did not make thorough work.

The Lord has a message for Dr. Kellogg. Holding up the Bible, one of authority said to him, "On this Book shalt thou meditate day and night. Then you will have much less confidence in your own wisdom and methods, and in the agreements and arrangements that you have formulated. You have greatly dishonored God. But He gives you another invitation. If you hear and obey His word, you will have power to become one of the sons of God. Make straight paths for your feet, lest the lame be turned out of the way. Unless in the cares of your accumulated responsibilities you take God as your guide, you will continue to act a part displeasing to God, and the blood of souls will be charged to your account.

---

*The 1899 General Conference session was held at South Lancaster, MA.
**The 1901 General Conference session was held at Battle Creek, MI.

"The Word of God is to be a lamp to your feet. That precious, sacred Word, is not to be appealed to to uphold any spiritualistic, philosophical views regarding God, for He is dishonored by such views.

"No greater deception could be presented to the minds of men than the representation you have made of God in the pleasing fables you have advocated. Souls will be lost through the sowing of the sentiments found in Living Temple. In presenting error you have united with the prince of darkness in his work of seducing souls to eternal ruin.

"The influence you have obtained with worldlings is not the credit to you that you have supposed it to be. Unless you change, decidedly change, your life will be a savor of death unto death instead of a savor of life unto life.

"Make the Word of God the man of your counsel. It will be a lamp unto your feet, and a light unto your path. Study the Word to see what God has revealed in regard to who He is. He is 'the Almighty,' 'from everlasting,' an unerring Guide. Upon whom else would you venture to depend in times of difficulty? What folly could be greater than to set aside the wisdom of God, and accept the wisdom of him who fell from his exalted position in heaven as a covering cherub, and who has become the head of an apostate race? Will you unite with the arch-deceiver? Will you receive his deceptive falsehoods? Shall it continue to be said of you, 'Thou art weighed in the balances of the sanctuary, and art found wanting'?"

My brother, heed the invitation of Christ, "Take My yoke upon you, and learn of Me; for I am meek and lowly in heart: and ye shall find rest unto your souls" (Matthew 11:29). Your safety depends on linking up with Christ, and learning from Him.

You have much to unlearn. Your example has not been in harmony with the example of Christ. You could do nothing more objectionable than to put aside the wisdom of God, and set up your own ideas as of greatest merit for healing diseased bodies and souls, belittling and disparaging the remedy prescribed by the eternal God, and superseding the divine instruction.

God is in earnest with you. You have sought to set aside God's revealed will, teaching for doctrine the opinions and the speculations of finite human agencies through whom Satan works to destroy. Let the Word of God be your lesson book. Guided by it, you will be led to think wisely; you will reveal steadfastness of purpose; and you will build upon the true foundation.

If you are transformed, and your character is formed after the character of Christ, it will be pleasing to God for you to remain in a position of responsibility. If you refuse to be transformed, if you look to men of the world, and cherish worldly ambition, turning from God to human beings, you will become an instrument of deception in the hands of Satan until at last you will have no power to break away from the snare. If you continue to work as you have been working, you will become one of the chief of sinners. But the eternal God has thoughts of mercy toward you, and He will abundantly pardon you through Jesus Christ if you will repent and turn to Him with full purpose of heart.

Christ does not want you to lose your soul. He wants you to take hold of His saving grace, that He may do a thorough work in your heart. Now is your opportunity to decide whether you will have eternal life or eternal death. It will be a tremendous struggle for you to make a thorough work of repentance. Those who have not seen the inwardness of your character will flatter and sympathize with you, seeking to establish you in your sins.

To such a man as Dr. Paulson the reception of spiritualistic ideas means much more than it can ever mean to you. When he realizes how near he has come to making shipwreck of his faith, when he sees that he has been giving heed to seducing spirits and doctrines of devils, it may cost him his life. He will ever feel the wound. It is hard for you, but tenfold harder for such men as Dr. Paulson to recover from the shock.

My heart is heavily burdened over these matters. The knowledge of what these things will mean to you unless you change has induced me to urge you to become intelligent in regard to your condition, and to take your position for the truth.--Letter 265, 1903, pp. 1-7. (To Dr. J. H. Kellogg and His Associates, November 26, 1903.)

White Estate
Washington, D. C.
November 12, 1981

TWO SPIRITS PRESENT AT THE MINNEAPOLIS MEETING AND FOLLOWING IT

The Holy Spirit Present at Various Meetings Attended by EGW--A meeting was conducted at Potterville by the Michigan ministers. I was urged by Brother Van Horn to attend the meeting. I was glad to do this, hoping that the prejudice would be removed. The Lord gave me of His Holy Spirit at that meeting. The Lord seemed to be close by my side and I had freedom when bearing my message to the people. On this occasion, when only our brethren were present in the morning meeting, I spoke plainly, stating the light that the Lord had been pleased to give me in warnings and in reproof for His people.--Ms. 30, 1889. p. 6.

I thought it was my duty to go to Des Moines, Iowa. I hoped to meet most of the ministers in that State. . . . I wished I had all the conference that I could address, for my heart was full of the Spirit of God just as it was at Minneapolis. The Spirit of the Lord came into our morning meetings and many humble testimonies were borne with weeping. I will say to the glory of God that He did sustain me and hearts were touched. I did hope to see some who had taken an active part in Minneapolis bend their proud wills and seek the Lord with their whole heart. I believed this would be done, but although the Lord was manifestly at work upon hearts, no thorough con- fessions were made. They did not fall upon the Rock and be broken, so that the Lord could put His mold upon them. Oh, if they had only yielded their pride, the light and love of God would have come into their hearts!--Ms 30, 1889, pp. 8, 9.

Light on the Covenants--I am much pleased to learn that Professor [W. W.] Prescott is giving the same lessons in his class to the students that Brother [E. J.] Waggoner has been giving. He is presenting the covenants. John thinks it is presented in a clear and convincing manner.

Since I made the statement last Sabbath that the view of the covenants as it had been taught by Brother Waggoner was truth, it seems that great relief has come to many minds.

I am inclined to think Brother Prescott receives the testimony, although he was not present when I made this statement. I thought it time to take my position, and I am glad that the Lord urged me to give the testimony that I did.--Letter 30, 1890, p. 2.

Wrong Spirit Manifested at Minneapolis--I cannot sanction the spirit that prevailed at Minneapolis, neither can I have confidence that those who were actuated by that spirit are walking in the light.

Suppose Dr. [E. J.] Waggoner did hold views that were not wholly correct, was it Christlike to manifest the spirit that was felt in that meeting? The rich blessing of God was hanging over that conference, but the Lord could not work upon hearts so full of misconceived opinions of His own messages and so barricaded with prejudice against them. The reports that were brought to Battle Creek were in accordance with the spirit that prevailed at that meeting.--Letter 22, 1889, pp. 11, 12.

Righteousness of Christ as Presented by A. T. Jones--I think that Elder A. T. Jones should attend our large camp meetings and give to our people, and to outsiders as well, the precious subject of faith and the righteous-

ness of Christ. There is a flood of light in this subject, and if he goes
to the canvassers' meetings only, how can the light come before the largest
number? You cannot expect that any of the canvassers can present this
matter in the light in which he presents it. I think that it is robbing the
churches of the light and the message for the present time for him not to
attend the camp meetings.--Letter 1, 1889, p. 6.

Spirit of God Needed--Now brethren I want to tell you when the Spirit
of God comes into our midst it will strike the minds that are ready to
receive it. But if their minds are not open to receive it, they are all
ready to pass judgment upon the messenger and the words spoken, and in the
place of coming to God and asking Him to give them a new heart and a new
mind, and that the transforming influence of the grace of God shall be upon
them, they commence to find fault and pick flaws. It does not strike them.
It must harmonize with their ideas. They will stand right there until these
things are culled out of the way, and they place themselves right there to
judge. This is the way it was at Minneapolis.--Ms. 2, 1889, p. 2.

EGW Shown Spiritual Condition of Many at Minneapolis--I related in the
Thursday morning meeting [at Ottawa, Kansas] some things in reference to the
Minneapolis meeting. I told them by what means the Lord had opened to me
the spiritual condition of many of those who came to that conference. They
came under a delusion, with false impressions upon their minds. This was
Satan's work, for the Lord was to revive His people and give them light in
clear distinct rays that would lead to the magnifying of Christ. The Lord's

command to His people through His messengers was, "Go forward." And now Satan determined to hold the people away from the light that the rich bless-ing of God should not come upon the delegates. . . . Satan raised an alarm. They thought the law in Galatians would come up and they would go armed and equipped to resist everything coming from those men from the Pacific Coast, new and old.

I never labored in my life more directly under the controlling influ-ences of the Spirit of God. God gave me meat in due season for the people, but they refused it for it did not come in just the way and manner they wanted it to come. Elders Jones and Waggoner presented precious light to the people, but prejudice and unbelief, jealousy and evil-surmising barred the door of their hearts that nothing from this source should find entrance to their hearts.--Letter 14, 1889, pp. 2, 3.

Different Spirits at Work in Chicago and S. Lancaster--We have traveled all through to the different places of the meetings that I might stand side by side with the messengers of God that I knew were His messengers, that I knew had a message for His people. I gave my message with them right in harmony with the very message they were bearing. What did we see? We saw a power attending the message. In every instance we worked, and some know how hard we worked--I think it was a whole week, going early and late, at Chica-go, in order that we might get these ideas in the minds of the brethren.

The devil has been working for a year to obliterate these ideas--the whole of them. And it takes hard work to change their old opinions. They think they have to trust in their own righteousness, and in their own works, and keep looking at themselves, and not appropriating the righteousness of Christ, and bringing it into their life and into their character. And we worked there for one week. It was after one week had passed away before there was a break and the power of God, like a tidal wave, rolled over that congregation. I tell you, it was to set men free; it was to point them to the Lamb of God which taketh away the sins of the world.

And there at South Lancaster, the mighty movings of the Spirit of God were there. Some are here that were in that meeting. God revealed His glory; and every student in the College was brought to the door there in confession, and the movings of the Spirit of God were there. And thus from place to place, everywhere we went we saw the movings of the Spirit of God. Do you think, like the ten lepers, I shall keep silent, that I shall not raise my voice to sing the righteousness of God and praise Him and glorify Him?--Ms. 9, 1890, pp. 7, 8.

Critics of J. H. Kellogg Should Help Him--Dr. Kellogg has done a work that no man I know of among us has had qualifications to do. He has needed the sympathy and confidence of his brethren. There should have been a tender compassion for him in his position of trust, and they should have pursued a course that would have gained and retained his confidence. God would have it thus. But there has been instead a spirit of suspicion and criticism.

If the doctor fails in doing his duty and being an overcomer at last, those brethren who have failed in their want of wisdom and discernment to help the man when and where he needed their help, will be in a large measure

responsible. There have been but few who faithfully warned him in kindness
and love for his soul. His brethren do at times really feel that God is using the doctor to do a work that no other one is fitted to do. But then
they meet so strong a current of reports to his detriment, they are perplex-
ed. They partially accept them, and decide that Dr. Kellogg must really be
hypocritical and dishonest. They do not consider the good he has done and
that he is doing. They do not look at his efforts to elevate the religious
and moral tone at the sanitarium and keep it up to a high standard. How
must the doctor feel to be ever regarded with suspicion? Can nothing be
done to change this order of things? Must it ever be thus? I know that it
is not right. . . .

Christ paid the redemption price for his soul and the devil will do his
utmost to ruin his soul. Let none of us help him in his work.--Letter 21,
1888, pp. 16, 17.

Minneapolis Spirit Made EGW's Labors More Difficult--Brethren you are
urging me to come to your camp meetings. I must tell you plainly that the
course pursued toward me and my work since the General Conference at Minne-
apolis--your resistance of the light and warnings that God has given through
me--has made my labor fifty times harder than it would otherwise have been.
I find that my words have far less influence upon the minds of our people
than upon unbelievers whose hearts have not been hardened by rejecting the
light. I have no word from the Lord to labor for you in the camp meetings,
to repeat to you, little by little, that which at great cost and labor I
have published for your benefit. As you feel no burden to obtain and circu-

late the books, I feel that my oral testimony would make no lasting impression.   I have no courage to meet you in camp meeting.   It seems to me that
you have cast aside the word of the Lord as unworthy of your notice.--Letter
1, 1890, p. 10.

White Estate
Washington, D. C.
November 12, 1981

LOVE, THE NEED OF THE CHURCH

"Charity suffereth long, and is kind; charity envieth not; charity vaunteth not itself, is not puffed up, Doth not behave itself unseemly, seeketh not her own, is not easily provoked, thinketh no evil" (1 Cor. 13: 4,5). Troubles exist between brethren in the church because they fail to understand what constitutes true Christian charity, brotherly affection, and Christlike love. Self-love and self-esteem lead professed Christians to measure themselves by themselves. They take for granted that all their surmisings and suspicions of others are correct. But it is because of suspicions and judging of one another that there is discord, strife, and an unhealthy condition of the church.

If brethren would meet together once or twice a week, and with humble minds, feeling their weakness and realizing their defects, would then ask the Lord to enlighten their understanding and fill their hearts with His love, examining not one another, but the Scriptures, Satan would be defeated. Many imaginary difficulties, mere molehills that have been magnified into mountains and have made barriers between brethren, would vanish, and love, compassion, and respect would take the place of jangling and accusation. When you begin to judge your brethren, you are doing a work God has not given you to do. You are not working with Christ. God did not place you upon the judgment seat to measure and pronounce sentence upon your brethren.

Satan is an accuser of the brethren, and when he can set the leaven of dissatisfaction to work in human hearts, he is exultant. When he can divide brethren, he has a hellish jubilee. I think if our brethren could see, as I have seen, how much wrong is done in speaking evil of our brethren, there would be an entire change in the way we treat one another. You do not understand yourselves, you misinterpret words and deeds, and you measure them from your own finite standpoint. Your imagination leads you astray. Your feelings, your tongues, which are not sanctified, are employed in a service and work that is anything but holy and Christlike.

We should bring the attractiveness of Christ into our Christian service. The soft beams of the Sun of Righteousness should shine into our hearts, that we may be pleasant and cheerful, and have a strong and blessed influence on all around us. The truth of Jesus Christ does not tend to gloom and sadness. Do not forget, my brethren, that we are in Christ's school to learn lessons of truth and love. We are taught in this school to have faith in our Redeemer. We must attend carefully to our own soul's necessity, improving every privilege provided for us to learn the meekness and lowliness of Christ.

We will have to learn that trials mean benefit, and not be discouraged under them. The heart must be disciplined, faith must be cultivated, the soul's endurance must be tested. The simplicity of faith and perfect confidence in God needs to be encouraged in our hearts. You must be constantly looking and talking on the bright side, and while the work of self-discipline must be carried on by every individual Christian, it must be in such a manner as to exalt and ennoble, and not to contract the mind and center it upon little things. Your thoughts should be the outgrowth of holy principles. Do not center your minds on objectionable things, and make a brother an offender for a word. Do not judge him by your own finite measurement.

Let the voice of simple, trustful, earnest prayer be heard in your dwellings. When our sisters visit one another, let them not speak words of criticism of their brethren. Let your minds dwell upon the attributes of God,
and tell of your experiences in the love of Jesus. The fullness of that
love will soothe the heart and cause us to forget disagreeable occurrences.

How much sweet peace we lose because we keep poring over the disagreeable items in ourselves and in our brethren. We must look away from the
disagreeable to Jesus. We must love Him more, obtain more of His attractive
beauty and grace of character, and cease the contemplation of others' mistakes and errors. We should remember that our own ways are not faultless.
We make mistakes again and again, and should others watch our every word and
every action as diligently as we watch them, they would present a catalogue
fully as dark as we are able to present against our brethren and sisters.
No one is perfect but Jesus. Think of Him and be charmed away from yourself, and from every disagreeable thing, for by beholding our defects faith
is weakened. God and His promises are lost from sight.

You need more of Jesus and less of self. Think no evil, talk no evil
of anyone. Keep your lips as with a bridle. You cannot measure others' experiences by your own. It would be a deplorable thing if everyone were of
the same mind. What if in some respects we do err, does the Lord forsake
us, and forget us, and leave us to our own ways? No, the Lord does not
treat us as we treat one another. May the Lord help you all to repent and
confess, and let the love of Jesus pervade your hearts. Jealousy is all
ready to spring into existence at the least provocation. Envy and evil
surmising are ready to flourish, ready to grow by being cultivated. Oh, how

many hurt the heart of Christ because they want their own way and their own will. War against these unenviable traits of character, and not against one another.

If the elements existed in the church which existed in the life of Christ, there would be a firm union among His professed followers. The world is working against the church, seeking to weaken and destroy it. Shall the church imitate the world in this matter? Shall we as church members destroy confidence in other church members because they do not meet a certain standard? The message of the angel to us is, "Press together, press together, press together." Let not Satan thrust himself between the members of the church. Do not give a stroke on the enemy's side of the question to weaken the influence of any member of the church. There will always be agents of the great adversary of souls who are doing their master's work of accusing those who profess to believe the truth. They will relate something that reflects upon the attitude and character of those who profess to be Christians.

The seed of evil surmising is frequently dropped into prepared soil, and it produces a harvest after its kind. Those who should guard the interests of those of like precious faith entertain suggestions and reports from the enemies of God and truth, and the root of bitterness defiles many. Could the state of every heart reputed as eminent for holiness be critically examined and developed there would be seen some dark chapters in the experience of those most highly honored. What erroneous ideas of Christian life we would find! What false ideas of God's prerogatives and of His moral government! What limiting ideas of the powers of the Holy One of Israel, what narrow ideas in regard to the agency of the Holy Spirit!

I know many are earnestly struggling after a higher life and seeking for clearer views of heavenly things, yet how very slow is their progress! How difficult for the mind to arise to the full assurance of hope that maketh not ashamed! In spite of all our efforts, we are often discouraged because the flesh warreth against the spirit. Let not the common, cheap, earthly things engross the mind that the presence of Jesus shall be withdrawn. The life of the church is communicated from Christ, and we help the church when we work in harmony with the life-giving power, losing sight of ourselves, and seeking to build one another up in the most holy faith.

God may choose instrumentalities that we do not accept, because they do not exactly meet our ideas. They do not work in the very line marked out as perfect, and in place of leaving them with God, for His Spirit to work with them, many begin to present difficulties, barricade the way, and cherish a grieved feeling because they see that they are doing a work that has not been done. Then begins the dissecting of character and the gathering up of tidbits of complaints, and faultfinding and slander, and magnifying of little occurrences and events into grave sins. This has been done in the church until we are weak, and we will always be weak unless this narrow order of things is changed. May the Lord show you all what to do that you may be filled with thanksgiving, gratitude and praise to God for the precious gift of the Son of God, and put away envyings, jealousies and rivalries, that true love and unity may exist.

Christ prayed that His disciples might be one even as He and His Father are one. In what does this unity consist? This oneness does not exist because everyone has the same disposition, the same temperament, and thinks in the very same channel. All do not possess the same degree of intelligence. All have not the same experience. In a church there are different gifts and varied experiences. In temporal matters there are a great variety of ways of management, and yet these variations in manner of labor, in the exercise of gifts, do not create dissension, discord, and disunion.

One man may be conversant with the Scriptures, and some particular portion of the Scripture may be especially appreciated by him; another sees another portion as very important, and thus one may present one point, and another, another point, and both may be of highest value. This is all in the order of God. But if a man makes a mistake in his interpretation of some portion of the Scripture, shall this cause diversity and disunion? God forbid. We cannot then take a position that the unity of the church consists in viewing every text of Scripture in the very same light. The church may pass resolution upon resolution to put down all disagreement of opinions, but we cannot force the mind and will, and thus root out disagreement. These resolutions may conceal the discord, but they cannot quench it and establish perfect agreement. Nothing can perfect unity in the church but the spirit of Christlike forbearance. Satan can sow discord; Christ alone can harmonize the disagreeing elements. Then let every soul sit down in Christ's school and learn of Christ, who declares Himself to be meek and lowly of heart. Christ says that if we learn of Him, worries will cease and we shall find rest to our souls.

The great truths of the Word of God are so clearly stated that none need make a mistake in understanding them. When as individual members of the church, you love God supremely and your neighbor as yourself, there will be no need of labored efforts to be in unity, for there will be oneness in Christ as a natural result. The ears will no longer be open to reports that will injure your neighbor, and no one will take up a reproach against his neighbor. The members of the church will cherish love and unity, and be as one great family. Then we shall bear the divine credentials to the world, that will testify that God has sent His Son into the world. Christ has said, "By this shall all men know that ye are My disciples, if ye have love one for another" (John 13:35). The divinity of Christ is acknowledged in the unity of the children of God.

Brethren, when you humble your hearts before God, you will see that there is danger of pharisaism in every church, danger of thinking and praying as did the self-righteous Pharisee: "I thank God that I am not as other men are." Oh, that there may be a breaking up of the fallow ground of the heart, that the seeds of truth may take deep root and spring up and bear much fruit to the glory of God! My brethren, when you would accuse one of the brethren, consider the words of Jesus, "He that is without sin among you, let him cast the first stone" (John 8:7). Your sin may not be the particular sin that is under consideration, but Jesus' words mean that when you are free from sin you may cast the first stone. When Jesus spoke these words to the accusers, their guilty consciences were aroused. They could not answer Him; they were convicted each in his own conscience, and they went out one by one, beginning at the oldest even to the youngest.

What can Christ who is so forgiving, so patient with all our mistakes, so rich in mercy and love, think of our hardhearted criticism and fault-finding? Love for your erring brethren will produce far greater effect in reforming them than all your harsh criticisms. Let all the faults and emotions of the heart be after Christ's order. Let self be put out of sight. The Lord would have the thoughts and the language and the experience of Christian life far more attractive than it is today. If they are not more like Jesus they can never be the light of the world. Our work is between God and our own individual souls. What are you thinking of, my brethren? There is work to be done in the saving of souls around you, and precious time is passing. The hours of probation will soon close. Is your work for the Master of that character that you will hear the words, "Well done, thou good and faithful servant" (Matthew 25:21)?

Remember that every soul striving to advance in the divine life finds every inch of ground disputed by an antagonistic force, and he must gird himself for the conflict by earnest prayer, and fight the good fight of faith. He is called to "wrestle not against flesh and blood, but against principalities, against powers, against the rulers of the darkness of this world, against spiritual wickedness in high places" (Ephesians 6:12). We cannot afford to be found warring against each other. If we make progress in spirituality, we must gird the loins of the mind about with truth, and we must have on the breastplate of righteousness, we must take the helmet of salvation, and the sword of the Spirit. Brethren, seek God. Seek Him while He is to be found, call ye upon Him while He is nigh.

Oh, what deep, rich experiences we might gain if we were devoting all our God-given ability to seeking knowledge and spiritual strength from God in the place of devoting our powers to hurting one another. Brethren, love one another as Christ has loved you. How little we really know of sweet

communion with God! How little we know of the mysteries of the future life!
We may know far more than we do know if all our powers are sanctified to
discern the character of Christ. There are heights for us to reach, depths
of experience to sound, if we are to be the light of the world. Then why
dishonor God by contention and strife? Why question and find fault with one
another? Why misinterpret and misconstrue the words and acts of your brethren?

Is there not better work for you to do than to discourage one another
and try to put out the light of your brethren? Oh, rather, let the mind ex-
pand that you may take in the heavenly beauties of the blessed promises.
Only believe in Jesus and learn in the school of the greatest Teacher the
world ever knew, and His grace will act mightily upon the human intellect
and heart. His teaching will give clearness to the mental vision. It will
give compass to the thoughts; the soul hunger will be filled. The heart
will be softened and subdued, and filled with glowing love that neither discouragement, despondency, affliction, nor trial can quench. God will open to
the mind's eye His preciousness and His fullness. Then let us love and
labor. I point you to Christ, the Rock of ages. You can be saved only
through Him. Let the praise of God be upon your lips when you meet together
in little companies to worship God. Let all take a part.

He who heard the voice of Christ and did His will was the wise man that
built upon a rock, and neither storm nor tempest could destroy this structure. Let us be workers with Christ for time and for eternity. Love one
another, forgive one another, even as God for Christ's sake has forgiven
you.--Ms. 24, 1892, pp. 1-9. ("Love, the Need of the Church," 1892.)

White Estate
Washington, D. C.
November 12, 1981

Manuscript Release #899

FILLED WITH THE SPIRIT OF CHRIST'S SECOND ADVENT

We are looking for the second coming of our Lord and Saviour Jesus Christ. We are not only to believe that the end of all things is at hand. We are to be filled with the spirit of Christ's advent, that when the Lord comes, He may find us ready to meet Him, whether we are working in the field, or building a house, or preaching the Word; ready to say, "Lo, this is our God; we have waited for Him, and He will save us" (Isaiah 25:9).-- Letter 25, 1902, p. 7. (To Those in Positions of Responsibility in the Southern Field, Feb. 5, 1902.)

White Estate
Washington, D. C.
December 10, 1981

Manuscript Release #901

GATHER UP THE FRAGMENTS

One thing I know--my wrestling in Australia has been as severe as any place I was ever in. Now my work is not to attend large meetings and wrestle as I have done. The publication of books is urged upon me. That, with the articles for the papers, is enough. I have so much precious matter. Light came to me, you remember, before you left for America, "Gather up the fragments. Let nothing be lost." [See John 6:12.].--Letter 200, 1897, p. 3. (To W. C. White, Nov. 25, 1897.)

White Estate
Washington, D. C.
December 10, 1981

PROXY VOTING

I have written out something in regard to votes by proxy. The way in which this matter has been managed should not be repeated. Those who, by the number of votes which they have accumulated, have placed men whom they have chosen in positions of influence, reveal that they are untrustworthy. They show just what they would do if they could. It may be that the Lord has suffered this thing to be, that He may awaken the understanding of His people. There must be faithful watchmen on the walls of Zion who will be ready to give the note of warning to the unruly elements who think that they have wisdom to run anything they choose. It is the privilege of all who are thus elected to say, I do not choose to serve in any position brought about by such unprincipled means.--Letter 45, 1898. (To W. C. Gage and wife, May 19, 1898.)

White Estate
Washington, D. C.
December 12, 1981

Manuscript Release #903

WARNING AGAINST CENTRALIZATION

As the work increases there will be a great and living interest to manage it by human instrumentalities. The work is not to be centered in any one place, not even in Battle Creek. Human wisdom argues that it is more convenient to build up the interests [of the work] where it has already obtained character and influence. Mistakes have been made in this line. Individual and personal responsibility are thus repressed and weakened. The work is the Lord's, and its strength and efficiency are not all to be concentrated in any one place.

Already it has been proved that there was a lack of faithfulness in the men placed in important positions of trust. The simplicity of the work was forgotten. The principles God had laid down were ignored. Self-denial and self-sacrifice were not maintained. Selfishness was indulged, because the men in positions of trust were not with heart and soul relying upon divine wisdom and power but walking after the imagination of their own hearts. This Scripture was presented to me as applicable: Jeremiah 7:1-14, 23, 24. --Letter 71, 1894, p. 8. (To the General Conference Committee and the Publishing Boards of the Review and Herald and the Pacific Press, April 8, 1894.)

White Estate
Washington, D. C.
December 10, 1981

GIFTS OF THE SPIRIT

Diversity of Gifts--In the ministration of the gospel of Jesus Christ the Lord uses diverse gifts. . . .

[Ephesians 4:11-14 quoted.]

All these gifts are to be blended in the work of building upon the foundation of the apostles and prophets. Jesus Christ Himself is the chief cornerstone, "in whom all the building fitly framed together groweth unto an holy temple in the Lord" (Ephesians 2:21). "Fitly framed together." Study these words, and seek to understand all that they comprehend. "Fitly framed together," each acting his respective part unitedly. Thus we grow "unto an holy temple in the Lord." Have a care how you build.--Ms. 108, 1899, pp. 1,2. ("He That Loveth Not His Brother Abideth in Death," August 2, 1899.)

Every entrusted gift is to be cultivated and employed in the Master's service.--Letter 195, 1899, p. 3. (To W. A. Colcord, G. B. Starr, and A. S. Hickox, November 29, 1899.)

Not All God's Servants Have the Same Gifts, But All Are His Workmen-- God's servants do not all possess the same gifts, but they are all His workmen. Each is to learn of the great Teacher, and then to communicate what he has learned. All do not do the same work, but under the sanctifying

influence of the Holy Spirit they are all God's instrumentalities, through
whom He works for the success of the work. God employs a diversity of gifts
in His work of winning souls from Satan's army.--Ms. 130, 1899, p. 9. ("The
Test of Obedience," September 8, 1899.)

Members of Christ's Body Given Such Gifts as Will Best Advance His
Kingdom--God will use you when you are willing to be used in His appointed
way. Remember that the church of believers constitutes the body of Christ,
and "that there should be no schism in the body; but that the members should
have the same care one for another" (1 Corinthians 12:25). God calls upon
you to unite with your brethren. He has assigned different gifts to the
different members of His body. He has given them such talents and opportunities as will best promote His glory and the advancement of His kingdom.
He is put to shame when the members of His body work contrary one to the
other.--Letter 19, 1901, p. 16. (To E. E. Franke, January, 1901; copied,
January 29, 1901.)

Gifts Dispensed as God Pleases--Today the Lord has called some to the
work of teaching others, to fit them for service in His cause. Let those who
are so called go cheerfully to their field of labor, following ever the
leadings of God.

God dispenses His gifts as it pleases Him. He bestows one gift upon
one, and another gift upon another, but all for the good of the whole body.
It is God's order that some shall be of service in one line of work and
others in other lines of work--all working under the self-same spirit. The

recognition of this plan will be a safeguard against carnal emulation, pride, envy, or contempt of one another. It will strengthen unity and mutual love.--Letter 60, 1907, p. 3. (To the Southern Union Conference Committee, February 24, 1907.)

Members to Respect Each Other's Gifts--What a lesson this scripture [1 Corinthians 12] teaches! There is to be an active exercise of the various gifts in one body, the head of which is Jesus Christ. Let no member of Christ's body entertain a spirit of self-sufficiency. Because two members do not act the same part, let not one member say to another member, I have no need of thee. Among the members of the body there is to be no crowding, no judging, no measuring of one gift by another. Many gifts are called for, yet all are members of one body.--Ms. 128, 1901, p. 4. ("The Principles That Should Control the Lord's Workers," December 24, 1901.)

Every Gift Essential to Success of God's Work--There is need for a variety of gifts in the Lord's work. Read carefully the fourth chapter of Ephesians. The entire chapter is a description of the Lord's manner of working. [Ephesians 4:11-13 quoted.] Every gift is to be acknowledged as essential to the success of the work.--Letter 8, 1899, p. 6. (To J. H. Kellogg, January 23, 1899.)

God Dishonored by Failure to Be Kindly Affectioned One to Another--No haphazard work is to be done by those who are laboring in the ministry or in medical-missionary lines. God's servants must seek to understand the words: [Romans 12:4-10 quoted.]

This instruction is of vital importance to everyone. At this time, above all other times in the history of the earth, these words should be practiced. But today they are to a great extent left out of the practice of professing Christians. This is the reason why God is dishonored by discord and strife, why He does not give to His people the power He would be pleased to impart. He desires to glorify His name before the world and before the heavenly universe. But church members are not doing the work they should do.--Ms. 69, 1901, pp. 2,3. ("The Unity of the Spirit," July 29, 1901.)

Each to Cultivate the Gifts Given Him--Brother and Sister Bourdeau should be united in their labor, and Sister Bourdeau may qualify herself to become a still more efficient laborer in the cause of God.

In the government of children many make a mistake and govern too much. They give so much counsel, so much direction, and want to manage so completely, that they are liable to destroy the will, the identity of their children, and they confuse their minds so completely that they give them no opportunity to act out the powers and develop the qualities God has given them as their endowment.

Just so it is with the family of God. There is diversity of operation of gifts and all by the same Spirit. These diverse gifts are illustrated by the human body from the head to the feet. As there are different members with their different offices, yet all of the body, so the members of Christ's body all center in the Head, but have different gifts. This is in the economy of God to meet the varied organization and minds in the world. The strength of one servant of God may not be the strength of another.--Letter 25, 1870, p. 1. (To D. T. Bourdeau and wife, cir. 1870.)

Those With Superior Talents Expected to Use Them Wisely--If God has given to one man superior talents and greater advantages, He has a right to expect that that man will use his gifts, not boastingly, but wisely.--Letter 10, 1884, p. 16. (To J. G. Matteson, May 3, 1884.)

God Brings Different Gifts Together Wherever an Interest Springs Up-- Wherever an interest is started, the Lord in His providence will bring different gifts in connection with the one or two who are bringing the truth before the people.--Ms. 21a, 1894, p. 8. ("Testimonies to Ministers," April 2, 1894.)

Need for Realizing Individual Responsibility--Women may accomplish a good work for God, if they will first learn the precious, all-important lesson of meekness in the school of Christ. They will be able to benefit humanity by presenting to them the all-sufficiency of Jesus. When each member of the church realizes his own individual responsibility, when he humbly takes up the work which presents itself before him, the work will go on to success. God has given to every man his work according to his several ability. It will not be an easy task to work for the Master in this age. But how much perplexity might be saved, if workers continually relied upon God, and duly considered the directions that God has given. He says, "Having then gifts differing according to the grace that is given to us, whether prophecy, let us prophesy according to the proportion of faith; Or ministry, let us wait on our ministering: or he that teacheth, on teaching; Or he that exhorteth, on exhortation: he that giveth, let him do it with simpli-

city; he that ruleth, with diligence; he that sheweth mercy, with cheerfulness" (Romans 12:5-8).

This is a subject that demands close, critical study. Many mistakes
are made because men do not heed this instruction. Many who are entrusted
with some humble line of work to do for the Master, soon become dissatis-
fied, and think that they should be teachers and leaders. They want to
leave their humble ministering, which is just as important in its place as
the larger responsibilites. Those who are set to do visiting, soon come to
think that anyone can do that work, that anyone can speak words of sympathy
and encouragement, and lead men in a humble, quiet way to a correct understanding of the Scriptures. But it is a work that demands much grace,
much patience, and an ever-increasing stock of wisdom.--Letter 88, 1895, pp.
4,5. (To J. E. White, July 7, 1895.)

Gifts to Be Blended--The Lord has given gifts differing according to
the grace that is given. Let no one suppose that his special gift is above
all other gifts. These gifts are to be made helpful by connecting them with
the gifts of others. Each is to fill his place with the gift appointed of
God. They are to be appreciated as essential for the advancement of the
cause of God.--Letter 57, 1898, p. 3. (To W. W. Prescott, June 19, 1898.)

Abuse of Gifts Offensive to God--Nothing can be more offensive to God
than to cripple or abuse the gifts lent us to be devoted to His service.--
Ms. 31, 1899, p. 3. ("Do All to the Glory of God," March 19, 1899.)

Our Service Made Acceptable by Christ's Merits--Our Saviour, during all His sojourn on earth, shared the lot of the poor and lowly. Self-denial and sacrifice characterized His life. All the favors and blessings we enjoy are alone from Him. We are stewards of His grace and of His temporal gifts. The smallest talent and the humblest service may be offered to Jesus as a consecrated gift, and with the fragrance of His own merits He will present it to the Father. If the best we have is presented with a sincere heart, in love to God, from a longing desire to do service to Jesus, the gift is wholly acceptable.--Undated Manuscript 74, p. 5. ("Our Duty in Ministering to the Poor.")

White Estate
Washington, D.C.
December 10, 1981

Manuscript Release #906

AN APPEAL FOR ACCEPTANCE OF THE MESSAGE OF CHRIST'S RIGHTEOUSNESS

Spirit of Unbelief Manifest by Some at Minneapolis and After--At the meeting in Minneapolis, at Potterville, and at Battle Creek, I presented general principles before you,* hoping that you might hear, be impressed, and be converted, that I might not be under the painful necessity of addressing you personally. But as you have had the privilege of hearing the message that God has given me and others to bear, and yet your doubts and unbelief have been strengthening instead of diminishing, I am alarmed for you. I know you and others in a similar position are not in the light. You are on the enemy's ground. Both of you are placing yourselves where the spirit of God can no more find access to your hearts than it could find access to the hearts of the Jewish people when they gave themselves up to unbelief. Through Christ, light is shining to man; heaven is connected with earth, and the angels of God are ascending and descending upon the mystic ladder. They bring messages of warning, reproof, instruction, encourage- ment, and love. The glory of God is above the ladder and shines down all its length. God will not devise some new way to reach the hearts of those who have shut themselves away from the light. It is at the peril of their souls that they refuse the light.

Parallels Between Christ's Rejection at Nazareth and the Rejection of Truth Today--Bro. B, you have encased yourself in an armor of unbelief and spiritual pride. You do not recognize Him whose goings forth have been from

---

*Ministers in the cause.

old, from everlasting. The King of glory appeared in the form of a servant, clothed in the garb of humanity. When He began His public ministry in Nazareth, there was a sad and terrible exhibition of what human nature can and will be when Satan works on the heart. Jesus proclaimed Himself to be the Anointed One. No man had before ventured to assume as much; not the learned or noble of the earth, not even the prophets or kings. He arose in the synagogue, and read from the prophet Isaiah these gracious words: "The spirit of the Lord God is upon Me; because He hath anointed Me to preach the gospel to the poor; He hath sent Me to heal the brokenhearted, to preach deliverance to the captives, and recovering of sight to the blind, to set at liberty them that are bruised, To preach the acceptable year of the Lord" (Luke 4:18,19).

The eyes of all in the synagogue were fastened upon Him, for divinity flashed through humanity, and with one voice they witnessed to the "gracious words" that proceeded from His lips. God had spoken to their hearts and given them a testimony which they acknowledged to be the truth. But soon doubt and unbelief arose. Who was this that claimed to be the Messiah? They did not expect Christ to come in this way. His family connections were humble, pious people, but not distinguished for riches, learning, rank, or power.

The Jews expected the Messiah to come with pomp and ceremony as a great king. They looked for Him to appear as a conqueror, to deliver Israel from the Roman yoke. They thought they would be able to cry, "This is the King that will reign on David's throne." But this Man, who made the claim that He was the anointed One of God, was from the humble walks of life, the son of Joseph and Mary. They had seen Him going up and down the hills. They had seen Him toiling daily at the carpenter's bench, and could He be the Messiah?

The very humiliation that Christ bore was foretold in the Scriptures as a specification of His divine character and mission, and should have commended Him to every home and heart in the land. But to proud and unbelieving Jews His humiliation was an offense.

The men of Nazareth refused the Prince of Life. The power of God that had stirred their hearts as He read and expounded to them the Scriptures, was resisted, and their passions were stirred as He spoke truths that revealed to them their real condition. . . .

The Lord has shown me that we are in just as much danger [of rejecting truth] in our day as were the people in the days of Christ. The Lord is speaking through His delegated messengers; but the same unbelief is exhibited. Men close their hearts against Jesus and hold themselves in the veriest bondage to Satan, supposing that they are preserving their dignity as free men; that they are maintaining their right to think and act for themselves, to believe or doubt; and like the despisers of the gospel in the apostolic times, they wonder and perish.

Those who on special occasions of controversy have taken a course similar to that of the men of Nazareth, should take heed lest they follow their example when a second opportunity is given to accept the gracious light of truth. After the first rejection, when excitement and confusion are over, you may again be called upon by the divine Messenger, and you should beware lest you harden your hearts in prejudice and pride, and in final rejection of the message that would work for your salvation.

You may encase yourselves in pride, and continue to reject Christ in the person of His messengers. . . .

We are less excusable than were the Jews, for we have before us their example of rejection of Christ and His apostles, and we have been warned not to fall after the same example of unbelief. . . .

Criticism of the Plans of Others--My brethren, the Lord is not pleased to have us settle down in unbelief, and question and quibble over matters of truth as you have done. . . .

When you receive the words of Christ as if they were addressed to you personally, when each applies the truth to himself, as if he were the only sinner on the face of the earth for whom Christ died, you will learn to claim by faith the merits of the blood of a crucified and risen Saviour in your own case. . . .

The Righteousness of Christ, Our Immediate Need--Many feel that their faults of character make it impossible for them to meet the standard that Christ has erected; but all such ones have to do is to humble themselves at every step under the mighty hand of God. Christ does not estimate the man by the amount of work he does, but by the spirit in which the work is performed. When He sees men lifting the burdens, trying to carry them in lowliness of mind, with distrust of self, and with reliance upon Him, He adds to their work His perfection and sufficiency, and it is accepted of the Father. We are accepted in the Beloved. The sinner's defects are covered by the perfection and fullness of the Lord our righteousness. Those who with sincere will, with contrite heart, are putting forth humble efforts to live up to the requirements of God, are looked upon by the Father with pity-ing, tender love. He regards such as obedient children, and the righteousness of Christ is imputed to them. . . . O, may the Lord imbue me with His Holy Spirit constantly that I may present the attractions of Christ so as to engross the whole mind of those for whom I labor! O, that my brethren might appreciate the promises of God in all their breadth and fullness! Then they might be saved from themselves, from self-confidence, criticism, unbelief, and pharisaism. Then self-exaltation would not be increasing, but decreasing; spiritual pride undone.

There are many who claim to believe in Christ who have not yet fallen upon the Rock and been broken. Self lives, and is exalted. To such Christ does not appear what He is, or what He will be to all those who believe on Him. . . .

Need for Independent Bible Study--A large number who claim to believe the present truth, know not what constitutes the faith that was once delivered to the saints--Christ in you the hope of glory. They think they are defending the old landmarks, but they are lukewarm and indifferent. They know not what it is to weave into their experience and to possess the real virtue of love and faith. They are not close Bible students, but are lazy and inattentive. When differences of opinion arise upon passages of Scripture, these who have not studied to a purpose, and are not decided as to what they believe, fall away from the truth. We ought to impress upon all the necessity of inquiring diligently into divine truth, that they may know that they do know what is truth.

Some claim much knowledge, and feel satisfied with their condition, when they have no more zeal for the work, no more ardent love for God and for souls for whom Christ died, than if they had never known God. They do not read the Bible [in order] to appropriate the marrow and fatness to their own souls. They do not feel that it is the voice of God speaking to them. But, if we would understand the way of salvation, if we would see the beams of the Sun of Righteousness, we must study the Scriptures, for the promises and prophecies of the Bible shed clear beams of glory upon the divine plan of redemption, [the] grand truths [of which] are not clearly comprehended.

. . .

Not for Us to Say How God's Message Should Come or Who Should Be Messenger--God has sent you a message that He wishes you to receive--a message of light and hope and comfort for the people of God. It is not for you to choose the channel through which the light shall come. The Lord desires to heal the wounds on His sheep and lambs through the heavenly balm of the truth that Christ is our righteousness. . . .

It is a grievous sin in the sight of God for men to place themselves between the people and the message that He would have come to them as some of our brethren are now doing. There are some who, like the Jews, are doing their utmost to make the message of God of none effect. Let these doubting, questioning ones either receive the light of the truth for this time, or let them stand out of the way, that others may have an opportunity of receiving the truth, that the wrath of God may not come on them because they are bodies of darkness, when He desires them to be bodies of light.

Those That Seek for a Sign Will Be Deceived as Were the Jews--Those who live just prior to the second appearing of Christ may expect a large measure of His Holy Spirit. If God has ever spoken by me, some of our leading men are going over the same ground of refusing the message of mercy as the Jews did in the time of Christ. If they turn away from the light, they will fail to meet the high and holy claims of God for this important time. They will fail to fulfill the sacred responsibility that He has entrusted to them.

The character and prospects of the people of God are similar to those of the Jews, who could not enter in because of unbelief. Self-sufficiency, self-importance, and spiritual pride separated them from God, and He hid His face from them. . . .

The Jews despised the good that was proffered them in the time of Christ, and after the long forbearance of God, the things that were for their peace were hidden from their eyes--that which, if received, would have been to them their greatest blessing became their stumbling block. Thus it is today among us. . . .

The light of truth is shining upon us as clearly as it shone upon the Jewish people, but the hearts of men are as hard and unimpressible as in the days of Christ, because they know not what they oppose. Many who claim to be standing in the light are in darkness, and know it not. They have so enshrouded themselves in unbelief that they call darkness light, and light darkness. They are ignorant of that which they condemn and oppose. But their ignorance is not such as God will excuse, for He has given them light, and they reject it. They have before them the example of the past, but they will not be warned, and unbelief is enclosing them in impenetrable darkness. They refuse to accept the testimonies they ought to believe, and are ready to accept tidbits of gossip and testimonies of men, showing their cred-ulousness and readiness to believe that which they want to believe.

There is an alarming condition of things in our churches. Says the Word of God, "Your iniquities have turned away these things, and your sins have withholden good things from you. For among My people are found wicked men: they lay in wait, as he that setteth snares; they set a trap, they

catch men. . . the prophets prophesy falsely, and the priests bear rule by

their means; and My people love to have it so: and what will ye do in the

end thereof?" (Jeremiah 5:25,26,31).   "They have healed also the hurt of the

daughter of My people slightly, saying, Peace, Peace; when there is no

peace" (chapter 6:14).   "And now, because ye have done all these works,

saith the Lord, and I spake unto you, rising up early and speaking, but ye

heard not; and I called you, but ye answered not; therefore will I do unto

this house, which is called by My name, wherein ye trust, and unto the place

which I gave to you and your fathers, as I have done to Shiloh, And I will

cast you out of My sight, as I have cast out all your brethren" (chapter

7:13-15).   God will surely fulfill His word to those who will not hear, will

not see, and refuse the light that He sends them.

Those Who Should Have Been Promoting the Message Found Resisting It--

The very men who ought to be on the alert to see what the people of God

need, that the way of the Lord may be prepared, are intercepting the light

God would have come to His people, and rejecting the message of His healing

grace.   Brethren, I beseech you to come into harmony with the work of God

for this time. . . .

God wants to put His Spirit upon you, but He cannot do this while you

are so full of self.   When self dies, you will feel the quickening influence

of the Spirit of God.   God's people are enjoined to seek for unity, that

they may be framed together into an holy temple for the Lord.   "Ye are God's

husbandry, ye are God's building" (1 Cor. 3:9). . . .

You will never have any greater evidence than you have had as to where

the Spirit of God is working.   The Lord never proposes to remove all occasion for men to doubt. He will give sufficient evidence to bring the candid mind to a right decision; but if you are determined to have your own way, if you are like Saul, unwilling to change your course because of pride and stubbornness of heart, because of ignorance of your own condition of spiritual destitution, you will not recognize the light. You will say with Saul, "I have performed the commandment of the Lord" (1 Sam. 15:13). . . .

Only Hope Is to Fall Upon the Rock and Be Broken--Selfish pride is holding you from good, and your only hope is to fall upon the Rock and be broken. As these words come to you, you will say, "Are there no others who need the same reproof?" There are many who need to see that the Laodicean message applies to them, who do not see it. I write out your case definitely, not merely that you may be benefited, but that many others may see [that] they are in the same condition, and that they, with you, may make decided changes in their attitude before God and before His people. . . .

The faith that works by love and purifies the soul, produces the fruit of humility, patience, forbearance, long-suffering, peace, joy, and willing obedience. Says the Scripture, "Whatsoever is not of faith is sin" (Romans 14:23). "He that cometh to God must believe that He is, and that He is a rewarder of them that diligently seek Him" (Hebrews 11:6).

The promises of God comprehend all the spiritual blessings needed by weak, sinful mortals, who cannot save or bless themselves. . . .

Christ has said, "I am the way, the truth, and the life" (John 14:6). If your good works were the way, then Christ would not have said, "I am the way." It is not our doings and deservings that will save us. If man could have gained heaven by his own efforts, Christ need not have died to make an atonement for our sins. Yet all who tread the narrow path that leads to heaven, will bear the fruits of godliness, and give evidence that they are the light of the world. . . .

The Lord commands His people to go forward, from light to a greater light. Some have had great light, they have been blessed, they have believed that God, for Christ's sake, forgave their sins, but there they have stopped, and have made no further advancement. They have not attained unto a greater faith or broader experience, because they have not received the light of the truth which is constantly unfolding to those who follow the Light of the world. The blood of Christ cleanseth from all unrighteousness, but just as soon as a soul ceases to walk by faith, he becomes enshrouded in darkness.

The only safety for any one is to advance, to increase in the knowledge of the truth, to be sanctified by it. Those who are content with preaching old discourses, and praying stereotyped prayers, fail to improve the talents that God has given them, and these talents will be taken from them. . . .

Brother B, you have heard the testimony which God has given me to bear, but while you have professed to believe, you have in spirit rejected the message. It is my duty to say to you that you have had all the evidence that the Lord will give you in regard to the special work He is doing at this time to arouse a lukewarm, slumbering church. Those who accept the message given, will heed the counsel of the True Witness to the Laodiceans, and will buy the gold, which is faith and love; the white raiment, which is the righteousness of Christ; and the eyesalve, which is spiritual discernment. Says Christ, "As many as I love, I rebuke and chasten: be zealous therefore, and repent. Behold, I stand at the door, and knock: if any man hear My voice, and open the door, I will come in to him, and will sup with him, and he with Me" (Revelation 3:19,20).

Results of Refusing to Heed the Warning--If the church refuses to hear the voice of the Heavenly Merchantman, refuses to open the door, then Christ will pass on, and it will be left destitute of His presence, destitute of true riches, but saying in self-righteousness, "I am rich, and increased with goods, and have need of nothing" (Revelation 3:17).

Many who refuse the message which the Lord sends them are seeking to find pegs on which to hang doubts, to find some excuse for rejecting the light of heaven. In the face of clear evidence, they say as did the Jews, "Show us a miracle, and we will believe. If these messengers have the truth, why do they not heal the sick?" These objections recall to mind what was said concerning Christ: [John 7:3-5 and Matthew 27:39-43 quoted.]

How can any of our brethren, who have before them the history of the Lord of life and glory, open their lips to utter words similar to the taunting words of the murderers of our Lord? . . .

When men close their eyes to the light that God sends them, they will reject the most evident truth, and believe the most foolish errors. . . .

The Lord has been appealing to His people in warnings, in reproofs, in counsels, but their ears have been deaf to the words of Jesus. Some have said, "If this message that Brother A. T. Jones has been giving to the church is the truth, why is it that Brother C and Brother D have not received it, and have not united with him in heralding it? These good intelligent men would surely know if this were the message of truth."

Sentiments similar to these were expressed in the days of Christ, when He came to bear to earth the tidings of salvation. The people looked to their leaders, and asked, "If this were the truth, would not the priests and rulers know it?" . . .

In the days of Christ there were many who incurred deep guilt because they denounced His teaching without carefully investigating its claims to their attention. . . .

We Are to Follow No One but Christ--When Christ told Peter what should come upon him because of his faith, Peter turned to John, and asked, "Lord, and what shall this man do?" The Lord said, "What is that to thee? Follow thou Me" (John 21:21,22). If Elder C or Elder D should reject the message of truth that the Lord has sent to the people of this time, would their unbelief make the message error?--No. We are to follow no one but Christ. If men who have occupied leading positions feel at liberty to despise the message and the messenger, their unbelief is no excuse for others. Our salvation is an individual work. Neither Brother C, Brother D, nor any other mortal man can pay a ransom for my soul or yours in the day of judgment. In that day there will be no excuse to offer for neglecting to receive the message the Lord sent you. . . .

We should take no man for our pattern, for we are to see and know for ourselves what is truth. It is of vital importance to us that we allow no one to come between us and our God. We should not accept any man's opinions and ideas unless through careful searching for ourselves we find that they bear the credentials of heaven. It is of the greatest importance that we individually open our hearts to the convicting power of the Holy Spirit. Let God speak to us through His Word. Let God impress the soul.

It is your duty to grasp every ray of light. . . . Sanctified resolution, self-control, supreme love for Christ, will place you in right relation to God and to humanity. God has sent message upon message to His people, and it has nearly broken my heart to see those whom we thought were taught and led by God, fall under the bewitching power of the enemy, who led them to reject the truth for this time.

Do not men know from the Word of God that just such a message as has lately been going to the churches must be given in order that the very work which has been going on among us might be accomplished? Some who ought to have been first to catch the heavenly inspiration of truth, have been directly opposed to the message of God. They have been doing all that was in their power to show contempt for both the message and the messenger, and Jesus could not do many mighty works because of their unbelief. However, truth will move on, passing by those who despise and reject it. Although apparently retarded, it cannot be extinguished.

The Message Will Triumph in Spite of Opposition--When the message of God meets with opposition, He gives it additional force that it may exert greater influence. Endowed with vital, heavenly energy, it will cut its way through the thickest barriers, dispel darkness, refute error, gain conquests, and triumph over every obstacle. I speak that [which] I do know. I testify of that which I have seen. Those who would triumph in the truth will have to act a part in the sight of the universe that will bring to them the reward of "Well done." They will be known as laborers together with God.

Misunderstanding, misapplication of the truth will alienate the hearts of those who have been brethren. But this would not be if self and self-esteem, if customs and traditions, were not disturbed by the message of truth. Patience, moderation, self-control, and carefulness of speech should ever be cultivated and manifested. But while we show these commendable traits of character, for Christ's sake let us cry aloud and spare not. Says the Word of God, "Lift up thy voice like a trumpet, and show My people their transgression, and the house of Jacob their sin" (Isaiah 58:1).

The watchmen on the walls of Zion are asleep. Many have no burden of the work; they have no positive warning to give. There are many who have heard the message for this time and have seen its results, and they cannot but acknowledge that the work is good, but from fear that some will take extreme positions, and that fanaticism may arise in our ranks, they have permitted their imagination to create many obstacles to hinder the advance of the work, and they have presented these difficulties to others, expatiating on the dangers of accepting the doctrine. They have sought to counteract the influence of the message of truth. Suppose they should succeed in these efforts, what would be the result?--the message to arouse a lukewarm church should cease, and the testimony exalting the righteousness of Christ would be silenced.

What Does the Opposition Have to Offer?--Suppose that prejudice should do its baleful work, suppose the work should be given into the hands of these opposers and faultfinders, and they should be permitted to give to the church the doctrine and the labor they desire to give; would they present anything better than the Lord has sent to His people at this time through His chosen agents? Would the message of the doubters arouse the churches from their lukewarmness? Would its influence tend to give energy and zeal to uplift the souls of the people of God? Have those who have opposed the light, openly or in secret, been giving the people the food that would nourish their souls? Have they been presenting the message which the time demands, that the camp may be purified from all moral defilement? Have they anything to offer to take the place of the truth that has been given with fervor and zeal to prepare the way for the Lord's coming?

The character, the motives and purposes of the workmen whom God has sent, have been, and will continue to be, misrepresented. Men will catch at words and statements that they suppose to be faulty, and will magnify and falsify these utterances. But what kind of work are these lookers-on doing? Has the Lord placed them on the judgment-seat to condemn His message and messengers? Why do not these opposers lay hold of the work if they have so much light? If they see defects in the presentation of the message, why do they not present it in a better way? If they possess such farseeing discernment, such caution, such intelligence, why do they not go to work and do something?

The world is a second Sodom; the end is right upon us, and is it reasonable to think that there is no message to make ready a people to stand in the day of God's preparation? Why is there so little eyesight? So little deep, earnest, heartfelt labor? Why is there so much pulling back? Why is there such a continual cry of "peace and safety," and no going forward in obedience to the Lord's command? Is the third angel's message to go out in darkness, or to lighten the whole earth with its glory? Is the light of God's Spirit to be quenched, and the church to be left as destitute of the grace of Christ as the hills of Gilboa were of dew and rain? Certainly all must admit that it is time that a vivifying, heavenly influence should be brought to bear upon our churches. It is time that unbelief, pride, love of supremacy, evil-surmising, depreciation of the work of others, licentiousness, and hypocrisy should go out of our ranks. . . .

Sincerity Does Not Guarantee Rightness--The idea is entertained by many that a man may practice anything that he conscientiously believes to be right. But the question is: Has the man a well-instructed, good conscience, or is it biased and warped by his own preconceived opinions? Conscience is not to take the place of "Thus saith the Lord." Consciences do not all harmonize and are not all inspired alike. Some consciences are dead, seared as with a hot iron. Men may be conscientiously wrong, as well as conscientiously right. Paul did not believe in Jesus of Nazareth, and he hunted the Christians from city to city, verily believing that he was doing service to God.

Appeal to Accept the Message of Christ's Righteousness--In view of these things, we can see that there is great need of seeking counsel of God, of searching the Scriptures with a humble, prayerful spirit, that the Lord may enlighten our understanding, so that we can carefully weigh every point of truth that is presented. We should watch the tendency of it, and see whether its fruit testifies that it is of God. . . .

The message of God has been presented to the people with clearness and force. It is the very message that God means that His church shall have at this time. Your refusal to listen to it, your rejection of it, while it will not stop the work, will result in great loss to your souls. Every ray of light that God has given to His people is necessary for them in the emergency that is to come. But if the rays of Heaven's light are not discerned, if they are not appreciated, accepted, and acted upon, you will lose the heavenly benefit yourselves, and keep the light from others whom God designed should receive it through you. . . .

The duty of setting a good example must be considered. We must weigh faithfully the results of our actions. If we think a certain course will do us no harm, we should then look at it from the standpoint of others and ask how it will affect them. There are sins of omission, as well as sins of commission, and all of us are influencing the course of others. A neglect when the work is laid before you, is as wrong as to perform some sinful action, for in neglecting your duty you fail to supply your link in the chain of God's great work. Your influence does not sustain His cause. . . .

In this time of danger, if Satan can work upon the unconsecrated elements of men's characters, so as to keep them quibbling and questioning until it is too late to rescue souls who are rapidly getting beyond the reach of help, he will do it. I have been shown that this is just what he is doing. He is holding men away from the work that they should do, holding them back from obedience to their Captain's orders, in subservience to their own supposed wise judgment and criticism of plans for the advancement of the work. There are many who preach discourses, lamenting the extensive and deplorable depravity now existing in the world, but they fail to do their part in shedding Heaven's light into the world's moral darkness. . . .

There is need that the converting power of God should come upon our ministering brethren, for many of the people are far in advance of them in experience in the things of God. The highest interest of souls both for time and eternity, is involved in a proper understanding of the work for this time.

We deplore the fact that men idolize their own opinions; that they are willing to be governed by their own preconceived ideas, rather than by a plain, "Thus saith the Lord." . . .

When men open their hearts to unbelief, they open them to the great deceiver, the accuser of the brethren. With the glorious light of truth emanating from God, with abundant evidence that the work for this time is ordained of Heaven, beware that you do not harden your hearts and ask for further proof, saying, "Show us a miracle." The rich man of the parable prayed that one might be sent from the dead to warn his brethren, that they might not come to the place of torment in which he found himself. He said, "If one went unto them from the dead, they will repent." But the answer came to him, as it comes to us today, "If they hear not Moses and the prophets, neither will they be persuaded, though one rose from the dead" (Luke 16:30,31).--Letter 4, 1889, pp. 7-13, 15-41.

White Estate
Washington, D.C.
December 10, 1981

ELLEN G. WHITE LETTERS TO J. H. KELLOGG

God Is Testing You; Keep Your Eyes Fixed on Jesus--Jesus loves you. The experience which you are having makes me glad, not because you are a sufferer, but because this is evidence to me that the Lord is testing and proving you to see if you will come to Him, to see if you will put your trust in Him, if you will find peace and rest in His love. I am praying for you, that Jesus will teach you precious lessons in coming to Him, the fountain of living waters. This is the experience every one of us must have if we ever dwell with Jesus in the mansions He has gone to prepare for us. You have lessons of the highest value to learn in the school of Christ, lessons that will lead you to work out your own salvation with fear and trembling.

If you are prospered, if all men speak well of you, then will be your danger. Be on guard, for you will be tried. My greatest fears for you have been that you would have too great prosperity, and fail to learn that your dependence is alone upon God. Your heavenly Father loves you. He is all-powerful. He would draw you to Himself by the very trials that seem to you so severe. You have been placed in a position of great trust and honor, and there has been danger of your becoming dizzy and not realizing your dependence upon God. You have been in a position where you could exert a wide, far-reaching influence if the eye were constantly single to the glory of God. While climbing the ladder of progress, if your eye sees God above the ladder, if you can see the messengers of light, angels of God, ascending and descending on this ladder of shining brightness; if you can see the Lord as the source of all power, and you as only His humble agent, walking in His ways, keeping the truth in the beauty of holiness, then the inducement is before you, the precious boon of eternal life--a home of rest and peace, a crown of glory that fadeth not away, riches that are exhaustless. . . .

You have One ready and able to help you whenever you shall call upon Him. He is at your right hand. If you try to carry your burdens alone, you will be crushed under them. You have weighty responsibilities, and Jesus knows all about them, but He will not leave you alone if you do not leave Him. He is honored when you commit the keeping of your soul to Him as unto a faithful Creator. He bids you hope in His mercy, believing that He does not desire you to carry these weighty responsibilities alone. Only believe, and you will see the salvation of God. . . .

Jesus sees every action of the children of men. He weighs thoughts and motives. You are carrying a heavy load. I wish that everyone could feel this as I do, and would be true and faithful to you, not to hinder, not to praise or extol and glorify you, but to look upon you as one whom God is using as His instrument to do a given work, and that they must not block the wheels, but put their shoulder to the wheel and help rather than hinder.

Again I say, Rejoice in the Lord. Weave Jesus into your daily experience and rest in Him. His power as a helper you need, and you may have it. Go forward firmly, valiantly, courageously. You may err in judgment, but do not lose your hold on Jesus.--Letter 8, 1886, pp. 2,3,7-10. (To J. H. Kellogg, July 16, 1886.)

Let Others Bear Responsibilities--You must never take the position that because you have an experience in your calling and practice that others have not, everyone must meet your exact measurement in all particulars before you can take them by your side and teach them all you know yourself, and have them obtain a practical knowledge of everything essential for the work [so] that you can leave the sanitarium [to] visit Europe and California, and give instruction to our young institutions there. . . .

You have been wonderfully successful in your career in doing a special work. God has raised you up as a man of opportunity to do this work. But if at any time you take the credit or glory to yourself, then the Lord will not work by you or through you. . . .

How thankful I felt when I read from your pen which traced the lines that you were enjoying more of the Spirit of God. No one could appreciate the blessing of God daily more than yourself. No one could estimate the knowledge of sins forgiven and the reconciled countenance of your Redeemer more than yourself, and this precious evidence and light from above will make you constantly a channel of light, a source of blessing to those with whom you are brought in contact.

I am so desirous that you should come off conqueror, that you should have the eternal weight of glory. I want you to live, not for this life, but for the future immortal life. You have transmitted to you traits of character that are not the most helpful, or helpful to you in the religious life, but these may be overcome. Now is our time to fit for eternity. You have a battle to fight with your own individual temptations and your marked traits of character which will seek constantly for the supremacy.--Letter 64, 1886, pp. 1,3,4. (To J. H. Kellogg, cir. 1886.)

Keep Your Eyes on Jesus--God is very near you in your work, angels are close in attendance; then let not any feelings or any words or works of human beings overwhelm you. Rise above all these difficulties so trying to human nature. Every day has its own troubles for every soul who lives. Then do not in any way, by feeling, word, or look, increase the temptations of Satan upon one soul. When tempted to be hasty or passionate, remember Jesus your Pattern. I want you to have the gift of eternal life, and I beg you to seek peace and harmony for your own sake as well as for the sake of those whom God loves, who have devoted their lives to His service. May the Lord help you, strengthen and bless you, is my prayer. . . .

I know that the Lord has helped you many, many times. I have the fullest confidence that He has made you a blessing to very many. May the Lord clothe you with His salvation. Walk in the light, press to the light, refuse to look at darkness or talk darkness. Talk of things that are calculated to uplift the soul; come close to Jesus, commune with Him. He will be your wisdom. He will preserve you still to do a good work for Him. Satan, you must know, will seek to hinder you in every possible way. He will delight to discourage you and shorten your life. I want your life spared; I do not want the devil to have his way. I want you to be a strong, well-balanced character because the grace of Christ is given you in large measure. I know it is your privilege to have the blessing of God daily, and you cannot fill your position unless you do have it. May you be of good courage in the Lord. Turn your attention from disagreeable things. By beholding you become changed. Talk of pleasant things, talk hope and courage, and you will have hope and courage.--Letter 46, 1887, pp. 4, 7. (To J. H. Kellogg, April 22, 1887.)

Book by Dr. Paquin* Questionable--Have you evidence that Dr. Paquin, who has written the book in question, has been standing where the bright rays of the Sun of Righteousness are shining upon him? Have you evidence that he is an instrument in the hands of God to bring in the rays of light essential for God's people in these last days, to increase their faith and confidence in spiritual things? . . .

Here, my brother, has been and will be your danger, in your scientific researches: Unless you are daily increasing in the knowledge and love of the truth, growing up into Christ your living head, you are in positive danger. I have not at present anything to say to you or Elder [E. J] Waggoner in regard to the author of the book published. I have not strength to give to these questions, but I know that the Lord has been pleased to show me, in clear lines, your danger in the past and at the present time. Be careful how you favor these things that limit the power of God. . . .

Once these young men# were willing to submit their wills and ideas to God's will and ways, but they became confused through your ideas of science. While you could start them on a track of investigation, you could not control their imagination. Human ideas, contracted, confused, and obscure, were to them like the bright shining of a candle at midnight. They were simply walking in the sparks of their own kindling. . . .

These men have fallen because of their human ideas of science. I know that if you had stood in the clear light; if you, in your position of trust, had felt that you needed to walk humbly and carefully before God; if you had daily felt the need of His grace, His power, His wisdom, you could have been

---

*Paul Paquin, M.D., The Supreme Passions of Man; or the Origin, Causes, and Tendencies of the Passions of the Flesh (Battle Creek, Mi., 1891) was reviewed favorably by Kellogg in Good Health, vol. 27 (Jan. 1892), 32, and more extensively in Good Health, vol. 27 (Feb. 1892), 64-65. Meanwhile, the Signs of the Times, vol. 18 (Jan. 18, 1892), 176, reviewed the book, labeling it "anitbiblical and therefore antichristian."

#Two young doctors who had received a reproof from the Lord.

as a light shining in a dark place, and could have guided these poor souls
to Jesus, their only hope. Now, I do not present this matter to discourage
you, but to warn you, that you may not make crooked paths for your feet and
lead others astray. You need to have divine enlightenment through an experimental knowledge of God and our Saviour. My much-respected brother, you
need the divine touch. . . .

There is a higher standard for you to reach in spiritual things, and I
greatly hoped that this sickness and your recovery through the gracious
mercy of God would clear away much of the fog that has obscured your spiritual vision. Much of the talk about science I know is a snare. Men have
erroneous views of science. They should be searching diligently to see if
they are accepting Christ as their personal Saviour. . . . It is not enough
for you and me to assent to the truth. We need to have a practical knowledge of the truth. Every believer in Christ is a believer in God's mercy.
The renewing of the heart is a far greater miracle than the healing of the
diseases of the body. . . .

The Holy Spirit's presence and power in the hearts of the professed
people of God is their only hope in these last days of peril. Let not the
impression be given to any minds that there is in human nature a power to
work out its purity and develop a beautiful character, for this is not true.
This is Satan's fallacy. "Without Me," said Christ, "ye can do nothing"
(John 15:5). The completeness of man is in Christ Jesus. . . .

Let me tell you, Dr. Kellogg, it is not safe for us to employ as instructors in our institutions those who are not believers in the present
truth. They advance ideas and theories that take hold of the mind with a
bewitching power which absorbs the thoughts, making a world of an atom, and
an atom of a world. . . .

Dr. Kellogg, I entreat you to come close to Jesus. You need Him every moment. I can say no more now, for this letter must go into the mail. But if the Lord gives me strength, I will write further upon this subject. Your own letter has called this out. I have not had a line from Dr. Waggoner or A. T. Jones since I came to Australia.

Please accept these hastily written lines from one who has the deepest interest in your prosperity.--Letter 18, 1892, pp. 2-10. (To J. H. Kellogg, April 5, 1892.)

Counsel to Look to Christ for Wisdom--Warn every student against placing dependence on you, for you are not beyond temptation. Even now, though doing the very work the Lord designs to have done, you are embracing too much. The light of Christian example and Christian instruction may be turned in wrong channels, and the work God would have done may become too scattered, thus bringing confusion and discouragement upon the workers.

The Lord alone must be your counselor. Remember that Satan has come down with great power to work with all deceivableness of unrighteousness in them that perish, because they yield to his plans. You are not above temptation. You are not to feel confidence in your own wisdom. Your only dependence must be in God. Lean hard on Jesus Christ. You have worked hard to bring about good results. Do not now make any mistakes and spoil your work. You must never, never seek to lift one pin, remove one landmark of truth, that the Lord has given to His people as truth.--Letter 126, 1898, p. 4. (To J. H. Kellogg, Dec. 18, 1898.)

J. H. Kellogg Warned He Is in Danger--Brother John Kellogg, my mother-heart goes out toward you with weeping, for by symbols I am warned that you are in danger.   Satan is making masterly efforts to cause your feet to slide, but God's eye is upon you. Fight these last battles manfully. Stand equipped with the whole armor of righteousness. By faith I lay you in earn-est prayer at the feet of Jesus. You are safe only in that position. Never for a moment suppose that you are in no danger.--Letter 132, 1898, pp. 4,5. (To J. H. Kellogg, Dec. 29, 1898.)

Greatness Dependent on Humility--You need never try to shape your reli-gious experience in order that you may be a great man before the world. Your greatness depends upon your humility. . . .

Put on Christ. In the closet, communing with Him who seeth in secret, lay hold by faith on His might. Put away your self-confidence. Make peace with Him and you shall in your simplicity make peace with Him. . . .

Walk humbly with God. Bear in humility all the honor God has seen fit to give you. Do not exalt yourself and demerit your brethren as. you have done, for then you show distinctly that the Spirt of the Lord is departing from you, and that you will be left to your own wisdom.--Letter 40, 1899, pp. 4,5,11. (To J. H. Kellogg, copied Feb. 23, 1899.)

J. H. Kellogg's Way and Spirit Not Approved by God--All I have to say now is that your way and spirit toward your brethren is not approved by God. He calls for unity. Variance and dissension are not created by the Lord. The Lord has given light to men that it may be a help to them and all con-nected with them. If the same spirit is manifested to justify and condemn that has been cherished in the past, settle it in your mind that Jesus Christ is not glorified. The softening, subduing influence of the Spirit of God is greatly needed. Nothing can dishonor God more than the independent self-sufficiency that marks the defections of your brethren and fails to see your own dangers and defects. I am afraid for you. I am afraid for my brethren in responsible positions.--Letter 55, 1899, p. 1. (To J. H. Kellogg, March 24, 1899.)

J. H. Kellogg Urged to Remain Loyal--If my words have wounded and bruised your soul, I am sorry, for I am wounded and bruised also. Our work, a strange work, a great work, given us by God, links us heart and soul together. You dare not throw off your armor. You must wear it till the end. When the Lord releases you, then it will be time for you to lay your armor at His feet. You have enlisted to the very close of the battle, and you would not disgrace yourself and dishonor God by deserting from the army. May the Lord open to you many matters which He has opened to me. Satan is watching his opportunity to dishonor the cause of God. I have been shown your peril and your guardian angel preserving you again and again from your-self, keeping you from making shipwreck of faith. Lift up the standard, lift it up, and be not fainthearted or discouraged. . . .

The Lord loves you, the Lord upholds you. In God you can triumph. I have appreciated the confidence you have ever maintained in my humble self, as the Lord's servant, who speaks and works His will. You have ever shown me respect. In return you have my sincere appreciation of the same.--Letter 73, 1899, pp. 5,6,8. (To J. H. Kellogg, April 17, 1899.)

Warnings of Dangers Have Not Been Overstated--I am writing much and the Lord gives me strength and grace. He has assured me that when at any time I have written to you in plainness, it has been to save you from making mistakes, and to place you under the leading of the Holy Spirit. Here I must leave the matter. Nothing has been overstated in regard to the dangers which threaten you.--Letter 129, 1899, p. 2. (To J. H. Kellogg, August 29, 1899.)

EGW Concerned for JHK-I love you and I pray for you, and I believe the Lord hears my prayers for you as verily as if they came from your own mother's heart. Hide yourself in Christ.--Letter 129a, 1899. (To J. H. Kellogg, Aug. 29, 1899.)

Why EGW Wrote Kellogg So Often-Why is it that I have written to you so often? Because there is none other whom you consider of sufficient authority to heed. . . .

May the dear Jesus reveal Himself to you as He has done to me, is my prayer. He is the One "altogether lovely," and "the chiefest among ten thousand." Believe, only believe. Commit the keeping of your soul unto Him as unto a faithful Creator. Jesus will forgive you, and make your character like His own pure character, if you will open the door of your heart and let Him in. He wants to give you His peace, His joy, His comfort. If you will let Him do this, He will cause you to triumph gloriously.--Letter 135, 1899, pp. 1, 9. (To J. H. Kellogg, Aug. 29, 1899.)

EGW Concerned for JHK--Your last letter expresses the thought that I have lost confidence in you. I do not know just how to reply to this statement. I am certainly deeply concerned for you, and it is most difficult to say anything because you do not take the matter as you should. I know that the Lord is your true friend, and He has presented your case before me as not directing the work correctly. . . .

You need to be counseled and to receive this counsel as a blessing, not as a curse. You are wearing out your powers. I need you to encourage and to help me in bearing the straightforward testimony that God has given me. The discouragement which you think I have brought upon you is not to be charged to me, for I have given you the Source of my message.--Letter 77, 1900, pp. 1,6. (To J. H. Kellogg, Dec., 1899.)

JHK Reproved--You were entirely out of place in making such sweeping censures of your brethren. The Lord did not give to you the work of laying a reproach upon them. Your actions in this respect pleased the evil angels, but the angels of God veiled their faces. Such manifestations are not prompted by the Spirit of God, but by another spirit. Your sarcasms, your witticisms, your play on words, which seemed so clever to some present, were an offense to God. You spoke sharp words to Christ in the person of His servants, who were appointed to do a special work for the Master. Sometimes they worked under great disadvantages. This was calculated to discourage them and to weaken their hands. Your inclination to chastise the ministers as you have done, and to break out upon them with a tirade of abuse, bears the rebuke of God. Unless you repent and make a thorough change, you will do more and more of this work. . . .

Oh, John, John, what are you doing, and what do you mean? The work that is coming from your hands is not pure and sanctified. The work that should be done is not done. The Lord does not endorse the work that you are doing. . . .

Dr. Kellogg, as you have dealt with others, so God will deal with you unless you repent and change your course of action. He cannot serve with injustice. There is not a vestige of justice in the position you so firmly maintained. Your wit and sarcasm were inspired by a spirit from beneath. Where you should have shown benevolence, kindness, love, and tenderness, as a representative man, you manifested traits exactly the opposite of these. I cannot find words to describe the way in which God regards such a course. --Letter 177, 1900, pp. 1,2,6,7. (To J. H. Kellogg, Jan. 21, 1900.)

JHK Warned Concerning Operation of Medical Work--I have had matter written for some time, but have not sent you all you should have. I have been in such dread to have the words I should speak come in to contradict your course of action that I have kept still, but since I have been having representations of the vast field, God's vineyard, it has been distinctly presented before me that you have been bringing in principles that will not be sustained or favored by the Lord. The case of Nebuchadnezzar was presented before me. I must now say I have the matter before me in distinct lines.

My brother, I am instructed to say to you that if you carry on the sanitarium and medical—missionary work as you are now doing, you will bring in a state of things that will be according to the wisdom of human minds, but not as God requires His work to be carried on.

Brother John, I tell you, your eternal interest depends upon a change in your heart in order that your head may work and plan so that all others may have a chance to accomplish the work, not after your devising, but after the wisdom given them individually of God.--Letter 188, 1901, pp. 1, 4. (To J. H. Kellogg, December 30, 1901.)

Ellen White Will Not Cease to Warn J. H. Kellogg--So long as the Lord presents before me your case and your dangers, I shall not cease to warn you. If you will not take heed, if you refuse to change, I must then present the instruction given to me to those in responsible positions, that the people of God may not be leavened by the influence of your erroneous position.

Dr. Kellogg, no one can appreciate more fully than myself the honor that God has bestowed on you in connecting you with His work as His chosen physician. I have a knowledge of you as a boy, and the Lord instructed me in regard to the dangers that threatened you, even in your childhood years, because of hereditary and cultivated tendencies.

One evening my husband and I talked about your case for a long time, and then joined in prayer for you. In the night season light was given that we were to make a way for you and two of your companions. We decided to invest three thousand dollars in this--a thousand dollars for each of you. Light was given me that my husband and I were to act the part of a father and mother to you. . . .

You need to be converted, to be born again, before you can cooperate with the Lord Jesus. . . .

You may close your eyes and ears to the messages that God sends, but after all, you do believe them. And you may depend on this: A mother could not hold more firmly to a child that she dearly loves than I shall hold to you. I expect to see you engaged in the work that God has given you, and I pray for you constantly, in private prayer and at family worship. Sometimes I am awakened in the night, and rising, I walk the room, praying, "O Lord, hold Dr. Kellogg fast. Do not let him go. Keep him steadfast. Anoint his eyes with the heavenly eyesalve, that he may see all things clearly."-- Letter 174, 1902, pp. 2,6,9. (To J. H. Kellogg, Nov. 11, 1902.)

EGW's Concern for and Appeal to JHK--My brother, I have the deepest interest in you, knowing the value of the human soul, and I entreat you to turn to the Lord with full purpose of heart. In the night season I am pleading with you to heed the Scripture, "Examine yourselves, whether ye be in the faith; prove your own selves. Know ye not your own selves, how that Jesus Christ is in you, except ye be reprobates?" (2 Cor. 13:5). I am waiting and longing to hear from you in regard to your individual experience. . . .

I beseech you to make an unreserved surrender to God, and to make it now, just now. When you make this surrender you will have an experience entirely different from the experience that you have had for many years. Then you will be able to say with the apostle Paul, "I count all things but loss for the excellency of the knowledge of Christ" (Eph. 3:8). "I delight in the law of God after the inward man" (Romans 7:22).

Every privilege is opened before you. Christ presents His loveliness of character for you to copy. When you make Him your example, your pride and self-assurance will be removed. You are becoming weak in spiritual power, through cherishing an unforgiving spirit and indulging wrathful feelings that place you under the control of Satan. These things are bearing sorry testimony against you. When you are converted, your masterly spirit, which leads you to judge and condemn and censure, will be changed.--Letter 65, 1903, pp. 1,2,5,6. (To J. H. Kellogg, April 19, 1903.)

EGW Prays That God Will Let JHK See Where He Stands--Last night, after going to rest, I wrestled in earnest prayer for you until eleven o'clock. Then I slept until three. I then rose and dressed, and continued my prayer that God would draw back the curtain and let you see where you stand. I have felt that it was of little use for me to write more to you, for the many letters that I have written do not seem to have that [effect] which I so much hoped they would accomplish. And yet my burden does not leave me, because you cannot see yourself as God sees you.

The words, "Thou hast left thy first love," describe your condition. God calls upon you to repent, else He will come to you quickly, and will remove the candlestick out of its place. You need the ministry of the great Physician to cure you of the disease which, unless cured, will result in spiritual blindness. Let the Spirit of God come in and take possession of your heart, purifying the soul-temple. God wants you to let your heart break before Him. He wants you to confess and forsake your besetting sins. --Letter 180, 1903, pp. 2, 3. (To J. H. Kellogg, May 5, 1903.)

JHK Reproved for Confederating with Worldlings--Is it possible that you do not realize that Satan is playing the game of life for your soul? You are certainly in danger.   You have not walked perfectly before the Lord.

You have been ambitious, and have opened before worldlings that which you

should not have opened to them.   You have made with them a confederacy

wholly displeasing to the Lord.--Letter 52, 1903, p. 1. (To J. H. Kellogg,

April 5, 1903.)

   Unscriptural Theories in "The Living Temple"-If ever there was a time

when the writings of every author needed to be criticized, it is now. God's

Word is to be our study book.   In this Word we do not find such representa-

tions of God as are presented in the Living Temple.   Had Christ thought it

essential for such theories to be given to human beings, He would have in-

cluded them in His teachings.

   To me it seems passing strange that some who have been long in the work

of God cannot discern the character of the teaching in Living Temple in re-

gard to God. All through the book are passages of Scripture. These Scrip-

tures are brought in in such a way that error is made to appear as truth.

Erroneous theories are presented in so pleasing a way that unless care is

taken, many will be misled. . . .

   I am called upon by God to stand in defense of the truth that has been

given us as we have followed the leading of Him who is the way, the truth,

and the life.--Letter 232, 1903, pp. 1,14,16. (To J. H. Kellogg, Oct. 16,

1903, marked "not sent.")

   "The Living Temple" Not Inspired by God--The book Living Temple is not to

be patched up, a few changes made in it, and then advertised and praised as

a valuable production.   It would be better to present the physiological parts in another book under another title. When you wrote that book you were not under the inspiration of God. There was by your side the one who inspired Adam to look at God in a false light. Your whole heart needs to be changed, thoroughly and entirely cleansed. . . .

My brother, I must tell you that you have little realization of whither your feet have been tending. The facts have been opened to me. You have been binding yourself up with those who belong to the army of the great apostate. Your mind has been as dark as Egypt. If you will fall on the Rock and be broken, Christ will accept you. . . .

I write to you as I would to a son. Break away from the enemy--the accuser of the brethren. Say to him, "Get thee behind me, Satan. I have committed a grievous sin in heeding your suggestions. I will no longer listen to them." I beg of you, for your soul's sake, to resist the tempter, that he may flee from you. Draw near to God, and He will draw near to you. You will lose heaven unless you fall on the Rock and are broken.--Letter 253, 1903, pp. 1, 12-14. (To J. H. Kellogg, Nov. 20, 1903.)

Fables Similar to Heresies in the Early Days of the Message Present in "The Living Temple"-The difficulties that have arisen have been very hard to meet, and they are far from being settled yet. One, and another, and still another are presented to me as having been led to accept the pleasing fables that mean the sanctification of sin. The Living Temple contains the alpha of a train of heresies. These heresies are similar to those that I met in my first labors in connection with the cause in Maine, New Hampshire, Vermont, then in Boston, Roxbury, Portsmouth, New Bedford, and other parts of Massachusetts. Through them the evil one worked upon the minds of men and women. . . .

I bore them a message similar to the message I have been bearing for the last two months. I was instructed that the ideas they had accepted were but the alpha of a great deception. I had to meet similar delusions in Portsmouth and in Boston.--Letter 265, 1903, pp. 1,2. (To J. H. Kellogg, Nov. 26, 1903.)

There Is Yet Hope--I am now bidden to say to you, "You may now come to the Saviour. Your opportunity is here. At the General Conference [session] held in Battle Creek in 1901, the Lord, in the testimonies borne in the Tabernacle, pointed out the way that you were to follow, but you did not choose to follow. At one time, after the [General] Conference [session] held at South Lancaster [1899], you broke down and you did see yourself, but in none too strong a light. Had you then kept the repentance that needeth not to be repented of, you would have boldly taken your stand under the banner of Jesus Christ. But it is not natural for you to yield, and you cherished a stubborn determination to carry out your own will and way. You would not yield to the Holy Spirit's guidance. You kept yourself under your own control, devising first one plan and then another plan, and working against the Lord's plans. . . .

If you could leave your work in the charge of some other physician and go away from Battle Creek for some months, with someone who understands your danger, you might break the spell. But this seems to be an impossibility. You do not realize the danger of your condition. . . .

I am moved by the Spirit of God to tell you to break with Satan's agencies. Come to Jesus. Make things right, even though this takes an effort that would seem to dissolve human nature. Take yourself in hand and go

straight to Jesus, your invisible Mediator. Go in spite of the opposition
of the flesh. Resist every inclination to draw back. Make the break. Die
to self. Then you will be able to say, "I thought on my ways, and turned my
feet unto Thy testimonies" (Psalm 119:59).--Letter 269, 1904, pp. 1,3,5.
(To J. H. Kellogg, May 22, 1904.)

Deceptive Power Working on J. H. Kellogg's Mind for Years--Christ says
to you, "Let him take hold of My strength, that he may make peace wth Me;
and he shall make peace with Me" (Isaiah 27:5). I plead with you to respond
to this invitation. You do not understand yourself, because for years a
deceptive power has been working upon your mind. . . .

I am at times in an agony of distress for your soul. . . .

The Lord does not acknowledge as pleasing to Him the course that you
have pursued at our general meetings. You may think that you have clothed
yourself with the garments of righteousness, but should you come thus
clothed to the marriage supper of the Lamb, it would be seen that you have
on the dress of a civilian.

The Lord Jesus was much displeased with your course of action at the
General Conference [session] held in Oakland [1903]. At one time it was
presented to me that evil angels clothed with beautiful garments were es-
corting you from place to place, and inspiring you to speak words of boasting which were offensive to God. Heavenly messengers were viewing all that
took place. They heard the words and witnessed the acts that were of a
nature to bring glory to men rather than to God.

At this time you were not led by the Spirit of God. Your threats that
you would bring the law to bear upon those who oppressed your track showed

-317-

that you were in the same condition as those to whom the Laodicean message
is addressed.

Should I be removed by death, I leave in writing this testimony that
you are not yourself. You are not particular to teach the truth, and unless
you are converted you will lead the people of God in strange paths. . . .

I, too, must speak the truth, even though it cut men to the quick. The
Lord has a controversy with those who make of no effect the testimonies of
His Spirit. He is dishonored by those who reject the light given concerning
The Living Temple, telling you that you have been misjudged. The warnings
given regarding this book should be received, believed, and acted upon.--
Letter 257, 1904, pp. 1-4. (To J. H. Kellogg, July 27, 1904.)

Not One Word to Destroy Hope--This morning I received a letter from
you. I would encourage you in the efforts that you are making to press into
the light. We pray for you, that you will work out your own salvation with
fear and trembling, knowing that it is God which worketh in you, both to
will and to do of His good pleasure. I would not say one word to destroy
hope. I know that the enemy will work diligently to dishearten right
effort.--Letter 361, 1904, p. 1. (To J. H. kellogg, August 25, 1904.)

Do Not Discuss God's Personality--Never allow yourself to be drawn into
discussion regarding the personality of God. On this subject, silence is
eloquence. . . .

Here are words given me to repeat to you: "Many prayers have been
offered up for you by those who would rejoice to see you converted in mind,
in thought, in writing."--Letter 283, 1904, pp. 4-6. (To J. H. Kellogg,
Sept. 10, 1904.)

Hope for Unity, If-- --If your faith in the Word of God is strengthened; if you will fully accept the truths that have called us out of the
world and made us a people denominated by the Lord as His peculiar treasure;
if you will unite with your brethren in standing by the old landmarks, then
there will be unity. But you remain in unbelief, unsettled as to the true
foundation of faith; there can be no hope of any more unity in the future
than there has been in the past.

I am instructed to say that you need to be re-taught the first principles of present truth. You have not believed the messages that God has
given for this time because they do not favor your sentiments. Think you
that while you remain in doubt and unbelief you can be fully united with
those who have stood for the truth as it is in Jesus and who have accepted
the light that God has given to us as a people?

Ask yourself candidly whether you are sound in the faith. Do all in
your power to come into unity with God and with your brethren. As a people
we cannot receive the full measure of the blessing of God while some who
occupy leading positions are continuously working against the truth that for
years we have held sacred, and obedient to the faith that has brought us
what success we have had.--Letter 23, 1904, pp. 1,2. (To J. H. Kellogg,
Dec. 1904, copied Jan. 16, 1905.)

Deceptive Influence Cultivated by JHK--I have a great burden of soul
for you, Dr. Kellogg. If I could see you in the road that leads onward and
upward, I should be more than thankful. Were you a child, I would say that
you had been spoiled through flattery, vain conceit, and self-exaltation.
That which makes your case so sorrowful, so hopeless, is that you are not a

man of truth. You frame for the occasion any sentiments that may come into your mind. You twist words; you misinterpret; and you make assurances that are false. You have cultivated this deceptive influence until you have become an unreliable man. With what grief and sadness the Lord has looked upon you! . . .

I have a word for you from the Lord. Take your stand for the right and cease to suppose that you are safe where you are now standing. You need to undergo a transformation that will give you an experience that is the opposite of the experience you now have. . . .

The Lord will not much longer allow Dr. Kellogg to pursue the course of deception that he has pursued for years. He will take his case in hand. He has borne long with him, but the medical-missionary work, so long controlled by him, shall not always bear the marks of his defection. God would have made Dr. Kellogg a man after His own mind, but he refused to place himself under God's control. His crooked ways and deceptive works are a great dishonor to the truth.

I have seen that Satan's power over him has not been broken. Those who choose to sustain the man who so greatly dishonors God and has stood directly in the way of His work, will themselves become so deceived that their work will not be accepted by God. I have felt reluctant to say these things, but I know the Lord would not have souls endangered any longer by Dr. Kellogg. Tares have been sown in the minds of God's people, and as a result of this some have given up the truth, some have become infidels. The misrepresentations that Dr. Kellogg has made of the work God has given me to do, have made them infidels.--Letter 116, 1905, pp. 1,3,10. (To J. H. Kellogg, April 22, 1905.)

FANNIE BOLTON

<u>Fannie Bolton's Experience With Ellen White</u>--The writings given you, you have handled as an indifferent matter, and have often spoken of them in a manner to depreciate them in the estimation of others. . . .

I mean now for your own good that you shall never have another opportunity of being tempted to do as you have done in the past. From the light given me of the Lord, you are not appreciating the opportunities which you have had abundantly, to be instructed and to bring the solid timbers into your character building. The work in which you have been engaged has been regarded as a sort of drudgery, and it is hard for you to take hold of it with the right spirit, and to weave your prayers into your work, feeling that it is a matter of importance to preserve a spirit wholly in harmony with the Spirit of God. Because of this lack, you are not a safe and acceptable worker. . . .

Every time I can distinguish a word of yours, my pen crosses it out. I have so often told you that your words and ideas must not take the place of the words and ideas given me of God.,..

You have come to think that you were the one to whom credit should be given for the value of the matter that comes from your hands. I have had warnings concerning this, but could not see how I should come to the very point to say, "Go, Fannie," for then you plead, "Where shall I go?" and I try you again. . . .

Just before coming to this country, in order to help Fannie,* I consented to make another trial after she had given me the assurance . . . that
her feelings in regard to the work had wholly changed. I followed my best
judgment, hoping that she had gained wisdom from God and would really love
the work.

I knew that she was naturally unbalanced in mind, but thought that
through the light given of God, the appeals constantly made presenting definite reproofs to some and general reproofs to others, she would learn the
lessons that it was her privilege to learn, and become strengthened in
character. Thus she would obtain wisdom to prepare the precious matter
placed in her hands, so that it might work for the saving of her soul as
well as the souls of others.--Letter 7, 1894, pp. 1-4, 16. (To Fannie
Bolton, February 6, 1894.)

Ellen G. White Writes Concerning Fannie Bolton's Experience--In Battle
Creek, Fannie pleaded hard and with tears to come with me to engage with me
in the work of preparing articles for papers. She declared she had met with
a great change, and was not at all the person she was when she told me she
desired to write herself....

I want not her life, or words, or ideas in these articles. And the
sooner this bubble is burst, the better for all concerned. . . . I have now
no knowledge of how we shall come out, and what I shall do. I am afraid
that Fannie cannot be trusted. . . .

---

*In this portion of the letter Ellen White addresses Fannie Bolton in the
third person.

If she has done the work as she has represented to other minds she has done, so that she thinks credit should be given her for her talent brought into my writings, then it is time that this firm be dissolved.

If she has done this work, which she has represented to others has been so much her talent, her production of ideas and construction of sentences as mine, and in "beautiful language," then she has done a work I have urged again and again should not be done, and she is unworthy of any connection with the work.-- Letter 88, 1894. (To W.C. White, February 6, 1894.)

Fannie Bolton Felt E. G. White Was Getting Credit for Her Work-- Well, I felt like a wounded, stricken deer, ready to die. I had been warned of this before, twice in Preston and three times in New Zealand. A similar warning was given me as in the case of Mary Clough, but this did not fully arouse me to the danger, and to the real situation. I will not take time to explain these warnings.

Not long before I left New Zealand, while in camp meeting, it was represented to me. We gathered in a room of quite a company, and Fannie was saying some things in regard to the great amount of work coming from her hands. She said, "I cannot work in this way. I am putting my mind and life into this work, and yet the ones who make it what it is, are sunk out of sight, and Sister White gets the credit for the work.". . .

A voice spoke to me, "Beware and not place your dependence upon Fannie, to prepare articles or to make books. She cuts out words that should appear, and places her own ideas and words in their stead, and because she had done this she has become deceived, deluded, and is deceiving and deluding others. She is your adversary."--Letter 59, 1894. (To O. A. Olsen, February 5, 1894.)

False Claims Concerning Beautifying E. G. White's Writings-- Fannie represented that she and Marian had brought all the talent and sharpness into my books, yet you were both ignored and set aside, and all the credit came to me. She had underscored some words in a book, Christian Education, "beautiful words," she called them, and said that she had put in those words, they were hers. If this were the truth, I ask, Who told her to put in her words in my writings. She has, if her own statement is correct, been unfaithful to me.

Sister Prescott, however, says that in the providence of God that very article came to them [Brother and Sister Prescott] uncopied and in my own handwriting, and these very words were in that letter. So Fannie's statement regarding these words is proved to be untrue....

If after this meeting Fannie shall come to Granville, you must not put one line of anything I have written into her hands, or read a line to her of the Life of Christ. I would not have any [advice] from her. I am disconnected from Fannie because God required it, and my own heart requires it. I am sorry for Fannie.--Letter 102, 1895. (To Marian Davis, October 29, 1895.)

EGW Regretted Not Heeding Warning That Fannie Bolton Was Her Adversary --I am now relieved from this fitful, skyrocket experience. She seems to swell up into such large measurements of herself, full of self-sufficiency, full of her own capabilities, and from the light God has been pleased to give me she is my adversary, and has been thus throughout her connection with me. . . .

Two years ago He revealed to me that Fannie was my adversary, and would vex my soul and weaken my hands, but I was so anxious to get out things that

I thought the people needed.   Then came other trials in N.S.W., one after another, that I was not able to bear it.

Oh, if I had only heeded the instruction given of God and let no other voice or influence come in to leave me in uncertainty, I might have been saved this last terrible heartsickening trial.   But I hope the Lord will forgive me and have mercy upon me, but to try this matter again is out of the question.   I am willing her talent shall be exercised for all it is worth, but it will never be in connection with me.   I have served my time with Fannie Bolton.--Letter 22a, 1895.   (To Marian Davis, November 29, 1895.)

Fifth Time Fannie Bolton Made False Claims--Fannie Bolton is discon-
nected with me entirely.   I would not think of employing her any longer. She has misrepresented me and hurt me terribly.   Only in connection with my work has she hurt me.

She has reported to others that she has the same as made over my arti-
cles, that she has put her whole soul into them, and I had the credit of the ability she had given to these writings.   Well, this is the fifth time this breaking out has come.

It is something similar to the outbreak of Korah, Dathan, and Abiram, only she has not those to unite with her because they know me and my work. She goes not only to those who believe and know me to tell her story, but she goes to those newly come to the faith and tells her imaginative story. The same sentiment is expressed as in Numbers 16:3. . . .

I could not possibly relate the suffering of mind while attending the camp meeting at Melbourne.--Letter 123a, 1895.   (To J.   E.   White, Dec. 9, 1895.)

Sacred Things Regarded as Common--I have tried to have her receive and appropriate the precious truths that were spread before her as a rich banquet, but while she handled these truths, she did not feast upon them. She regarded it all as a common thing.

The warnings, the appeals, the precious light given, the jewels of truth were apparently of no value to Fannie. She was feeling so rich in her supposed treasure of talent, that she wanted nothing. Sacred things were of no more value to her than the common fire, and she worked and walked in its light.-- Letter 104, 1895. (To Addie and May Walling, Dec. 11, 1895.)

EGW Instructed to Re-employ Fannie Bolton--Friday, March 19, I arose early, about half-past three o'clock in the morning. While writing upon the fifteenth chapter of John, suddenly a wonderful peace came upon me. The whole room seemed to be filled with the atmosphere of heaven. A holy, sacred presence seemed to be in my room. I laid down my pen and was in a waiting attitude to see what the Spirit would say unto me. I saw no person. I heard no audible voice, but a heavenly Watcher seemed close beside me. I felt that I was in the presence of Jesus.

The sweet peace and light which seemed to be in my room it is impossible for me to explain or describe. A sacred, holy atmosphere surrounded me, and there was presented to my mind and understanding matters of intense interest and importance. A line of action was laid out before me as if the unseen presence were speaking with me. The matter I had been writing upon seemed to be lost to my mind and another matter distinctly opened before me. A great awe seemed to be upon me as matters were imprinted upon my mind.

The question was, "What have you done with the request of Fannie Bolton? You have not erred in disconnecting with her. This was the right thing for you to do, and this would bring to her mind conviction and remorse which she must have. She has been tempted, deceived, and almost destroyed. Notwithstanding her perversity of spirit, I have thoughts of mercy and compassion for her. . . .

"Take this poor deluded soul by the hand, surround her with a favorable influence, if possible. If she separates now from you, Satan's net is prepared for her feet. She is not in a condition to be left to herself. She feels regret and remorse. I am her Redeemer. I will restore her if she will not exalt and honor and glorify herself. If she goes from you now, there is a chain of circumstances which will bring her into difficulties which will be for her ruin. . . .

"You are not to wait for evidence of transformation of character. The Holy Spirit alone can do this work, and mold and fashion this child's experience after the divine similitude. She has not power, if left to herself, to control a temperament that is always a snare to her, unless she keeps in the love of God, unless she humbles herself under the hand of God, and learns daily the meekness and lowliness of Christ.". . .

I . . . shall work accordingly. I have taken Fannie to my home here at Sunnyside, Avondale, Cooranbong. I shall do all I can to help her heavenward.-- Ms 12c, 1896. (Concerning Fannie Bolton, March 20, 1896.)

Fannie Bolton's Perversion of Facts Regarding Her Work on EGW's Writings--The work which you have done here in Australia has yielded a harvest which is widespread. You denied having said to Sr. Malcolm that which they told me, and insisted upon, you had said. You afterward visited Sister

Malcolm, and denied having said that Sister White was a very ignorant woman, who could not write, and whose writings you had to make all over, and that it was your talent in connection with the work that made the articles in the papers and books what they were. My only course has been to dismiss you from my employment several times. . . .

Then after the Brighton Camp Meeting we had that long, disheartening revelation made to us that you thought that Marian and yourself should be recognized as the ones who were putting talent into my works. I had a talk with Sisters Colcord and Salisbury, when I related to them the trouble I had experienced with your perversion of facts in regard to your work on my writings. These sisters told me that you had told them the same story. You also told it to Sister Miller. The same words which Sister Malcolm told me you had said to her, you repeated to Sister Colcord. . . .

Now these words were positively untrue, and as the result of your report, Sister Miller has repeated them to the Andersons. You have also, I learn, repeated the same to others. You claimed that it was your superior talent that made the articles what they were. I know this to be a false-hood; for I know my own writings. You yourself have adopted much of them, and interwoven them with your own articles [submitted for publication in Youth's Instructor] which I recognize.

I have met this again in the work you have done in your misrepresenta-tions to Brother McCullagh. . . .

The work in Adelaide was left for Brethren McCullagh and Hawkins to finish, and I think it was a finish. Brother McCullagh has given up the truth largely, and taken Brother Hawkins with him. The whole church had gone with them, but had not fully taken sides when these brethren sent in

their resignation, saying that they did not believe in Mrs. White's visions
or mission. . . .

Brother McCullagh has reported your words of information given him from
house to house, saying that I have very little to do in getting out the
books purported to come from my pen, that I had picked out all I had written
from other books, and that those who prepared my articles, yourself in particular, made that matter that was published. This is the way you became my
adversary.

When Brethren Colcord and Daniells visited from house to house, they
met these very same statements. . . .

Now, this is the state of things. You can see by this what a harvest
your leaven of falsehood and misrepresentation have produced. You opened
your mind to Brother and Sister McCullagh, which has changed their feeling
toward me. The leaven worked until it carried with it one whole church.
But thank God they are recovered. And now my way is clear to make statements just as they have been coming from you, and I will cut off the influence of your tongue in every way that I can.

I will say that much of the time that you were in Australia, you surely
did not know what manner of spirit you were of. Satanic agencies have been
working through Fannie Bolton.--Letter 25, 1897. (To Fannie Bolton, April
11,1897.)

EGW Responds to Fannie Bolton's Charges--Your words regarding me and my
writings are false, and I must say that you know them to be false. Never-
theless, those unacquainted with you take your words as being the words of
one who knows. Because you have been acquainted with me, and connected with
me, you can state what you please, and you think that your tracks are so

covered that they will never be discovered. But my writings have not stopped. They go out as I have written them. No words of my copyists are put
in the place of my own words. This is a testimony that cannot be controverted. My articles speak for themselves.

When I heard that A had apostatized, I said, "I am glad that all my
connection with him has been of the tenderest character." I thought that
there was nothing they could have to say against me. But both he and his
wife bore the same report that Sister B bore to me. A stated in a large
congregation that it was reported by one who knew that I picked up things
written in books, and sent them out as something the Lord had shown me. At
the Bible Institute in Cooranbong, A told me that you had made a statement
to him and his wife similar to the statement made to Sr. B. Your sowing is
producing its harvest. Many in Melbourne have been repeating the same
things, things which you have told them, and which they thought must be
true.--Letter 24, 1897, p. 4. (To Fannie Bolton, June 25, 1897.)

Fannie Bolton's Vacillations Between False Accusations and Contrite
Confessions--I regard Fannie as one who cannot retain a spirit of contrition
for any length of time. She is so inflated with Fannie Bolton that she does
not know herself a few moments after she has expressed deep humiliation
because of her own course of action. She springs into life speedily, and
blossoms out wonderfully, dwelling on the goodness, love, mercy, and forgiveness of God toward her, taking all the promises to herself.

In the past she has expressed wonderful sorrow for her wicked course of
action, but she does not stay penitent. She does not continue to be contrite in heart. She flashes forth, thinking she is inspired by God. While
she was praying the Lord that if it was right for her to marry Caldwell, his

wife might get a divorce from her husband, she told me that as she talked
and gave Bible readings, the people turned pale to hear her talk, and she
thought she was inspired by God. Her imagination is very strong, and she
makes such exaggerated statements that her word is not trustworthy. . . .

When she was in my family, it seemed that Satan used her as his agent
to invent those things that would make the whole household miserable. She
would have her times of confession, and would then say all that one could
ask another to say. But she would go over the same ground again and again,
each time worse than before, until I decided that Satan's temptations,
working upon her desire for recognition, were so strong that she had no
power to escape from the snare. She was one with the enemy, working in his
service.

Now, my brother, if it had not been for these articles in the Review, I
would have held my peace. I thought that if Fannie would only keep away
from me, and trouble me no more, I would not expose her, but would let the
poor, deluded, misshapen character alone. But when she figures so largely
in our papers, I must speak. I dare not keep silent. Such productions do
no one any good, and the blessing of the Lord cannot attend them.--Letter
115, 1897, pp. 1, 2. (To G. C. Tenney, July 5, 1897.)

Reason EGW Was Instructed to Re-employ Fannie Bolton--I now see why I
was directed to give Fannie another trial. There were those who misunder-
stood me because of Fannie's misrepresentations. These were watching to see
what course I would take in regard to her. They would have represented that
I had abused poor Fannie Bolton. In following the directions to take her
back, I took away all occasion for criticism from those who were ready to
condemn me.--Letter 61, 1900. (To G. A. Irwin, April 23, 1900.)

Fannie Bolton's Claims Totally Untrue--I have read what you say in regard to Fannie Bolton. There is no truth in the statement that I told Fannie to write a letter or testimony to A. R. Henry. My testimonies to the churches, and to individuals have never been written in that way. . . .

All through her experience, Fannie's light has been too much like that of a meteor. It flashes up, and then goes out in darkness. Her feelings are counted as her religion. What a pity that she has so much confidence in her brilliant flashes. Her mind is so full of an emotional religion that she knows not what the genuine article is. . . .

I tell you that there is not a semblance of truth in her statements. My copyists you have seen. They do not change my language. It stands as I write it. . . .

As I have stated, Fannie has been strictly forbidden to change my words for her words. As spoken by the heavenly agencies, the words are severe in their simplicity; and I try to put the thoughts into such simple language that a child can understand every word uttered. The words of someone else would not rightly represent me.

I have written thus fully in order that you may understand the matter. Fannie Bolton may claim that she has made my books, but she has not done so. . . .

Wherein do my articles in the papers now differ from what they were when Fannie was with me? Who is it that now puts in words to supply the deficiencies of my language, my deplorable ignorance? How was this done before Fannie Bolton had anything to do with my writing? Cannot people who have reason see this? If Fannie supplied my great deficiency, how is it that I can now send articles to the papers?--Letter 61a, 1900. (To G. A.

Irwin, April 23, 1900.)

White Estate
Washington, D. C.
December 12, 1981

Attending and Acting in Theatrical Performances

Dear Sister: We had some conversation in reference to your accompanying your daughters to the theater. Last night I was commissioned to speak to you, saying, "Come out from among them, and be ye separate" (2 Cor. 6:17). [2 Cor. 6:14-18 quoted.]

My sister, you are to be connected with Jesus Christ. Our Saviour, in His example, has led the way which every sinner who turns from sin must follow. By taking the requisite steps--in conversion, in repentance, in faith, and baptism--he is to fulfill all righteousness. Christ has shown that repentance, faith, and baptism are the steps that all must take if they would follow His example. All who in obedience to Christ's command follow in this ordinance, in the name of the Father, and of the Son, and of the Holy Ghost, signify that they are dead to the world. They are buried in the likeness of Christ's death, and raised again from the water in the likeness of His resurrection. Says the apostle Paul: [Colossians 3:1-4 quoted].

Christ is the light of the world. All who are born into the kingdom of God, Christ adopts into the household of faith. If you have been converted, then the whole tenor of your life is changed. You have been convicted by the Word of God. You have accepted unpopular truth. But now comes your danger. As a mother you have not felt your responsibility to so educate and train your children that they would consider themselves a part of the family firm, to take hold with their mother in their education and become efficient in learning a trade. This is essential for practical life, and this is work

-334-

that devolves upon the parents. They are to educate and train their children in this probationary time, that they may not remain in disobedience and
transgression, standing under the banner of the prince of darkness, and
uniting their God-given powers with the enemy of righteousness.

My sister, you have decidedly failed in the duties which every mother
should do in the fear of God, in training her children to lift with her the
burdens that come with every child that is born into the family. You have a
work to do even now, and God will help you if you will take up your work in
your home life. Your children are God's property, and they should not be
left to become estranged from Him. True, you have had large odds to contend
with, but you have not maintained the surrender you made of yourself to the
Lord. Had you followed on to know the Lord, you would have better understood what it means to give up your way and will to the Lord. But the temptation and snare of the enemy came to your children, and through them to
yourself, and as a family you are in constant peril of the loss of your
souls.

Had you, my sister, followed on to know the Lord, you would during this
period of time have had enlightenment from the Sun of Righteousness. Your
only safety lay in following in His footsteps. But in not decidedly taking
your stand to give no sanction by your presence to the theatrical performance of your children, you have encouraged them in their choice of the use
they have made of their talents. Their capabilities and power belong to
God, but they are not now being used to gather with Christ. All their talents were lent them to use to the honor and the glory of God, that they
might win souls away from everything that pertains to this class of fascina-
ting amusement that absorbs the mind and draws it away from God and from

heavenly things. But they have not had an experimental knowledge of what is truth. The principles of truth have never been stamped upon their souls. The deceptive temptation that they can be a blessing to the world while serving as actresses is a delusion and a snare, not only to themselves, but to your own soul. Said Christ, "Without Me ye can do nothing." Can the Lord Jesus Christ accept these theatrical exhibitions as service done for Him? Can He be glorified thereby? No. All this kind of work is done in the service of another leader.

My sister, you cannot have an experimental knowledge of the love of God in the soul, and the joy of true obedience to your Lord, who has bought you and your family with the price of His own blood, while you join yourself to these things. Your family do not understand as do you the reasons of the faith that leads away from all such pursuits. You can never be free in Jesus Christ and yet have a divided heart. My sister, you need now to consider that your influence in accompanying your daughters to the theater is decidedly against Christ. He declares that "he that loveth son or daughter more than Me is not worthy of me" (Matt. 10:37).

The Word of God is free. Under its hallowed power of influence you may with the disciple John say, "Behold, the Lamb of God, which taketh away the sin of the world" (John 1:29). Thus you may cooperate with God in saving many souls to Christ. You may be a savor of life unto life by becoming a living influence in your family to save them from Satan's deceptive snares. But if you are not steadfast, rooted and grounded in the truth, self-delusion will place you where God cannot use you as a vessel unto honor. The light that comes from God is the light which guides the human soul to God, and the Lord calls for every power He has lent the human agent to be exercised strenuously on Christ's side of the question, to rescue the souls deceived and infatuated with just such service as your daughters have entered upon--to amuse and delight the senses and endeavor to supply a necessity in which Christ has no part.

You can see, my dear sister, that the blessing which attends the cheerful, consecrated sons and daughters of God cannot be realized by those who work with a divided heart. You do not feel the freedom, the rest, and the joy of believing in Christ because your mind is largely taken up with worthless things. Your work, and the work that God has given your children to do, you are not doing. They have consented to work up a counter-attraction that has no Christ in it.

If the truth as it is in Jesus is brought into actual contact with the souls that are ready to perish, it will produce good works. The talents of your daughters should be brought into the home life to make a model home. They should use their God-given powers to reform, to restore, and to bring order and discipline and sound principles into the home life. This would be the beginning of the work represented in the Word of God as bringing to the foundation gold and silver and precious stones, which are imperishable. This work will bring the approval of God. Angels of God in the heavenly courts would rejoice to see such a work done.

The "form of sound words" is to be prized, for it leads to right actions. The souls of your children cost the greatest sacrifice our God could make. He gave His Son to die that they might not perish. They have souls that Jesus loves. But if they follow a course of disregard for the truth and the commandments of God, they cannot enter into the kingdom of heaven. If they accept the only One who can save them from ruin, He will accept them and their service. And angels of God will be their escorts as they use their powers in guiding lost and perishing souls to a haven of rest. The power of the truth will elevate the nature, refine the taste, sanctify the judgment, and give them characters after the divine similitude. They will become members of the royal family, children of the heavenly King.

There is an abundance of theatrical performances in our world, but in its highest order it is without God. We need now to point souls to the up-lifted Saviour. Deceptions, impositions, and every evil work are in our world. Satan, the wily foe in angel's garments, is working to deceive and destroy. The object of the death of Christ was to declare His righteous-ness, and no man, woman or child can do this in his own strength, or by his own words.

Paul declared: [Ephesians 3:8-11 quoted].

To make known "unto the principalities and powers in heavenly places . . . the manifold wisdom of God." Righteousness is made known in that man-ifold wisdom, for nothing that is unrighteous can be wise. The wisdom of God and the power of God are waiting every human agency. God desires that we shall put to the tax every spiritual nerve and muscle, that we shall strive for an entrance into that city which hath foundations, whose builder and maker is God. All who win eternal life will arm themselves for the con-flict against every influence that would obstruct the way. They must bring their minds up to noble and elevated thoughts. While they offer humble prayer to God, they are to search to know what is truth.

Does my sister place herself in a position where the Lord can come close to her to manifest His presence? What do the angels see in your house on the Sabbath day? All who become members of the heavenly family will have a

philosophy and faith that is founded on a true faith in Jesus Christ. His
life alone is to be our guide. His life, His attributes, are to become
woven into all our life and all our works. God speaks from heaven, "This is
my beloved Son, hear ye Him."

Christ did not come into the world to disparage education, for He Himself was the greatest Teacher the world has ever known. Christ came to call
the minds of His redeemed people to learn of Him. He will sanctify the
human talents that are employed for His glory. He came to make human learning strong and pure and ennobling, and of such a character that He could
commend. He came to give it a foundation upon which to stand--a knowledge
of Himself. Christ declared, "Think not that I am come to destroy the law,
or the prophets: I came not to destroy, but to fulfil" (Matt. 5:17). He
came to give every specification of the law a depth and meaning which the
Pharisees had never seen nor understood. Christ is the originator of all
the deep thoughts of true philosophy, of every line of that education that
will be retained through sanctification of the spirit. True education is
that which will not be left behind when He shall come to be admired in all
them that believe.

Every member of your family is deciding his own destiny. Those who will
be rewarded with the gift of eternal life in the kingdom of God will be
those who are learning here of the great Teacher. You do not have peace and
joy because you have not consecrated yourself to God. To you the voice of
your children is above the voice of Jesus Christ, and in not taking your
stand firmly you are being led away from God and His holy requirements. In
becoming their escort and companion to go where they choose, you are making
yourself one with them. You endorse the ambitious enterprise that is

perverting their talents so that God cannot sanctify them. And the food you thus give to your soul, in seeing and hearing, is making its impression upon the mind. Should the heavenly intelligences offer you the bread of heaven, you would have no relish for it.

Just that which you give your soul to feed upon will determine the character of your experience. If you place yourself in objectionable positions where the Lord is not honored or glorified, you disqualify yourself for enjoying wholesome, heavenly instruction that would make you wise unto salvation. You are bought with a price. The plan of salvation is so vast that it brings into action the attributes of the divine nature.

If we will let Him, the Lord by His Holy Spirit will put every part of our entrusted capabilities into His service. He will cause us to feel our deep need of the grace of Christ, that we may feel His love constraining us to declare that, could we multiply our powers a thousandfold, they should all be invested in the work and cause of God. Our testimony would be, "Of Thine own we give Thee" (1 Chron. 29:14). When we have a soul hunger for Christ, we shall be filled with His fullness.

My sister, I have an intense interest that you shall have the rich manna of heaven upon which to feed. Read the sixth chapter of John. You are choosing whom you will serve. If you keep before your eyes and in your ears the transactions of the theater, you will find in your heart no soul hunger for God. It is a question of life or death with you. The Lord has appointed means whereby you may gain spiritual strength and comfort. But if you close the door of your heart to the rays of light from the throne of God and give your mind to the performances of the stage, you can have no peace, no joy, no hope. Gradually you have been losing the spirit of assurance. Your

love for Bible religion is dying out. You cannot serve God with a divided
heart.

I have a message for your daughters: You are not feeding upon the bread
which came down from heaven, but upon husks. All the praise and glory you
receive from human beings is of no value. Repent ye, for the kingdom of
heaven is at hand. Christ, the Sent of God, gave His life a sacrifice that
the world might have a second probation in which to return to their loyalty
to God. When Christ was threatened by His foes, He said, "My kingdom is not
of this world (John 18:36). It is not My mission to recognize caste and
human theories, or to establish political interests. My kingdom is not to
be set up by the power of human armies or the sword. If My kingdom were of
this world, then would My soldiers fight. No human power can weaken or
overthrow My kingdom through the enemies of God."

Who are the subjects of the kingdom of heaven? Daniel tells the world
the name by which they shall be called. "The saints of the most High shall
take the kingdom, and possess the kingdom for ever, even for ever and ever"
(Daniel 7:18). And Paul writes to the Philippians: [Phil. 1:1, 9-11; Eph.
2:18-22 quoted].

All who are enrolled as citizens of the heavenly country are required
that their behavior shall be such as the gospel of Christ can approve. And
it is our privilege to claim the rights and privileges of subjects of the
kingdom of heaven. But to everyone who accepts Christ as his personal
Saviour, He says, "Come out from among them [the world] and be ye separate."
We are to conform to the Lord's requirements, and not disgrace our citizen-
ship before the angels of heaven or before men. We are to render to God
cheerful service. Christ does not speak to those who are no more to wrestle

with temptation; who are not in any danger of being drawn away from Christ and overcome by the wiles of Satan, when He says: "Let your conversation be as becometh the gospel of Christ. . . . Stand fast in one spirit, with one mind striving together for the faith of the gospel; . . . For unto you it is given in the behalf of Christ, not only to believe on Him, but also to suffer for His sake" (Philippians 1:27,29). There is to be no strife or vainglory, no selfishness or murmuring, no disputing, nothing impure or dishonest found in the characters of the followers of Christ.--Letter 58a, 1898, pp. 1-11. (To Mrs. Gorick, July, 1898. Copied July 19, 1898.)

White Estate
Washington, D. C.
December 10, 1981

MAKE THE SECOND ADVENT PART OF LIFE

The Lord is soon coming. Talk it, pray it, live it! Make it a part of the life. You will meet lifeless, doubting, objecting faith, but this will give way before firm, consistent trust in God. When objectionable features arise, lift the soul to God in songs of thanksgiving. Preach the truth with boldness and fervor.--Letter 66, 1901, p. 6. (To R. M. Kilgore, June 26, 1901.)

White Estate
Washington, D. C.
December 10, 1981

INSIGHTS INTO THE INCARNATION

Nature of Christ a Combination of Divine and Human--The nature of Christ was a combination of the divine and the human. Having all the attributes of God, He also represented the excellencies of humanity and showed that all who believe in Christ as their personal Saviour will perfect a character after Christ's likeness and be qualified to become laborers together with God. By precept and example He uplifts those who are depraved, for through the virtues of Jesus Christ he has become the son of God. His life is like Christ's life, his work is like Christ's work, and he will not fail nor be discouraged, because he is vitalized by the Spirit and power of Jesus Christ. Christ is the Son of God in deed and in truth and in love and is the representative of the Father as well as the representative of the human race. His arm brought salvation. He took humanity, was bone of our bone and flesh of our flesh, and submitted to all the temptations wherewith man would be beset. He showed in the great controversy with Satan that He was fully able to remove the stigma and discount the degradation of sin which Satan had placed upon the human family. By taking humanity and combining it with divinity, He was able to meet every demand of the law of God, to overcome every objection which Satan had made prominent, as standing in the way of man's obedience to God's commandments.--Letter 11a, 1894, pp. 7-8. (To Captain Christiansen of the Pitcairn, Jan. 2, 1894.)

Why Christ Could Speak Forgiveness to the Dying Thief--He could, as the propitiation for the sins of the whole world, speak these words of forgiveness, which meant so much to the dying criminal. Divinity was doing its work while humanity was suffering from the hatred and revenge of a God-hating people, because Christ had acknowledged Himself the Son of God. He alone could respond to the poor suffering thief.--Ms 84a, 1897, p. 2. ("Christ on the Cross," August 15, 1897.)

The Plan of Redemption--In the councils of heaven, before the world was created, the Father and the Son covenanted together that if man proved disloyal to God, Christ, one with the Father, would take the place of the transgressor, and suffer the penalty of justice that must fall upon him.

"For God so loved the world, that He gave His only begotten Son, that whosoever believeth in Him should not perish, but have everlasting life" (John 3:16). Christ did not come to change the Sabbath of the fourth commandment. He did not come to lessen the law of God in one particular. He came to express in His own person the love of God. He came to vindicate every precept of the holy law.--Ms 145, 1897, p. 4. ("Notes of Work," Dec. 30, 1897.)

Christ's Human Nature Like Unto Ours--The human nature of Christ was like unto ours. And suffering was really more keenly felt by Him; for His spiritual nature was free from every taint of sin. The aversion to suffering was in proportion to its severity. His desire for the removal of suffering was just as strong as human beings experience.--Ms 42, 1897, pp. 9, 10. ("In Gethsemane," May 16, 1897.)

White Estate, Wash. D. C.
January 4, 1982   -345-

Manuscript Release #912

COUNSEL REGARDING GHOST WRITERS

Edson, do not, I beg of you, write books and get this one and that one to write them for you, and then sign your name to them, even if you say these men have helped you. It hurts you as an author. You can write in simplifying the truth, but do not engage any man or woman to write for you. With close application you can read the Scriptures and make the thoughts your own. The Lord will help you if you will only take time for careful study. You have ideas; do not employ others to put their fingers and brains into the work. We want you here to plan on books. Come right along [to Australia] as soon as possible and escape the hard winter. I want you to take this matter to the Lord yourself, and pray about it. The Lord will teach all who seek Him earnestly.-- Letter 240, 1899. (To J. E. White and wife, July 30, 1899.)

White Estate
Washington, D. C.
February 7, 1982

INSIGHTS ON INSPIRATION

Bible Writers Inspired, Not Extinguished--The Lord takes the instrument that will submit to the Holy Spirit's influence. He works through the human instrument that accepts that holy influence. He works in giving the heaven-ly mold, but He waits for the human agency to cooperate with the divine. The Holy Spirit inspired John; He did not extinguish John. He inspired Matthew, but He did not make Matthew into some other person.

We have a whole far—reaching history. Christ's prayer is: "Sanctify them through thy truth"--that is, make the human agent holy through the sanctification of Thy Word. The human agent is not to take Christ's place, or to receive the glory that was to be His living ministration. He was to behold and bear witness to the Light, pointing out the way, a witness attest-ing to the glory--a voice in the desert, "Behold the Lamb of God." That you may understand more clearly, John [the Baptist] says he was not that Light, but was appointed for this office, to bear witness of that Light.

Here is to be a lesson for all ministers who wish to fill the place Christ would have them fill. The minister of the gospel is to keep his hearer's attention to the fact he is a witness crying in the wilderness, "Behold the Lamb of God." He was the True Light.--Ms. 228, 1902. ("Bible Writers Inspired, Not Extinguished," cir. 1902).

Providence and Revelation Will Guide--If you watch and wait and pray, Providence and revelation will guide you through all the perplexities that you will meet, so that you will not fail nor become discouraged. Time will outline the beauty and grandeur of Heaven's plan. It is difficult for human minds to comprehend that God in His providence is working for the world through a feeble instrument. To know God in the working out of His providence is true science. There is much knowledge among men, but to see the designs of heavenly wisdom in times of necessity, to see the simplicity of God's plan revealing His justice and goodness and love, and searching out the hearts of men --this many fail to do. His plan seems too wonderful for them to accept, and thus they fail to be benefited. But Providence is still in our world, working among those who are grasping for the truth. These will recognize the hand of God. But His word will not be revered by those who trust in their own wisdom.--Letter 348, 1906, p. 6. (To G.I. Butler, Oct. 30, 1906

Handwritten Draft of a Vision. [From Diary #16, pp. 321,322, Nov. 20, 21, 1890. Ms. 29, 1890 and Ms. 29a, 1890 are copies of this diary material as edited by Mrs. White's literary assistants and approved by her. The diary passage shown here is also shown in its typewritten form from Ms. 29, 1890 immediately after this handwritten material. In Ms. Release #237 and #701 all of the material shown here is released]

my weakness and I am pleading with God forbear
to restore me and I believe that he will do it
I am reaching out for stronger faith.

Nov 21 During the night Seasons I have had
special exercises of the Spirit of the Lord, my soul had
been drawn out in earnest supplication to God I was
distressed on account of the backslidings of his people I was
pleading with the Lord while upon my bed unable to sleep
for the burden was that was upon me I fell asleep and in the
night Season I was taught of God, My guide said I have to
a work for you to do speak the words which you will have to
speak from the Lord, After these words are spoken your duties
done here you are not required to enter into details before individuals whatever may be their position or work, if they do not
hear if they do not recognize the voice of God in the message that
you bear, that God has given you to bear in his name, all the
particulars you enter into with individuals weaken the
message God gives you to bear . . .
the Lord that speaks through you . . .
. . .
and Set speak the words I shall give you however painful
it may be to you. All ways God leads his people are generally
mysterious, you have asked . . . Gods way you have your
supplications answered God knows better than you what
is good and essential for his children he never leads them
otherwise than they would wish him to lead them if they were able

to see as clearly as he does their necessities and what they must-
do to establish characters that will fit them for the heavenly
courts above. The people whom God is leading must venture
upon his word.

Ellen White's Duty Done Once She Delivers God's Messages--I spoke this evening at eight o'clock, and the Lord gave me great freedom. I feel my weakness, and I am pleading with God to restore me. I believe that He will do it. I am reaching out for stronger faith.

Nov. 21. During the night season I was specially moved upon by the Spirit of God. My soul had been drawn out in earnest supplication to God. I was distressed on account of the backsliding of His people. While lying in bed, unable to sleep because of the burden resting upon me, I was pleading with the Lord. I fell asleep, and in the night season I was taught of God. My guide said, "I have a work for you to do. You must speak the words given you by the Lord. After these words have been spoken, your duty here is done.

"You are not required to enter into details before individuals, whatever may be their position or work, if they do not recognize the voice of God in the message He gives you to bear in His name. All your efforts to remove their doubts will be of no avail if they gather the clouds of darkness about their souls. If you enter into particulars, you weaken the message. It is not you speaking, but the Lord speaking through you. Those who want to know the will of God, who do not desire to follow their own will and judgment, will be easily entreated. They will be ready to discern the right way.

"The whys and wherefores are concealed from you, yet speak the words I give you, however painful it may be to you. The ways in which God leads His people are generally mysterious. You have asked to know God's way. Your supplication has been answered. God knows better than you do what is good

and essential for His children. He never leads them otherwise than they would wish to be led if they were able to see as clearly as He does what they must do to establish characters that will fit them for the heavenly courts. The people whom God is leading must venture out upon His word."
--Ms. 29, 1890.   ("Diary," November 20, 21, 1890).

White Estate
Washington, D.C.
February 4, 1982

DANGER OF FOLLOWING "IMPRESSIONS AND FEELINGS"

In [Testimony] No. 9, you will see a note in regard to the East. I was shown that, as God revived His work, those who had formerly been in fanaticism would be in danger of crediting their impressions and feelings, and the devil would use them to push poor souls into the fire. Satan uses some as long as he can push souls into the waters (into cold formality), and then when he has accomplished all he wishes in that direction, he will give them a blind zeal and lead them to be moved by feelings and impressions, and through them will push souls into the fire to be consumed by fanaticism. The Paris people have been first pushed into the fire, next into the water, now again into the fire.

My soul is sick and discouraged in regard to those who have been so long rebellious in Waukon. "For rebellion is as the sin of witchcraft, and stubbornness is as iniquity and idolatry" (1 Sam. 15:23). Souls in Waukon have rebelled and stood fast in their rebellion, and very recently they have professed to see themselves, and their stubbornness is changed to a spirit of witchcraft or divination. I call upon all who have the cause of God one particle at heart to rise in the name of the Lord and put down the manifestations among them.

In the last vision I was shown that some in Waukon were just beginning to see themselves, but they had been in the snare of the devil so long, and been influenced by evil angels so many years to resist the testimonies God had sent them, that they could not recover themselves from Satan's snare at once; and that such ones would have to walk in deep humility, and live a life of continual repentance before they could redeem the past. I saw that their former experience has been so dark and evil that they had not discernment enough to know the work and spirit of Satan. They would as soon call darkness and error light, and reject the true light and think themselves very near to God, when Satan was controlling them. Therefore it was not safe for them to follow their own judgment or to attempt to lead or dictate in the least; but they must submit to do what their stubbornness has made exceeding difficult for them to do--be led by the judgment of others who have been true to the cause of God. . . .

This work which you think may be of God is directly from evil angels. Beware of it. Resist it. Be afraid of it as you would of a rattlesnake. We will not give it the least quarter. . . .

I have written in great haste, in great earnestness, for I feel that the case demands a speedy and severe remedy. Be assured that God will not use individuals who have traveled much in darkness to direct and teach His children. These are perilous times. God works through those who have walked carefully and in humility before Him; those who have been true; those who have moved understandingly and in His fear.--Letter 2, 1863, pp. 1,2,4. (To a leading worker, June 20, 1863.)

White Estate
Washington, D. C.
February 4, 1982

WORK THE CITIES WHILE THERE IS TIME

Our faith is small. We need more earnestness in prayer. A heaven full of blessings awaits our demand. These blessings will be given in answer to the fervent, effectual prayer that asks with an earnestness that will not be denied. The firm hold of a wrestling Jacob is called for now. The holding power of unquestioning faith needs to come into the lives of God's people. God's work needs men who will say, "I will not let Thee go except Thou bless me." It needs men who will consecrate themselves unreservedly to God. Genuine, earnest faith will prepare the heart for the reception of God's power.

Is it true that the end of all things is at hand? What mean the awful calamities by sea--vessels shipwrecked and lives hurled into eternity without a moment's warning? What mean the awful accidents by land--fire consuming the riches men have hoarded, much of which has been accumulated by oppression of the poor? The Lord will not interfere to protect the property of those who transgress His law, break His covenant, and trample upon His Sabbath, accepting in its place a spurious rest day. As Nebuchadnezzar set up an image on the plains of Dura, and commanded all to bow before it, so this false sabbath has been exalted before the world, and men are commanded to keep it holy. But it has not a vestige of sanctity. Nowhere in God's Word are we commanded to reverence the first day of the week.

Thus men will continue to disobey their Maker. And the plagues of God are already falling upon the earth, sweeping away costly structures as if by a breath of fire from heaven. Will not these judgments bring professing Christians to their senses? God permits them to come that the world may take heed, that sinners may be afraid and tremble before Him.

"Curse ye Meroz, said the angel of the Lord, curse ye bitterly the inhabitants thereof; because they came not to the help of the Lord, to the help of the Lord against the mighty" (Judges 5:23). Let the indifferent ones arouse and do their part in the work of the Lord, lest this curse be spoken against them. Let all who can, give themselves to the long-neglected work in our cities, a work that has been looked at, and then passed by on the other side, as the wounded man was passed by by the priest and Levite. Take up the work in the cities wholeheartedly, intelligently, unselfishly.

I am instructed to encourage decided efforts to secure helping hands to do missionary work, to give Bible instruction, and to sell the books containing present truth. Thus skillful work may be done in hunting and fishing for souls. Young men, your help is called for. Make a covenant with God by sacrifice. Take hold of His work. He is your sufficiency. "Be strong, yea, be strong."

Not only men, but women, can enter the canvassing field. And canvassers are to go out two by two. This is the Lord's plan.

My brethren, will you use the talent of speech in earnest persuasion to lead our people to see the importance of the work? We must arouse the zeal and earnestness of the canvassing agents, calling on them to take the light into the dark places of the earth. There is no release for any who have talents and capabilities. They are required to be the Lord's instruments, required to cooperate with the Lord Jesus in shedding the light of heaven into this sin-darkened world.

To secure your present and future good, Christ gave Himself as a sacrifice. Will you draw back from making a covenant with God by sacrifice? Christ died on the cross to save the world from perishing in sin. He asks your cooperation in His work of soul-saving. You are to be His helping hand, to do the work that needs to be done, to place the truth before as many as possible. "Ye are not your own; for ye are bought with a price; therefore glorify God in your body, and in your spirit, which are God's." (See 1 Corinthians 6:19,20.)

"We are laborers together with God." Lay hold of His work with clean hands, a pure heart, and holy, consecrated endeavor. Press forward to gain the triumphs of the cross of Christ. Are you not striving for a crown of immortality, for a life that measures with the life of God? Oh, put your whole heart into the work. Let nothing cause your zeal to flag.

Let us press forward unitedly to the help of the Lord, all of one heart and of one mind. Let us not depend on human wisdom. Let us not lean on man. Look beyond human beings to the One appointed by God to carry our griefs and sorrows, and to supply our necessities. Taking God at His word, move forward with steadfast, persevering faith. Christ's presence and His Word, "Lo, I am with you alway," is our wisdom and righteousness. It is the living Presence that makes the living Word. The kingdom comes to us, not in word only, but in power. It is unwavering faith in Christ's presence that gives power.--Letter 21, 1902, pp. 4-7. (To A. G. Daniells and E. R. Palmer, February 16, 1902.

White Estate
Washington, D. C.   -356-
March 4, 1982

MAKE CHRIST YOUR CONSTANT COUNSELLOR

We received your letter last night and we were very glad to hear from you. We feel sorry to hear that you feel lonely. We were not sorry to learn that our absence is felt. This would be only natural. We hope, my son, that you will not depend upon any one or any surroundings for happiness. Look aloft, my boy, look aloft. There is a heaven full of consolation for those who seek it. You have an Advocate with the Father, Jesus Christ the righteous. He pleads your cause before His Father. He has invited you to come to Him and cast all your care upon Him.

The invitation is to you, "Come unto me, all ye that labour and are heavy laden, and I will give you rest. Take my yoke upon you, and learn of me; for I am meek and lowly in heart; and ye shall find rest unto your souls: for my yoke is easy and my burden is light" (Matt. 11:28-30).

Your only safety and happiness are in making Christ your constant Counsellor. You can be happy in Him if you had not another friend in the wide world. Your feelings of unrest and homesickness or loneliness may be for your good. Your heavenly Father means to teach you to find in Him the friendship and love and consolation that will satisfy your most earnest hopes and desires. I fear that you are striving to carry your own burden. It is too heavy for you. Jesus bids you cast it upon Him that He may carry it for you. There is an experience for you to gain in faith and trust in God. He is faithful who hath promised. You must exercise faith in the promises of God.

Do not be overanxious about anything. Go quietly about your duty which
the day brings you. Do the best you can; ask God to be your helper. Do
what you can, and do not neglect to pray and watch thereunto and in no case
neglect your religious duties. Never let your studies interfere with your
religious exercises. You want to be obtaining a more thorough knowledge of
the will of God as well as to advance in the sciences. If one must be
neglected, let it never be religious duties. Go on from day to day doing
what you well can, and be content with that. You may say, I do the best I
can today and leave what I cannot do without worriment or care. And when
tomorrow comes I will, in the fear of the Lord, do what I can on the morrow.
Thus from day to day pursue your course of duty, trusting in God to be your
helper and to give you quick perception and heavenly wisdom that you may be
fitted to honor Him with your talents.

Have you fully consecrated yourself to the Lord? Feel every day, "I am
doing my work for God. I am not living for myself, to glorify myself, but
to glorify God." Oh, trust in Jesus and not in your own heart. Cast your
burdens and yourself upon Him. If you feel no joy, no consolation, do not
be discouraged. Hope and believe. You may have a precious experience in
the things of God. Wrestle with your discouragements and doubts until you
gain the victory over them in Jesus' name. Do not encourage grief, despondency, and darkness. Cast your burden upon Jesus and be sure not to with-
hold yourself.

Is not God's Word sufficient for you with the assurance of emotion or
joy? Can you not trust Him and believe without feeling? Repose in the
broad, sure promises of God. Rest in these promises, without a doubt. Find

time, my son, to comfort some other heart, to bless with a kind, cheering word someone who is battling with temptation, and maybe with affliction. In this blessing another with cheering, hopeful words, pointing him to the Burden bearer. you may unexpectedly find peace, happiness, and consolation yourself.

But I entreat of you to drop your burdens upon the Burden bearer. You will not then be drifting away from God, for by faith you are anchored upon His promise. You cannot doubt the love of your dear Saviour for you, my son, even for you. You cannot distrust His mercy. Only believe He has spared you to work for Him. Seek for a deep and living experience in the things of God and learn of Him who is meek and lowly of heart and you will find rest to your soul.--Letter 2b, 1874, pp. 1-3. (To her son, W. C. White, 19 years of age.)

White Estate
Washington, D. C.
March 11, 1982

ELLEN WHITE'S GENEROSITY IN AUSTRALIA

In this country I have found destitution and poverty everywhere, and had I not means to relieve the distressed, to clothe the naked, to take the youth who are too poor to help themselves and place them in schools, and to help the churches in building houses of worship, we should have left the field long ago; for it would be useless to attempt to do anything, hampered on every side. In a letter of mine copied by someone at the Pacific Press, the statement appears that I had spent $100 to educate students. It was $1,000, and $2,000 has been used in helping in different places where help was really needed.

Suppose that my brethren at the Review and Herald had been able to bring me to their terms in the publication of my books; what could I have done among this poverty-stricken people? I not only tell them what must be done, but shoulder a large part of the burden myself. I know that God sent me here, but if I had been more closely bound about for want of facilities, I might have worn my life out, and died in disappointment that I could not relieve the situation. I will have Emily Campbell give you the figures showing what I have expended solely for the education of students in our school. I am satisfied with the outlay. It pays, thank God, it pays.--Letter 5, 1895, p. 19. (To "Brethren in Responsible Positions in America," July 24, 1895.)

White Estate
Washington, D. C.
March 11, 1982

CITIES DESTROYED BY "BALLS OF FIRE"

In the night I was, I thought, in a room but not in my own house. I was in a city, where I knew not, and I heard expression after expression. I rose up quickly in bed, and saw from my window large balls of fire. Jetting out were sparks, in the form of arrows, and buildings were being consumed, and in a very few minutes the entire block of buildings was falling and the screeching and mournful groans came distinctly to my ears. I cried out, in my raised position, to learn what was happening: Where am I? And where are our family circle? Then I awoke. But I could not tell where I was for I was in another place than home. I said, Oh Lord, where am I and what shall I do? It was a voice that spoke, "Be not afraid. Nothing shall harm you."

I was instructed that destruction hath gone forth upon cities. The word of the Lord will be fulfilled. Isaiah 29:19-24 was repeated. I dared not move, not knowing where I was. I cried unto the Lord, What does it mean? These representations of destruction were repeated. Where am I? "In scenes I have represented that which will be; but warn My people to cease from putting their trust in men who are not obedient to my warnings and who despise My reproof, for the day of the Lord is right upon the world when evidence shall be made sure. Those who have followed the voices that would turn things upside down will themselves be turned where they cannot see, but will be as blind men.

These words were given me from Isaiah 30: "Now go, write it before them in a table, and note it in a book, that it may be for the time to come for ever and ever: That this is a rebellious people, lying children, children that will not hear the law of the Lord: Which say to the seers, See not; and to the prophets, Prophesy not unto us right things, speak unto us smooth things, prophesy deceits." [Isaiah 30:8-15 quoted.]. . . .

I was instructed that light had been given me and that I had written under special light the Lord had imparted.--Ms 126, 1906. (Diary, August 23, 27, 1906.)

White Estate
Washington, D. C.
March 11, 1982

THEMES FOR MEDITATION

Let Jesus Be Lifted Up--The truly converted soul is illuminated by the light shining from the Sun of Righteousness. That light tells upon hearts, lightens the pathway, dispels the darkness, because it comes from Him who says, "I am the way, the truth, and the life" (John 14:6). Let everyone, to a man, now rise, and let his light so shine before men that they may see his good works, and glorify our Father which is in heaven. (See Matt. 5:16.) Do what you can, and do it at once, cheerfully, heartily, prayerfully, joyfully, not as unto men, but unto God. Settle it in your hearts, that you are not on the earth to exalt self, to make a great name, but to sink self wholly out of sight in Jesus Christ. Let Jesus be lifted up. Let the great truths connected with the salvation of man be the theme of your meditation day and night. Your work, both by precept and example, is to hold forth the word of life, to seek with all your power to bring souls to the knowledge of the truth.--Letter 38, 1890, p. 8. (To "Brethren Church and Bell, and All the Church in Fresno," Feb. 21, 1890.)

What Jesus Has Done For Us--Say to the youth, If you have not given your heart to Jesus, make Him the offering ere the year 1892 shall close. What has Jesus done for you? He has given His precious life for you. If God had not loved you He would have retained Jesus in heaven. "God so loved the world, that He gave His only begotten Son, that whosoever believeth in Him should not perish, but have everlasting life" (John 3:16). Do not allow the enemy to crowd this out of your mind. It is the most important theme for your meditation. What have I done to show that I appreciate this great love? What have I given to Jesus? The gift that will be a precious and fragrant offering to Him will be yourself. You that have not made your decision to be sons and daughters of God, I beg of you to do this without any delay. Place your will on the side of God's will. He delights in mercy. "Who is a God like unto Thee, that pardoneth iniquity, and passeth by the transgression of the remnant of His heritage? He retaineth not His anger forever, because He delighteth in mercy" (Micah 7:18). Have you decided to become a part of the heritage of the Lord? "Ye are God's husbandry, ye are God's building" (1 Cor. 3:9). Come to Jesus just as you are, weak and sinful, ignorant and unworthy and He will receive you. He says, "A new heart also will I give you" (Ezek. 36:26).

Among the Jews was a remembrance made of sins every year, and they felt that sin needed a fresh sacrifice. Sins forgiven in Christ are remembered no more. Saith God, "I will remember their sin no more" (Jer. 31:33). The Lord accepts the sinner that comes to Him in contrition, repenting of His sins; and treats Him just as if he were innocent. Again, He says our sins are covered. Will the youth think seriously and begin to inquire, What shall I do to be saved? "Behold! The Lamb of God which taketh away the sin of the world" (John 1:29). The more your mind is educated and trained to think of Jesus, to talk of Jesus, the less power will Satan have over your mind. He cannot bear to belong in the company of those who will meditate upon the love of God, and Jesus Christ.--Letter 43, 1892, pp. 5,6. (To Elder S. N. Haskell, Sept. 18, 1892.)

Why Christ Came--When the human family received the deadly wound caused by Adam's transgression, it became needful for the sinless Son of God, One equal with the Father, to take our nature upon Him, and come to the world to live in our behalf a perfect life, making it possible for man, through His ministration, to become a partaker of the divine nature, and thus escape the corruption that is in the world through lust. It was as our Redeemer that He came, that those who believe in Him may receive from Him the strength and the virtue that will enable them to overcome in the struggle with evil. For this reason the Word was made flesh and dwelt among us. As in Adam all die, even so, through accepting Christ as a personal Saviour, all may be made alive. "He that believeth on the Son hath everlasting life: and he that believeth not the Son shall not see life; but the wrath of God abideth on him" (John 3:36).

To the astonishment of all heaven, the proclamation was made that God so loved the world that He gave His only begotten Son to a life of humiliation and suffering. By an amazing sacrifice the Son of the infinite God displayed His love for the fallen race. He did this as the only means of manifesting the love of God for disobedient human beings. He made an offering that could not possibly be exceeded in value. The love of God was manifested in and through Christ. The Son of God suffered the penalty of sin, reconciling the world unto Himself. He who knew no sin became a sin-offering, that fallen, sinful human beings, through repentance and confession, might receive pardon. He became our propitiation, that man, repentant, humbled, receiving the merits of Christ, might be made the righteousness of God in Him.

We who have fallen through the transgression of the law of God have an Advocate with the Father, Jesus Christ the righteous. The way is open for everyone to prepare himself for the second appearing of Jesus Christ, that at His appearing we may be vindicated, having put away all evil, and having overcome through the cleansing blood of Christ. Through the intercession of Christ, the image of God is renewed in mind, and heart, and character. Through the blood of the only-begotten Son of God, we obtain redemption. We are accepted in the Beloved, made like unto Christ in character, receiving His wisdom, His righteousness, His sanctification, His redemption, if we hold the beginning of our confidence firm unto the end.

We are in this world to honor God; and from all devising that would in any way tempt us to dishonor our Redeemer, we must turn away. In Christ we have before us the Pattern of all righteousness.--Letter 72, 1906, pp. 3,4. (To Brother and Sister Farnsworth, Feb. 19, 1906.)

White Estate
Washington, D. C.
April 1, 1982

Manuscript Release #920

THE LOST SHEEP, LOST COIN, AND LOST SON

I have not been able to sleep past half-past four a.m. It has been impressed upon my mind that if we realized in a deeper sense the love of God for sinners, much more would be done in the name of Christ to seek and to save that which is lost. The parables of the lost sheep, the lost coin, the prodigal son, bring out in distinct lines God's pitying love for those who are erring and straying from Him. Although [following] their own course of action in turning away from God, He does not leave them in their misery. The Lord is full of lovingkindness and tender, pitying love to all who are exposed to the temptations of the artful foe.

How few bear in mind that the tempter was once a covering cherub, a being whom God created for His own name's glory. Satan fell from his high position through self-exaltation; he misused the high capabilities with which God had so richly endowed him. He fell for the same reason that thousands are falling today, because of an ambition to be first, an unwillingness to be under restraint. The Lord would teach man the lesson that, though united in church capacity, he is not saved until the seal of God is placed upon him, and he is made complete in Christ.

Those who use their God-given intellect to separate themselves from their Maker and lead others into sin need to be searched after and helped. Christ used the parable of the lost sheep to teach a lesson to the hardhearted scribes and Pharisees. The rebuke of God was upon these men because of their self-righteousness and pride. They did not appreciate the attri-

-367-

butes of Christ, His mercy, His goodness and truth. These were in marked contrast to their representation of piety, and they were therefore continually misunderstanding His mission and work.

Christ came to seek and to save that which was lost, but they found fault with Him for receiving sinners and eating with them. Christ did not rebuke them openly, lest He should close the door of their hearts against Him, but He gave them a symbol which they could carry with them, and through which some would be convicted. Upon these, after His resurrection and ascension to heaven, the Holy Spirit would come, and they would unite with the disciples in church capacity.

What did the disciples do under the influence of the Holy Spirit's working? They called nothing which they possessed their own. All their earthly goods they used to support the poor believers. And this is the influence the Holy Spirit will have upon the hearts of those who believe today. They will not be improvident with the property lent them in trust. They will remember that it is not their own, and will use the Lord's goods to advance His work. They will publish the glad tidings of the gospel. They will work to relieve the needs, to help the helpless. It was this class for whom Christ manifested the greatest pity, the most tender compassion.

By the parable of the lost piece of silver Christ sought to impress upon the minds of His hearers the necessity of arousing the sensibilities of those within the home to seek for those who were straying from God. Not one member of the family is to be forgotten. The one wayward child is to be sought for. The candle, the Word of God, is to be lighted, and diligently used in examining everything in the house, to see why this one child is lost to God. Parents are to search their own hearts, to examine their own habits and practices. They are answerable for their management of God's property. Have they done their work well? Are the fathers and mothers who claim to belong to God training their families to serve and honor and glorify Him?

The Lord works with those who are sinners. These are the ones who need most the help of the great Physician; yet, like the lost piece of silver, they are unconscious of their state. The soul unaroused is in a state of impiety, even at an early age. The woman who begins her search for the piece of silver sweeps the house until she finds it. She removes everything that will obstruct her search. She seeks diligently until she finds it. Then, rejoicing in her success, she calls her friends together, saying, "Rejoice with me, for I have found the piece which I had lost" (Luke 15:9). In every home let the candle be lighted. Fathers and mothers must bring the Word of God into their practical life if they would save the souls of their children.

Every soul is the object of the loving interest of Him who gave His life that He might bring men back to God. This earnest, persevering interest expressed by our heavenly Father teaches us that the helpless and outcast are not to be passed by indifferently. They are the Lord's by Creation and by redemption. If we were left to ourselves to judge, we would regard many who are degraded as hopeless. But the Lord sees the value of the silver in them. Though they do not look for help, He regards them as precious. The One who sees beneath the surface knows how to deal with human minds. He knows how to bring men to repentance. He knows that if they see themselves as sinners, they will repent and be converted to the truth. This is the work we are to engage in. It lies before us in this locality, and in every place around us.

In the parable of the prodigal son is presented before us the Lord's dealing with those who have once known the Father's love, but who have allowed the tempter to lead them captive at his will. The love of God is still strong for the one who has chosen to separate from Him, and He sets in operation influences to bring him back to the Father's house. Although he has grieved the Lord, yet if he repents, the Father will receive him. This work is to be done by us more thoroughly than it has been done. The work now being done in America in medical missionary lines is recognized as bearing the signature of heaven. The pearls buried beneath the rubbish of human invention are to be discovered; and when this work is done there will be rejoicing in the heavenly courts. The Lord is represented as joying over His people with singing.

In this parable Christ shows us that any class of sinners who will return to God He will receive with joy, and cover with His robe of righteousness. As this work is carried on, Satan is disappointed, and imbues with his spirit the elder brother, who apparently has been faithful in the service of his father. When the elder brother saw the joy that was expressed at the return of the prodigal, he felt that he was insulted; for he had never left his father's house. This spirit is a spirit of selfishness and jealousy. He is now prepared to watch that brother, to criticize all he does, to accuse him for the least deficiency. He will not forgive as the Lord forgives.

If the restored son makes mistakes, the elder brother marks every defect. He magnifies every wrong action into a large matter. This he does to justify his own unforgiving spirit. This accuser acts out the spirit of Satan to create disunion and heartburning. He sees the mote in his brother's eye that needs to be plucked out, but he does not discern the beam that is in his own eye. And that beam prevents him from coming close to his brother and adjusting the difficulty. The Spirit of God is not working in that suspicious mind. All this misinterpretation of his brother is placing the accuser where God cannot give him the light of His countenance.

Men often commit wrong through ignorance or want of judgment. In many instances there is no premeditated wrong; it is caused through a lack of thoughtfulness. The one who treats this as sin is himself a sinner. There is with many a keen imagination that makes them offender for a word or action. But often the one judged is innocent in the sight of God. The accuser, who has permitted the tempter to ruffle his feelings, needs to humble his soul before God, to be purified and refined by the Holy Spirit, to love as brethren, be kind, be courteous. The promise to all is, "Resist the devil, and he will flee from you. Draw nigh to God, and He will draw nigh to you" (James 4:7). If one errs, remember that this is no more than you yourself have done. Put away evil surmisings. Christ says, "All ye are brethren" (Matt. 23:8).

The Spirit of the Lord is grieved by those who partake of the feelings of the elder brother. Christ alone can take away suspicion and surmising of evil. It is for His glory to have these things put away, to have self purified. He can then work to mold and fashion the one who has erred. The

Saviour's love can find him and restore him to God, that his capabilities may be exercised for good, his life spent in honoring God and blessing his fellow men.

"The son of man is come to seek and to save that which was lost" (Luke 19:10). There is a prescription for all who are so rigid in regard to a brother's wrong, when their own record stands in the books of heaven charged with unconfessed sins. You may ask, What can I do? Listen to the Great Teacher: "How think ye? If a man have an hundred sheep, and one of them be gone astray, doth he not leave the ninety and nine, and goeth into the mountains, and seeketh that which is gone astray? And if so be that he find it, verily I say unto you, He rejoiceth more of that sheep, than of the ninety and nine which went not astray. Even so it is not the will of your Father which is in heaven, that one of these little ones should perish" (Matt. 18:12-14). The lessons of this chapter it is for the interest of all to study and practice.

There are those who act out the spirit of the servant in the parable who was forgiven much, but who revealed an unforgiving spirit. After his lord had forgiven his great debt, he [Matthew 18:28-35 quoted].

Personal piety can only bear its testimony in a wise and unconditional surrender to God. It can only be obtained by asking of God. We are to shut our doors to all outward activity, and kneel before our Maker. Away from human beings, we are to consider our duty in the light of the Word of God. "I pray not," said Christ in His prayer to the Father, "that Thou shouldest take them out of the world, but that Thou shouldest keep them from the evil" (John 17:15). The soul that seeks after God will find Him. And the life will be full of goodness, love, and truth.   The conversation will be of heaven, from whence we look for our Saviour.   Our religion will tell, in its influence, in our personal deeds.   [1 John 3:10-22; 2:4-7 quoted.]

The word given from the beginning is the holy law, spoken from Sinai in majesty and glory.   (Exodus 20.) In the words of Christ to the lawyer, we see how important it is that we keep the commandments of God.   Said Christ, "Thou shalt love the Lord thy God with all thy heart, and with all thy soul, and with all thy strength, and with all thy mind; and thy neighbour as thyself" (Luke 10:27).

The Lord has a work for us all to do.   And if the truth is not rooted in the heart, if the natural traits of character are not transformed by the Holy Spirit, we can never be co-laborers with Jesus Christ.   Self will constantly appear, and the character of Christ will not be manifested in our lives.   The Saviour represented the Word of God by a pearl of great price. When He sent His disciples forth, He warned them: Cast not your pearls before swine.   (See Matt. 7:6.)   They understood His meaning.   He had placed in their possession truths of the highest value.

The question is asked, "What advantage then hath the Jew?   Or what profit is there of circumcision?   Much every way: chiefly because that unto them were committed the oracles of God" (Rom. 3:1,2).   God had made the Jewish nation the repositories of His holy oracles.   Had they been faithful stewards of the sacred trust, the Lord would have delighted in His people, and would have made them the praise of the whole earth.   But they transgressed the law, and broke the covenant of God.   They had despised the riches of His goodness, His forbearance, His long-suffering, not knowing that the goodness of God leadeth to repentance, and in so doing they treasured up to themselves "wrath against the day of wrath and revelation of the righteous judgment of God; Who will render to every man according to his deeds: to them who by patient continuance in well doing seek for glory and honor and immortality, eternal life: . . . Not the hearers of the law are just before God, but the doers of the law shall be justified" (Rom. 2:4-7, 13). The Jews were the chosen nation. They were favored with the oracles of God. But they did not appreciate the pearl of great price. The apostle asks, "What if some did not believe? Shall their unbelief make the faith of God without effect? God forbid: yea, let God be true, but every man a liar; as it is written, That thou mightest be justified in thy sayings, and mightest overcome when thou art judged" (Rom. 3:3,4).--Letter 80, 1898.

White Estate
Washington, D. C.
April 1, 1982

Scripture Index

Scripture Index

Subject Index

Subject Index

Boston, EGW met heresy in 315-316

Bourdeau, Brother and Sister, to be united in their labor 277

Brain, proper labor safeguards against taxation of 174

Bread of heaven, one who perverts talents has no relish for 340, 341

Breed, A. J., letter to, re school land 164

Brethren, if in harmony with heaven, will be in harmony with 27

Brigs, Sister, EGW letter to, re Sabbathkeeping 30-31

Brown, Martha: and family, story of 18-19
    EGW urged, to attend camp meeting in New Zealand 12-13

Buena Vista, California, good site for school 167

Building, spiritual lessons from 38-39

Burrel, Brother, invited EGW to camp meeting in East 65

Business principles, church to adopt correct 77

Business training, essential for students 181

Butler, G. I.: at Newton, Iowa, camp meeting 131
    counsel to, re decentralization 79-80
    EGW met, in Chicago 57
    letter to, re sanitariums near schools 168

Caldwell, W. F., Fanny Bolton wanted to marry 330-331

California, EGW's travels in 62-65, 119, 129-132, 135, 139, 145, 148-152

Calvary, cross of, is the great center 101

Camp meeting: in California 63-64
    in Dakotas, first 61
    in Kansas 58, 61, 232
    in Newton, Iowa 130-131
    in Wellington, New Zealand, important to have 7-19

Campbell, Emily, gave *Review* information re EGW's donations 360

Canright, D. M.: discussed where to have tent meetings 129
    tided over points with assertions 231

Caro, Margaret, Dr., extracted teeth of EGW 3

Centralization: of power, not wise 41-47, 76-81
    warning against 273

Character: Christ can make one's, like His own 308
    Christ gives a new, to all believers 172
    Christlike, self-distrust is characteristic of 169
    forming of, likened to building a church 38-39
    perfection of, means perfection in unity 179
    self alone is not able to perfect 112, 304
    Spirit works from heart outward to develop 35

Charity, trouble exists among brethren because of lack of 261

Chicago, EGW proclaimed Christ's righteousness in 257

Chick, Mrs., letter to, re Avondale College 162

Children: are God's property 335
    need restraint 41
    parents not to overly govern 277

Christ: abide in, how to 38-39
    Advocate with the Father 357, 366
    Anointed One 282
    as Burden-bearer, trust in 357-359
    as faithful Creator, commit soul to 308
    as invisible Mediator, go straight to 316-317
    as our propitiation, forgives sins 344-345
    attractiveness of, to be shown to others 262
    attributes of 367-368, 339
    blood of, cleanses from unrighteousness 290
    came to restore moral image of God in man 173
    Captain, need to obey orders of 297
    completeness of man is in 304
    condescension of, without parallel 87
    constant Counselor, to be made one's 357-359
    conversation of, at transfiguration 101
    cooperation with, comes when converted 311
    correct conception of, needed 108
    death of, object of 338
    divinity flashed through humanity of 282
    dwell in, by faith 34
    example of: in soul-winning 219-220
        is for all to follow 334
    first coming of, reason for 365-366
    follow no one but 292
    follower of, how to be a 334-342
    friend of all 219
    gentleness of, to cherish 210
    great Head of the church 219
    Great Healer 187
    Great Teacher, listen to 372
    greatest physician 98
    greatest Teacher ever known 339
    Heavenly Merchantman 291
    Holy One of Israel 264
    human nature of, was like ours 345, 365
    humiliation of, showed his divine mission 283
    incarnation of 344-345
    Intercessor, be thankful to still have 242
    is rejected, when messenger rejected 284
    is representative of human race 344
    joy of, to do good to men 26
    King of glory 282

Subject Index

Subject Index

makes works consistent with faith 11
mind to be open to receive 237-238
mind sharpened by 49
most important promise to disciples 34-36
natural traits transformed by 373
need of 40, 307
not discerned at Minneapolis 227
not to have narrow ideas re 264
power and efficiency received through 220
reach highest standard, when sanctified by 110
SDA church guided by counsels of 153
to be filled with the, ready for second coming 270
truth planted in heart by 91
will put every capability into God's service 340
Home, parents need divine touch in 11
Howe, F., letter to, re sports in schools 160-161
Hughes, C. B., provided cottage for Pocock
    family 92, 94, 95
Human beings, See Man
Humility: God works through those who walk in 353
    greatness depends on 306
    living before God in, one has clearer view of
        Jesus 240-241
Idleness, greatest curse is 181
Ignorance: cannot be excused, if given light 287
    is a crime 171
Illinois, EGW's travels in 57, 68, 131, 149
Image of God, renewed in mind through Christ 366
Imagination, not to mold self by own 242
Impressions, danger of following 352-353
Incarnation, of Christ 344-345
Infidel, EGW met, when on train 120-121
Influence: power of 25-26
    religious, to radiate from the wise 184
Ings, Jenny, EGW asked that, be matron at
    St. Helena 146
Inspiration, insights on 347-351
Institutions: accounts of, review frequently 52
    SDA, not to centralize 41-47, 76-81
Instructors, See Teachers
Integrity, Christian, in the ministry 82-91
Intellect: becomes unbalanced when envious 244
    See also Mind
Interpretation, of Bible, differences re 234-235
Iowa, EGW's travels in 56, 130-131, 137, 141
Iowa Conference, weak leadership of 235
Irwin, Brother, letter to, re school debt 162
Irwin, G. A., letter to, re school degrees 165

Israel, M. C.: at camp meeting, Wellington,
    New Zealand 17
    house of, site of meetings in New Zealand 3
Jealousy: and evil surmising, are ready to grow if
        allowed to 263
    barred hearts, at Minneapolis meetings 257
    builds barriers between one and God 80-81
    grieves Holy Spirit 84
    intellect unbalanced by 244
    is of spirit of Satan 235
    minister who has, breaks God's law 83
    shown in prodigal's brother 370-372
    to be put away 265
Jesus Christ, See Christ
Jewish nation: evil surmising brought weakness to 243
    made repository of God's oracles 373-374
Jews: great work to be done for 105
    humiliation of Christ was offense to 283
    made message of none effect, like some
        today 286-287
    manifested stubbornness in rejecting Christ 243
    one is less excusable than, in rejecting Christ
        today 284, 286-287
    we are in no better condition than the 238
John, the disciple, imitated Christ's character 26
Jones, A. T.: counsels to 208-210
    EGW in harmony with 33
    false theories of, dishonor to God 214
    message of, to be told to all 231
    needed Spirit 248-249
    presented precious light to people 257
    to speak to all, re Christ's righteousness 255-256
Jones, Edwin, understood Christ's righteousness 244
Joy: God receives repentant sinners with 370
    let light shine heartily and with 363
    there is no, for those not consecrated to
        God 339, 340
Judging: one another, is of spirit of Satan 235
    the brethren, God did not give any the
        work of 261, 262
Judgment, no mortal can ransom another's soul
        in the 292
Kansas, EGW's travels in 57-58, 60-61
Kellogg, J. H.: commendations, warnings,
    advice to 299-320
    did work God gave to the church 217
    donated funds for Sydney sanitarium 222
    EGW and James to act as parents to 311

-383-

Subject Index

is of great value 219
rely on God rather than 205
Management, of sanitarium, not to rest on doctor 78
Manual arts, list of, to be included in curriculum 180-181
Manual training, sports not a substitute for 160-161, 168
Massachusetts, EGW met heresy in 315-316
Masters, Brother, canvasser in Dunedin, New Zealand 3
Matteson, J. G., heavy work load of 76-77
McCullagh, Stephen: apostasy of 206-207
    gave up the truth, and discounted EGW 328-329
    worked in Ormondville, New Zealand 3-4
McEnterfer, Sara, went through storm to help
    sick child 93-97
Mechanics, to be taught in SDA schools 156
Medical-missionary work: bears heaven's signature 370
    is best reason to start a school 192
    is essential for students 181
    keeps churches healthy 217
    to be done to glory of God 276-277
    to be hand and arm of gospel 98
    to be throughout world 45-46
    training needed in 187-189
Meditation, John 3:16 most important theme for 363-364
Men, See Man
Merriam, Flora, EGW learns of death of 30
Message, testing, Satan's purpose to obscure 100
Messenger, of God, not for us to say who should be 286
Michael, leads armies of Lord's host 248
Michigan, EGW's travels in 149
Milner, Sister, EGW hoped to see, in Iowa, but not
    home 141
Mind: and body, close relation between 197-198
    Christ came to ennoble 173
    counsel on development of 110-111
    one cannot force, of another 266
    one needs a clear, to do good work 198
    proper exercise, safeguard against taxation of 174
    to be cultivated to do thorough work 183
    to be expanded to take in blessed promises 269
    to be in constant repose in God 24
    when thinking, talking of Jesus, Satan has less power
        over 364
    See also Intellect
Ministers: at Minneapolis, many spiritually blind 227, 230
    spiritual, appeal for 98-104
    training of, no absolute rule for 72
Ministry: Christian integrity in the 82-91
    needs God's converting power 297

qualifications for the 179
work of, to be done to glory of God 276-277
Minneapolis, church at, is lukewarm, slumbering 290
Minneapolis General Conference: and its
    aftermath 227-246
    and law in Galatians 233
    compared to Christ's day 291-292
    EGW full of Spirit at 254, 257
    EGW lost confidence in brethren at 228
    Holy Spirit not discerned at 227
    Lord wanted to revive people at 256-257
    many pastors spiritually blind at 227, 230
    prejudice barred hearts at 257
    reformation needed at 229-230
    repentance and confession needed at 230, 232
    spirit of: pharisaism at 235
        unbelief shown at 281-298
    spiritual condition of those at 256-257
    two spirits present 254-260
    work of EGW 50 times harder after 259
    wrong spirit manifested at 255
Minnesota, EGW's travels in 134
Minor, Mrs., advocated sentimental sophistries 247
Miracle, renewing of heart is greater, than healing of
    body 304
Mission work, to be everywhere, not just America 6-7
Missionary work: educate children to do 191
    most acceptable, to obey God in everything 198
    to be done in neglected cities 354-356
Missions, EGW chose cheaper mode of travel, to
    save for 151
Missouri, EGW's travels in 136-137, 145-146
Moore, W. H., in party of 30 in Texas 59
Morrison, J. H., re leadership of Iowa Conference 235
Moses, on Mount of Transfiguration 101
Mountain, Brother, only SDA of means in Wellington 2
Music, more than, needed for spirituality 99-100
Napier, New Zealand, EGW spoke at 15
Nashville, school to be established near 166-167
Nature, book of: EGW sees God's love in 133
    how to teach lessons from 170
    lessons to be learned from 37, 177-178,
        183-184, 186
    students to study 186
Nebraska, EGW's travels in 68, 125, 130-131, 136-138,
    140-141
Negroes, See Blacks

Subject Index